To Sue.
Wishing you
and a we
love, Kane.

Divine Revelation

Edited by

Paul Avis

WILLIAM B. EERDMANS PUBLISHING COMPANY
GRAND RAPIDS, MICHIGAN / CAMBRIDGE, U.K.

First published 1997 in the U.K. by
Darton, Longman and Todd Ltd
1 Spencer Court
140-142 Wandsworth High Street
London SW18 4JJ
and in the United States of America by
Wm. B. Eerdmans Publishing Co.
255 Jefferson Ave. S.E., Grand Rapids, Michigan 49503

Printed in the United States of America

02 01 00 99 98 97   7 6 5 4 3 2 1

ISBN 0-8028-4219-4

Contents

Notes on Contributors

WILLIAM J. ABRAHAM is Albert C. Outler Professor of Wesley Studies at the Perkins School of Theology of the Southern Methodist University, Dallas. He has worked extensively on the topic of revelation. His recent publications include *The Logic of Evangelism* (Hodder).

PAUL AVIS is a parish priest and Sub Dean of Exeter Cathedral, Vice-Chairman of the Church of England's Faith and Order Advisory Group, Honorary Research Fellow in the Department of Theology of the University of Exeter and Director of the Centre for the Study of the Christian Church. His recent publications include *Authority, Leadership and Conflict in the Church* (Mowbray) and *Faith in the Fires of Criticism: Christianity in Modern Thought* (Darton, Longman and Todd). He has also edited *The Resurrection of Jesus Christ* (Darton, Longman and Todd).

RICHARD BAUCKHAM is Professor of New Testament Studies in the Department of Divinity of the University of St Andrew's, a member of the Church of England's Doctrine Commission and of the Doctrine Committee of the Scottish Episcopal Church. His recent publications include *The Theology of the Book of Revelation* (CUP), *The Climax of Prophecy* (T. & T. Clark) and *The Theology of Jürgen Moltmann* (T. & T. Clark).

GAVIN D'COSTA is Senior Lecturer in the Department of Theology and Religious Studies of the University of Bristol. He has recently edited *Christian Uniqueness Reconsidered* (Orbis) and *Resurrection Reconsidered* (Oneworld).

GABRIEL DALY is an Augustinian priest and teaches theology at Trinity College, Dublin and the Irish School of Ecumenics. He has published *Transcendence and Immanence: A Study in Catholic Modernism and Integralism* (Clarendon) and *Creation and Redemption* (Gill and Macmillan).

CHARLES DAVIS was formerly Professor of Religion at Concordia University, Montreal. His publications include *Theology and Political Society* (CUP) and *Religion and the Making of Society: Studies in Social Theology* (CUP).

JAMES D. G. DUNN is Lightfoot Professor of Divinity in the Department of Theology of the University of Durham. His recent publications include the Word commentary on Romans, *The Parting of the Ways: Between Christianity and Judaism* (SCM), *Christian Liberty* (Paternoster) and *The Theology of Paul's Letter to the Galatians* (CUP).

LESLIE HOULDEN is Emeritus Professor of Theology at King's College, London. His recent publications include *The Public Face of the Gospel* (SCM). He has edited *The Interpretation of the Bible in the Church* (SCM) and jointly edited the *Companion Encyclopedia of Theology* (Routledge)

TERENCE PENELHUM is Professor in the Department of Religious Studies of the University of Calgary. His recent publications include *Reason and Religious Faith* (Westview Press).

ESTHER REED lectures in the Department of Theology of the University of Exeter and is a member of the Faith and Order Committee of the Methodist Church of Great Britain. Her publications include *A Theological Reading of Hegel's* Phenomenology ... *Salvation in a Social Context* (Mellen).

MAURICE WILES was Regius Professor of Divinity in the University of Oxford. His recent publications include *Christian Theology and Interreligious Dialogue* (SCM) and *Archetypal Heresy: Arianism through the Centuries* (OUP).

Foreword

Divine revelation is one of the most fundamental of all theological questions. We could even say that it is revelation rather than suffering (as Muriel Spark suggests) that is 'the only problem'. For if we could be clear about whether there is a revelation from God, where it is located, what form it takes and who has the authority to interpret it, all other theological problems could be quickly solved! That is precisely the approach of traditional scholastic theology, both Protestant and Roman Catholic, an approach that is still maintained by fundamentalist Protestants, who appeal to the bare text of Scripture without taking into account what biblical scholarship can tell us about its context and meaning, and by official Roman Catholic theology, promulgated by the Vatican. The latter maintains that the formal teaching of the Church's Magisterium, in explicating the content of original revelation, enjoys the same clarity and security as that original revelation and, moreover, that the tradition of the Church's teaching is unassailable by the conjectural conclusions of the historical–critical method.

Modern Christian theology, dating from Kant, Schleiermacher and Coleridge at the beginning of the nineteenth century, does not, however, find that 'knock down' appeal to revelation convincing. The answer that modern critical theology gives to this most basic of theological questions is somewhat more nuanced and tentative: modern theologians tend to concur that there is indeed a revelation from God, but that it is not of such a nature as to be clearly specifiable. You cannot pinpoint revelation: it is given through a history of the engagement of individuals and communities with God, from the patriarchs and prophets of ancient Israel to the apostles of the New Testament Church. It is embodied supremely and definitively in the person and ministry of Jesus Christ. However, the consensus is that we do not have direct, unmediated access to this original revelation; it is mediated to us through a body of literature – the Bible – that reflects the thought-forms of its time and is itself the product of a complex process of oral transmission of traditions and editorial redaction.

Although it has an overarching unity of theme – the wonderful works of the God of Israel and the Father of Jesus Christ – the Bible is marked by a chronic diversity of literary forms and theological standpoints.

Because revelation is given in these personal, historical and communal modes, we cannot say, 'Here is where revelation begins and here is where it stops; this is revelation but that is human interpretation.' Revelation, as it is understood in modern theology, for example in Rahner, Tillich or Pannenberg, is integrated with the whole of significant human experience and is not locked away in some hermetically sealed compartment. Modern theology is generally anti-dualistic and seeks for a holistic understanding of the truth of God. That does not mean that revelation can be reduced to human experience or to general human religiosity. Revelation takes place within the medium of experience (as it must), but – as Barth above all has reminded us – it transcends and judges that medium. Revelation remains elusive and mysterious, for it is always the action of a sovereign, transcendent God.

Although the question of revelation is recognised to be crucial, it has not received the attention commensurate with its strategic significance in theology. The ground-breaking dogmatic treatments of revelation by Barth, Rahner and Pannenberg, for example, are conducted at an advanced level of abstraction and sophistication and are definitely not for beginners. There are worthwhile discussions of the concept of revelation in modern theology, of varying length and profundity, by individual theologians, such as Abraham, Baillie, Gunton, Niebuhr, Thiemann and Ward. But there is a lack of comprehensive resources on this topic for the student of theology in universities, colleges and seminaries, for those attending training courses for the priesthood or ministry and for lay Christians and the interested private individual.

This volume, which has taken several years to prepare, aims to redress that deficiency. The distinguished contributors represent a spectrum of religious traditions and theological views from England, Scotland, Ireland, the United States of America and Canada. The aim is to provide biblical, historical, contemporary and reflective resources on the ways in which divine revelation has been previously understood in the history of Christian theology and is now understood in theological discussion. It is hoped that this book will enable the student to think constructively about this topic in a way that is conducive to a critical, informed and living faith.

Paul Avis, Editor
Stoke Canon Vicarage, Exeter, England

1

Biblical Concepts of Revelation

James D.G. Dunn

The Term 'Revelation'

According to the *Oxford English Dictionary*, the first or primary meaning
of the term 'revelation' is 'the disclosure or communication of knowledge
to man by a divine or supernatural agency'. This indicates the lasting
influence of the word's origin, that is, as a term borrowed directly from
the Latin *revelatio* ('uncovering, laying bare'). For the Latin gained its
particular significance from its use in the Vulgate and ecclesiastical Latin
to translate Greek *apokalypsis* ('revelation, disclosure'). And the Greek
is used typically in the New Testament to denote the unveiling, from
heaven or by divine agency, of hidden truths, particularly about God,
the cosmos and/or the future. Lying behind this usage in turn is an
understanding which pervades the Old Testament, that God has made
himself and his will known, and has done so most clearly to the people
chosen to be his people, Israel. This concept of 'revelation' runs consistently through both Testaments of the Christian Bible. So we can indeed
speak quite properly of '*biblical* concepts of revelation'.

The traditional way of analysing these concepts is to distinguish
'general' revelation from 'particular' or 'special' revelation. And this still
provides a useful indication of what we might call the spectrum of
revelation. Since it is the 'concept(s)' of revelation which is our primary
consideration we will be focusing on the *means* or *mediums* of revelation,
rather than on the *content* of revelation.

Revelation Through Nature/Creation

The spectrum begins with revelation through creation. Best known, but
typical of the attitude, are the words of the Psalmist (Ps. 19:1):

> The heavens are telling the glory of God;
> and the firmament proclaims his handiwork.

The words of the Psalmist are one of the earliest expressions of what came to be known as the teleological argument for the existence of God: the design and artistry manifest in creation speak clearly of the designer and artist who brought it about.

In the earlier Ps. 8:3–4, the response is one of awe and humility:

> When I look at your heavens, the work of your fingers,
> the moon and the stars that you have established;
> what are human beings that you are mindful of them,
> mortals that you care for them?

This early sense of humankind's littleness before a greatness vast beyond human comprehension is one which has often recurred in human history. More striking still is the psalmist's sense of God manifesting his power through the wonder and terror of a great storm (Pss. 18:6–15; 29; 77:16–18).

In the New Testament, Paul echoes the same basic conviction that God has made himself known through what he has made – most strikingly in Rom. 1:19–20:

> ... what can be known about God is evident to them [human beings]. For God has shown it to them. For the invisible attributes from the creation of the world are perceived rationally in the things which have been made, both his eternal power and deity, so that they are without excuse.

The thought is basically the same. God is not know-able in himself. But he has put something of himself into what he has made, so that something of God can be known through what he has created. Creation is, as it were, the 'shadow' cast by God, by means of which the Creator may to some extent be discerned. Presumably tied into this is the thought of humankind as 'the image of God' – homo sapiens as the highest form of creation reflects God more clearly than inanimate creation – though the precise significance of this 'image' language has never been finally clear.

The thought of Rom. 1:19–20, it should be noted, is by no means exclusively Jewish and Christian. On the contrary, Paul's language reflects insights and arguments which we find in Platonic and Stoic philosophy of the time – including the thought that divine reality can be 'rationally perceived', is 'visible to the eye of reason' (NEB). Some twentieth-century theologians have been unhappy with the thought of such a 'natural theology'. But a biblical theology need not be *exclusively* biblical in order to be genuinely biblical. As did others of their day, the biblical writers recognised that the cosmos requires an explanation which lies outside of itself; at the end of the day it is not self-explanatory. That this appears to be a 'reasonable' deduction is neither to undermine other claims to revelation, nor to over-exalt human reason.

At the same time a full theology of revelation would no doubt hope to be able to say more about God and his purpose for creation and for humankind. In comparison with the clearer light of particular revelation, creation may indeed be as a mere shadow. Nevertheless, Paul evidently thought, the outline of God's character and purpose can be discerned clearly enough through the cosmos as creation and by created beings. And discerned clearly enough to put the person who denies and ignores that insight (cosmos as creation) in the wrong – 'so that they are without excuse'. Here already we begin to touch on the moral consequences (for everyone) of acknowledging or failing to acknowledge the character of the world in which we live.

Revelation Through Providence and History

Revelation through providence is closely related to revelation through creation. Here the thought is not so much of the wonder and beauty of creation as of its provision for human need, and of the constitution of human society. The thought is most clearly expressed in the two speeches of Paul to Gentile audiences in the Acts of the Apostles.

First, in Lystra, Acts 14:15–17:

> The living God, who made the heavens and the earth and the sea and all that in them is . . . has not left himself without a witness in doing good – giving you rains from heaven and fruitful seasons, and filling you with food and your hearts with joy.

The passage is resonant with Old Testament language. 'The living God who made heaven and earth and the sea and everything that is in them' (14:15) is a classic expression of Jewish monotheism (Exod. 20:11; Neh. 9:6; Ps. 146:6). And the description of God's providential care (14:17) also echoes the typically (but again not exclusively) Jewish reflection on

God's goodness as expressed in the fruitfulness of creation (Lev. 26:4; Ps. 147:9; Jer. 5:24).

What again is worthy of note is the theological or moral corollary which the speech draws. Those who recognise God in those terms should also recognise (14:15) that neither is God like mortal human beings nor can he be adequately imaged in idols made of wood or stone ('worthless things' – Jer. 2:5; Wisd. 13). The abundance of nature's provision is image enough! Jesus too had earlier on drawn similar deductions regarding the character of God and of God's provision for human need by his well known reflection on the provision evidently made for 'the birds of the air' and 'the lilies of the field' (Matt. 6:25–31). It is interesting to note that here too the reflection is accompanied by a disparagement of 'the Gentiles who strive for all these things' (6:32). Earlier in the Sermon on the Mount he is also recalled as drawing deductions for social relationships and mutual obligations from the providence of sun and rain (Matt. 5:44–5).

The second Acts speech, in Athens itself, develops a closely related point (Acts 17:26–9), again echoing familiar Jewish beliefs. Humankind is made from one common stock (17:26; Gen. 1:27–8; 10:32), an idea less familiar in Greek thought. God fixed the seasons and the boundaries of the nations (17:26; Gen. 1:14; Deut. 32:8; Ps. 74:17; Wisd. 7:18). His objective was that they should seek God (17:27; Deut. 4:29; Isa. 55:6) – the point being, presumably, that only in relation to and dependence on this beneficent and overseeing God would they be able to recognise their status and function as individuals and peoples.

The verbs used in 17:27 ('if perhaps they might grope for him and find him') capture well the sense of uncertain reaching out in the dark of those moved and motivated by such considerations of natural theology (God at work in the world, but manifest thereby only in an obscure way). The world is full of people with such unformed and indistinct religious feelings and aspirations. Here more clearly than before we see both the affirmation of the positive role of general revelation but also an appreciation of its inadequacy.

The clinching consideration is that this Creator God has not created a hunger for God within humankind only to leave it unsatisfied (17:27–8). This same sovereign Lord 'is not far from each one of us'. Once again the thought is drawn immediately from the (Jewish) scriptures (Ps. 145:18; Jer. 23:23). But precisely at this point two sayings from Greek poets can be cited as voicing the same insight. The first has an unknown source: 'In him we live and move and are'. The second is drawn from the Stoic poet Aratus: 'For we too are his offspring' (*Phaenomena* 5).

4

Here again the similarity of Jewish and traditional Greek sentiments provides a bridge over which early Christian apologetic can cross. But here again the recognition of common ground is followed up by the theological and moral corollary, so fundamental to Jewish perception of God, that such a God can hardly be represented by images of gold, silver or stone, or indeed by any work of human imagination (17:29; Deut. 4:28; Isa. 40:18–19; 44:9–20; Wisd. 13:10). Even the most indistinct perception of God carries with it consequences for the understanding and ordering of life.

A more specific case of this form of revelation may be revelation through history. This was a popular theme in the middle of the century – 'the God who acts'. Particularly in mind here was the revelatory force of the exodus from Egypt and the provision of food and drink in the wilderness. Already this comes to expression in the ancient 'songs of Moses' (Ex. 15:1–18; Deut. 32) or in recital psalms like Pss. 78 and 105. The Christian equivalent is the revelatory significance of Jesus' death (and resurrection) described, not insignificantly in Luke 9:31, as Jesus' 'exodus'. Acts in particular develops the theme in terms of the divine purpose behind the events of salvation and the divine necessity for them to take place (Acts 1:16; 2:23; 3:21; 4:12, 28; etc).

At this point, however, we are already moving from general revelation to particular revelation. For in the case of providence, the appeal can be made to the experience of humankind generally. Whereas revelation through history makes a specific claim regarding particular people and individuals. This also means that more than in the case of providence, the revelation claimed in and through history requires an interpreting word. History by and large is even more ambiguous than providence by and large. In which case the revelation is better described as coming through event *and* word.

Revelation Through Moral Consciousness

A noteworthy feature of Ps. 19 is that it comes in two parts. The first, as we have seen, meditates on the revelatory voice of creation. The second lauds the revelatory force of the law – not least its role in warning against wrong conduct and informing the conscience (19:11–12). For the psalmist, the two obviously went hand in hand; both were important in providing instruction as to the character of God and of his will for humankind; like Kant he was filled with wonder and awe at these two

5

things, 'the starry heaven above me and the moral law within me'. It is the latter to which we now turn.

To speak of the law itself would mean a major jump along the spectrum of revelation. The point here, however, is that the writers of the Old Testament recognised that a law which was external to individuals would in itself never be enough. For knowledge and performance of God's law to be effective it was necessary for the law to be written in the heart. This is the point already being made in Deut. 30:11–14: 'the word is very near to you; it is in your mouth and in your heart for you to observe'. And the importance of the point is reinforced in the famous promise of 'a new covenant' in Jer. 31: 'I will put my law within them, and I will write it on their hearts . . .' (Jer. 31:33). The equivalent point was made by the same authors in insisting that circumcision of the flesh was not enough; what really counted was circumcision of the heart (Deut. 10:16; Jer. 4:4). What should be noted here is that this experience of an 'inner law' was not something anticipated only in the future. Deut. 30:14 witnesses to a reality already known in the present. And the same feature of at least some Old Testament piety is clearly enough attested in Psalms like 19:7–14 and penitential psalms like Ps. 51 – as clear an expression of moral consciousness as one could look for.

In the New Testament it is once again Paul who bears clearest testimony to the fact and importance of moral consciousness within humankind generally. In Rom. 2:14–15 he speaks of 'Gentiles who do not have the law', but who nevertheless 'do by nature what the law requires', and who can therefore be said to be

the law for themselves, who demonstrate the business of the law written in their hearts, their conscience also bearing witness, while their thoughts bring accusation or even make defence among themselves.

The line of reflection here obviously follows on from the earlier thought of humankind having some knowledge of God (1:19, 21). And again it shares the wider sensitivity on the part of the Stoics that there is a universal or 'unwritten law' by which humans can live, that 'right reason' should serve as the rule of life. What is particularly interesting at this point is Paul's use of the term 'conscience'. It was a term which belonged more to Greek usage than to Hebrew thought. But it had begun to come into usage in the writings of Greek-speaking Jews, usually in terms of consciousness of wrongdoing (as in Wisd. 17:11). So elsewhere in Paul (e.g. 1 Cor. 8:7, 10, 12), though it also occurs in the more positive sense of a good conscience, that is, a moral consciousness lacking the painful sense that one's attitude or action is wrong (e.g. Rom. 9:1; 2 Cor. 1:12).

What should also not be ignored here is Paul's clear sense that this consciousness of what is good and bad, right and wrong, is a sufficient ground on which final judgement can be made on a human life. Paul ends his indictment of human conduct in Rom. 1:18–32 with the sobering comment (1:32):

> Although they (human beings in general) have known the just decree of God, that those who practise such things deserve death, they not only do the same but approve of those who practise them.

And the vivid trial scene in 2:15–16 makes the same point. There is in humankind and society generally what might be called a 'natural' sense of moral responsibility. The conflict of conscience, the conflict within the human heart, bears abundant testimony that the human being is not autonomous, but recognises, however unwillingly, an obligation to a higher power and a greater authority. Whether we speak of such consciousness as 'revelation', as 'the voice of God within', the fact remains that the biblical writers regarded it as having equivalent force in the evaluation of human character and conduct.

Revelation Through Wisdom

Wisdom has a role similar to that of moral consciousness in the spectrum of revelation. For it is evident from the proverbial wisdom of Proverbs and Ecclesiasticus, not to mention many of the aphorisms and epigrams of Jesus, that much wisdom is the fruit of long experience of human character and society – the wisdom of the ages. It is well known, for example, that Prov. 22:17–23:14 is most probably drawn from an earlier Eygptian wisdom collection (*Teaching of Amenemope*). As something of God may be 'read off' creation, so valuable lessons about right living and good practice can be drawn by those who have long experience of human foibles, ambition, social policy, manipulation, and so on. That is why ancient societies usually linked wisdom with age: the elders should be respected for their wisdom, that is, because they were able to advise their younger citizens or compatriots by virtue of their great experience.

Examples of such wisdom are easily given:

Prov. 10:19: 'When words are many, transgression is not lacking; but the prudent are restrained in speech.'

Prov. 12:1: 'Whoever loves discipline loves knowledge, but those who hate to be rebuked are stupid.'

Prov. 15:1: 'A soft answer turns away wrath, but a harsh word stirs up anger.'

Ecclus. 9:10: 'Do not abandon old friends, for new ones cannot equal them. A new friend is like new wine; when it has aged, you can drink it with pleasure.'

Ecclus 13:1: 'Whoever touches pitch gets dirty, and whoever associates with a proud person becomes like him.'

Matt. 6:21: 'Where your treasure is, there your heart will be also.'

Matt. 6:27: 'Can any one of you by worrying add a single hour to your span of life?'

Matt. 7:18: 'A good tree cannot bear bad fruit, nor can a bad tree bear good fruit.'

Such wisdom can properly be placed within the spectrum of revelation, because, like conscience, it bears testimony to the moral constitution of society. That is to say, the fact that such lessons not only can be but are drawn by human beings testifies to the given character of human beings and human society; they have been created thus. Which is also to say that the wisdom thus expressed unveils (reveals) the moral character of the personal and social structure of God's creation. That presumably is why in the wisdom literature of the Old Testament and in the wisdom teaching of Jesus there is no clear distinction between human wisdom and divinely given wisdom within the range of wisdom taught therein.

That being said, however, one of the most important features of the biblical wisdom tradition is the conviction that there is a higher (or deeper) wisdom than simply the wisdom of human experience. Humans sense this and search for it. But it is beyond their reach. It can only be given from without, from God. The poem in Job 28 is a powerful expression of this sense of frustration at human inability to attain this wisdom and of recognition that God alone can provide it. Human beings can uncover the most deeply hidden of nature's resources (Job 28:1–11).

> But where shall wisdom be found?
> And where is the place of understanding?
> Mortals do not know the way to it,
> and it is not found in the land of the living.
> The deep says, 'It is not in me',
> and the sea says, 'It is not with me'.
> It cannot be got for gold,
> and silver cannot be weighed out as its price. . . .
> It is hidden from the eyes of all living (Job 28:12–21).

Then comes the denounement:

> God understands the way to it,
> and he knows its place. . . .
> And he said to humankind,
> Truly, the fear of the Lord, that is wisdom;
> and to depart from evil is understanding (Job 28:23–8).

The intertestamental book Baruch expresses the same conviction regarding wisdom:

> Who has gone up into heaven, and taken her,
> and brought her down from the clouds?
> Who has gone over the sea, and found her,
> and will buy her for pure gold?
> No one knows the way to her,
> or is concerned about the path to her.
> But the one who knows all things knows her,
> he found her by his understanding (Baruch 3:29–32).

In the New Testament we find the equivalent sentiments in Matt. 11:25 and 1 Cor. 2.

> Jesus said, 'I thank you, Father, Lord of heaven and earth, because you have hidden these things from the wise and the intelligent and have revealed them to infants' (Matt. 11:25).

Here again we find the recognition that the acquiring of real wisdom is not a matter of human achievement or human ability. Its channels are different from those of human media; humanly judged success might prove in the event to be a barrier to it (similarly James 1:5).

9

In his penetrating treatment of wisdom in 1 Cor. 1–2 Paul presses the point still more strongly. There is a human wisdom which is actually unable to comprehend divine wisdom, since the two operate on different scales of value (1 Cor. 1:17–2:5). At the same time, there is a 'secret and hidden wisdom of God', which 'God has revealed to us through the Spirit; for the Spirit searches everything, even the depths of God . . .' (1 Cor. 2:6–16). Here again we find the same testimony: there is a wisdom which the world values, a wisdom measured by polished rhetoric and social status; but there is also a wisdom from God which illuminates the eyes of the spiritually discerning to the relative values of the two wisdoms (similarly James 3:13–18).

Where shall this wisdom be found? Here the two streams of biblical testimony diverge. On the one hand, it is clear from a passage like Deut. 30:11–14, as indeed from the very structure of the Jewish scriptures (the Old Testament), that the Torah (the Law) is to be seen as the epitome or expression of that Wisdom. The claim is explicit in the intertestamental books, Ecclesiasticus and Baruch:

> All this [regarding Wisdom] is the book of the covenant of the Most High God, the law that Moses commanded us as an inheritance for the congregations of Jacob (Ecclus. 24:23).

> She [wisdom] is the book of the commandments of God,
> the law that endures for ever.
> All who hold her fast will live,
> and those who forsake her will die.
>
> (Baruch 4:1)

This is a conviction which the New Testament writers share in turn. Hence the continued positive evaluation of the law, not only in passages like Matt. 5:17–20 and James 2:8–26, but also in Paul (despite popular views to the contrary), in such passages as Rom. 3:31, 8:4 and 1 Cor. 7:19.

At the same time, however, the first Christians were clear that the revelatory force of divine Wisdom expressed in and through the Law had been overtaken or eclipsed by the fuller revelation in Christ. And to that claim we must turn in due course.

10

Revelation Through Inspiration/Prophecy

The overlap between traditional wisdom and wisdom given by God takes us beyond the transition point in the spectrum to what we might call revelation proper, revelation as it has been understood historically. With prophecy we are firmly on that further side – prophecy as inspired speech, as the uttering of words crafted not by human artifice but coming to and through the mind unbidden, or in a word, prophecy as revelation (1 Cor. 14:6, 30). Of course, the experience of inspiration can today be interpreted as a welling up from the subconscious of unconscious impressions or folk archetypes. But inspiration, whether artistic or religious, is usually experienced as from without, often with a sense of commission. The point is worth making at the outset, since the concept of 'prophecy' has often been elided in discussion of the subject into preaching or even into merely bold, politically controversial comment. But in biblical terms, prophecy is nothing if it is not inspired speech.

This character of prophecy was established early on within the history of Israel. It is typified by the archetypal figure of Balaam, who was repeatedly instructed to prophesy against Israel, but who in the event could only speak what was given him to speak (Num. 23–24): 'Must I not take care to say what the Lord puts in my mouth?'; 'What the Lord says, that is what I will say' (Num 23:12; 24:13). So too when prophecy emerged within Israel itself it was as ecstatic prophecy, words uttered in a state of ecstasy (1 Sam. 10:5; 19:20–4), where by means of music and probably dancing the prophet laid himself open to the Spirit that spoke through him. Later on there seems to have been some reaction against the potential abuse of prophecy so conceived, so that in Israel's classical prophets the inspiration is attributed to the hand of the Lord (e.g. Isa. 8:11; Jer. 15:17; Ezek. 1:3) or the word of the Lord (e.g. Isa 38:4; Jer. 1:2, 4, 11, 13; Ezek. 1:3; 3:16; Hos. 1:1; Joel 1:1; Mic. 1:1) but the sense of divine compulsion to speak what one was bidden is still as clear.

> The lion has roared; who will not fear?
> The Lord God has spoken; who can but prophesy?
>
> (Amos 3:8)

> 'Whenever I said, "I will call him to mind no more,
>   nor speak in his name again",
> then his word was imprisoned in my body,

11

like a fire blazing in my heart,
and I was weary with holding it under,
and could endure no more'

(Jer. 20:9)

It is interesting to observe that Paul's discussion of charisms in 1 Corinthians focuses principally on the different kinds of verbal inspiration – speaking in tongues, where the inspiration bypassed the mind (a form of ex-stasy), and prophecy, where the inspiration engages the mind also (1 Cor. 14:13–19).

The religion of the Bible is through and through prophetic in character. That is to say, it is understood to have been given by God, a religion of revelation. It is largely, though by no means exclusively, a religion of words. And the most essential words are inspired words – insights regarding God, human society and the practice of religion which were not merely the sum or climax of human wisdom, but which were understood from the first as given by divine inspiration. The point is enshrined in the characterisation of Moses, the undisputed founder of Israel's religion, as himself a prophet – one in whose mouth God put his words, one who spoke everything that God commanded (Deut. 18:18). No room was to be left for any suggestion that within Israel's religion law and prophecy could be posed as competing principles.

For the first Christians, it could be said, however, that Israel's prophetic tradition was the more important. Central to their convictions and apologetic regarding Jesus was the claim that he had fulfilled the prophetic hope of Israel. Hence Matthew's repeated formulation: 'this happened in order that what was spoken through the prophet might be fulfilled' (Matt. 1:22; 2:5, 15, 17, 23; etc.). Hence too the climax of Luke's gospel where the risen Jesus begins with Moses and all the prophets and interprets to his bewildered disciples all the things about himself in the scriptures (Luke 24:27, 44–5). Equally significant is Luke's characterisation of the Pentecost experience as the fulfilment of Joel's prophecy – Acts 2:17–18:

In the last days it will be, God declares,
that I will pour out my Spirit upon all flesh,
and your sons and your daughters shall prophesy . . .
in those days I will pour out my Spirit;
and they shall prophesy.

Luke's addition to Joel's text of the second '[they] shall prophesy'

12

emphasises the point 'the new movement of Jesus' disciples fulfils the ancient aspiration of Moses himself: 'Would that all God's people were prophets, and that the Lord would put his spirit on them' (Num. 11:29). Nor is it either accidental or surprising that Paul should value prophecy as the most prized of spiritual gifts (1 Cor. 14:1), or that Eph. 2:20 should describe the Church, 'the household of God', as 'built upon the foundation of the apostles and prophets, with Christ Jesus himself as the cornerstone'. In such passages there is the deliberate claim both that Christianity is in full continuity with the religion of Israel and that this religion is essentially prophetic in character.

We should not ignore the fact that there is something unnerving about such dependence of a religion so directly on revelation, on prophecy. For, by definition, such a religion is not easily contained within regular structures and rubrics. The episode just alluded to, in Num. 11:16–30, makes the point archetypally: the order and administration of the assembly of God must allow for the Spirit of prophecy to fall upon others not included within the ordered structure. The religion of Israel must allow for an Amos to be called to prophesy, despite his lack of official recognition ('no prophet') or training ('nor a prophet's son') (Amos 7:14–15). So too Jesus was called upon to justify the authority with which he acted (Mark 11:27–33), and Paul had to defend his claim to apostolic status because of its unprecedented character (1 Cor. 15: 8–10; Gal. 1:11–12).

At the same time the biblical tradition is acutely conscious of the danger that inspiration/revelation may be misconceived or falsely claimed. Throughout the Bible the recognition that prophecy is crucial is accompanied by the recognition of the danger of false prophecy (e.g. Jer. 23:16). Tests which clearly distinguish true from false are not easy to come by: the false prophecy might be very similar to the true (cf. Deut. 13:2 with 18:22); and the issue would not often be so clear-cut as in Mic. 3:5. Classic illustrations of the difficulty of discerning aright are given in 1 Kings 22 and Jer. 28. In Matt. 7:22 Jesus gives a similarly sobering warning. And the problem continued through and beyond the New Testament, as we see in 1 John 4:1–3 and Didache 11.

It is noteworthy, then, that Paul who valued prophecy so highly, was also so sensitive on this point too. Prophecy must be accompanied by 'discernment' (1 Cor. 12:10). When one prophet prophesied, the rest should evaluate what had been said (1 Cor. 14:29). The Spirit should not be quenched; prophecy should not be despised; but everything (said) should be tested, and only what was good should be retained (1 Thes. 5:19–22). As examples of the tests which he himself used we can refer to 1 Cor. 12–14, where in succession he uses the confession of Jesus' lordship, the character of love, and the upbuilding of the assembly, as tests which determine the reality and value of claims to inspiration and charism (1 Cor. 12:3; 13; 14:3, 5, 12, 26).

Revelation in the form of prophecy, revelation as inspired utterance, thus stands at the very heart of biblical religion, at the centre of the spectrum of the biblical concept of revelation. In consequence it follows that a perennial question which any religion claiming to be rooted in the Bible must ask itself is whether its theology and praxis still gives expression to that insight as a living truth. Is it enough to claim that the Spirit of prophecy came to a definitive expression in scripture or even in scripture and tradition? Can a prophetic religion survive unless it is open to the Spirit of prophecy to inspire afresh and to reveal new things?

'I still have many things to say to you, but you cannot bear them now. When the Spirit of truth comes, he will guide you into all the truth; for he will not speak on his own, but will speak whatever he hears, and he will declare to you the things that are to come' (John 16:12–13).

'Pursue love and strive for the spiritual gifts, and especially that you may prophesy ... [for] those who prophesy build up the church' (1 Cor. 14:1–4).

Revelation Through Dream and Vision and Apocalypse

The idea of prophecy as inspired speech merges into the idea of revelation proper, that is the unveiling of things that were previously hidden, the opening of eyes to see what had previously been unseen. To the prophet was given the privilege of standing in the council of the Lord (Jer. 23:18), to see visions (e.g. Jer. 1:11–12; Amos 7:1–9), even of the Lord himself (1 Kings 22:19–23; Amos 9:1).

Revelation in this sense is itself a spectrum. At one end we can speak of an intellectual illumination. Thus, for example, in Ps. 119:18 the psalmist prays, 'Open my eyes, so that I may behold wondrous things out of your law'. And in 2 Cor. 3:14 the image is of a veil which lies over the minds of those who read Moses being taken away so that new truth can be seen. Or the thought can be of a revelation which gives guidance at a point of decision (as in 1 Sam. 9:15 and Gal. 2:2). This presumably is the sort of revelation which Paul had in mind when he spoke of revelation (through prophecy) in the assembly (1 Cor. 14:6, 26, 30), or in the prayer for a 'spirit of wisdom and of revelation' (Eph. 1:17). At the other end of the spectrum could be placed eschatological revelation – both in positive terms, when 'the earth shall be full of the knowledge of the Lord as the waters cover the sea' (Isa. 11:9), and in negative terms, when the day of the Lord would bring an unexpected and unwelcome revelation in judgement (classically expressed in Amos 5:18–20). One of Jesus' more enigmatic aphorisms points in the same direction (Mark 4:22/Luke 8:17; Matt. 10:26/Luke 12:2). And Paul similarly looks toward a final unveiling, in both positive (Rom. 8:18–19; 1 Cor. 1:7; 2 Thes. 1:7; cf. 1 Pet. 1:5, 7, 13; 4:13; 5:1) and negative terms (Rom. 2:5; 1 Cor. 3:13; 2 Thes. 2:8).

Characteristic within this inner spectrum is the idea of revelation through dream and vision. Israel did not follow the more typical pattern of other religions in seeking revelation through omens and auguries. Dependence on the mysterious 'Urim and Thummim' and on lots is limited to the early days of both Israel's religion and Christianity (Exod. 28:30; 1 Sam. 14:41–2; Acts 1:26). Presumably it is no coincidence that revelations of God as such (theophanies) early on seem to have been conceived in tangible ways – the anthropomorphisms in the garden (Gen. 3), the angel of the Lord (Gen. 16:7–12; 21:17; 31:11; Judg. 2:1), the theophanies in the burning bush and at Sinai (Exod. 3:2; 19:16–25; 24:9–11). We may contrast the more subtly conceived self-revelation of God already to Moses in Exod. 33:17–23, and subsequently to Elijah (1 Kings 19:11–12). The vision of God from early on was regarded as the climax of religious experience (Exod. 33:18; Pss. 17:15; 42:2), but was granted only occasionally, as in the visions of Isaiah (Isa. 6) and Ezekiel (Ezek. 1:26–8) which served as archetypes for subsequent mysticism.

At the same time, however, Israel and early Christianity seem never to have lost faith in an understanding of revelation through dream and vision. From early Old Testament tradition we may cite the paradigmatic dream of Jacob in Gen. 28:10–22. But equally at the far end we have a Joel who prophesies that 'your old men shall dream dreams and your young men shall see visions' (Joel 2:28), and a Daniel whose chief fame was as an interpreter of dreams (Dan. 2; 4; 5:12). And in earliest Christianity, Acts has no qualms about narrating how important developments in his account of Christian beginnings stemmed directly from dreams (e.g. Acts 9:10–16; 10:1–16; 16:9–10), and Paul freely confesses to his many visions and revelations from the Lord (2 Cor. 12:1, 7). It is a somewhat sobering thought to recall that it took the rise of psychology to help a more 'modernist' world to re-appreciate that dreams can have a significance beyond that of a disturbed night. At the same time we should recall that revelation could come equally through the sights and experiences of everyday life – the potter at his wheel (Jer. 18:1–11), Hosea in his tragic marriage, the parables of Jesus.

More characteristic and distinctive of Israel is the claim that God revealed himself through his name. As the brief account of Exod. 6:2–8 makes clear, Israel's sense of a special calling from God and covenant with God was bound up with the revelation of his name YHWH. It was precisely in his character as YHWH that God had committed himself to Israel (Ezek. 20:9), and precisely his obligation (righteousness) as YHWH that he sustain and vindicate his people (e.g. Ps. 98:2; 143:11; Isa. 45:21; 63:1, 7). It is this sense of God revealing his righteousness as an act of salvation which Paul took over directly in his own great account of God's righteousness in Romans (Rom. 1:17; 3:21).

Particularly important is the link between revelation and mystery, revelation as the unveiling of a mystery. It is already suggested in the thought of Deut. 29:29. But it comes to clearest expression in Daniel – 'God is .. a revealer of mysteries' (Dan. 2:28–9) – especially in the belief that the chief mystery previously hidden and now to be revealed is that concerning the unfolding of God's purposes in and for the future. The claim that God's hidden purpose had thus been revealed was common to both the Qumran community (e.g. 1QS 3:23; 4:18; 1QpHab. 7:5) and to the first Christians (Rom. 16:26; 1 Cor. 2:7). Notable is Paul's claim that he had been specially privileged in this respect. To him had been made known the mystery of God's purpose (from the first) to include Gentiles with Jews in his salvation, and to Paul had been given the privilege of preaching this gospel to the Gentiles (Rom. 11:25; Eph. 3:1–11; Col. 1:25–7).

It is this concept of revelation which gives its name to a whole genre of literature – the apocalypse. It is not unimportant to remind ourselves that 'apocalypse' means 'revelation' – hence the alternative names, the Apocalypse/Revelation of John. For the derivative term 'apocalyptic' has been a much abused term during the twentieth century. In popular usage it tends to evoke horrific images of catastrophe, the catastrophe expected to bring the present age (or the world itself) to an end. But, to repeat, the principal term ('apocalypse') means primarily the unveiling of heavenly mysteries. So the visions seen in a typical apocalypse include insights into how the cosmos functions, though it is true that the most striking and memorable visions in most apocalypses are those which preview the future and not least the eschaton (end). Only one apocalypse proper found its way into each of the two Testaments – Daniel and Revelation – but these are part of a sequence of texts from the overlapping period of early Christianity and early Judaism which include different tracts attributed to Enoch (1 Enoch) as well as documents known as 4 Ezra (= 2 Esdras 3–14 in the Apocrypha) and 2 Baruch.

Such an understanding of revelation is as unnerving for most Jews and Christians as is ecstatic prophecy. But the fact that it was found important to retain an apocalypse within both canons of scripture is a salutary reminder that religion needs to allow room for the apocalyptic. Among its more positive features are the power to fire jaded imaginations and the affirmation that reality should not be limited to what is visible, that the driving force behind history is God's purpose, that the present has to be evaluated in the light of the future, and that humans are ultimately responsible before a higher court. It is no surprise, then, that within the history of the West, it has been from within apocalyptic that the seeds of revolution have most often sprung. Like fire, an apocalyptic spirit will be a better servant than master.

The Revelation of Christ

Quite where this final form of revelation is to be located on the spectrum of revelation is not immediately clear. It is the only mode of revelation which is not fully shared between the Testaments and between Jews and Christians. But it is biblical in another sense in that, from a Christian perspective at least, the revelation of Christ sums up in itself all the other forms of revelation. Or to be more precise, from a Christian perspective, the revelation of Christ is the climax of all previous revelation and the key to making sense of all other revelation.

The point is most immediately obvious with regard to prophecy. The first Christians were convinced that Jesus was the fulfilment of Israel's expectation for a messianic saviour. We have already noted, for example, how much weight Matthew put on the repeated formulation, 'in order that what was spoken through the prophet might be fulfilled' in his version of the good news of Jesus. It evidently mattered little that Jesus had not fulfilled all messianic expectations: after all, the popular expectation of the royal Messiah was that he would be a warrior figure who would restore Israel as a nation by force of arms. Not surprisingly, then, an early concern of Christian apologetic was to demonstrate that Jesus fulfilled prophecies which had not previously been recognised as such – particularly as a messiah who would carry out his saving role

17

through his own suffering (e.g. Acts 17:3; 1 Pet. 1:11). At the same time it is worth noticing that the category of 'prophet' was little used in reference to Jesus (cf. Luke 24:19; John 4:19; 6:14); it was early on perceived to be inadequate to spell out the full significance of the revelation which was Christ.

Similarly the claim is deeply rooted within the New Testament that Jesus was the fulfilment and climax of God's providential purpose from the beginning. The claim probably goes back to Jesus himself: Mark was able to begin his summary of Jesus' preaching with the words, 'The time is fulfilled' (Mark 1:15). In the Areopagus speech in Acts Paul moves quickly from the common ground of Jewish scripture and Stoic poet to his principal assertion, that God

> has fixed a day on which he will have the world judged in righteousness by a man whom he has appointed, and of this he has given assurance to all by raising him from the dead (Acts 17:31).

Paul himself trumpets Jesus' mission of redemption as happening 'when the fulness of time had come' (Gal. 4:4). And the 'mystery' which is unveiled in Col. 1:27 is 'Christ in you, the hope of glory', 'God's mystery, that is, Christ himself' (2:2), 'the mystery of Christ' (Eph. 3:4).

A number of New Testament authors use what has been called a 'revelation-schema', centring on the verb *phanerousthai* ('to be manifested, appear'). The verb regularly has the connotation of a manifesting of what was previously hidden (e.g. Mark 4:22; John 1:31; Rom. 16:26; Col. 1:26). Consequently when used of Christ, particularly in 1 Pet. 1:20; Heb. 9:26 and 1 Tim. 3:16, the implication is that Christ himself, and not merely his message, was a revelation of what had previously been hidden. This is usually taken to mean that Christ himself had previously been hidden, in a pre-existence unknown to God's creation. But the motif could simply be a way of speaking about the hidden purpose of God now manifested in and as Christ (cf. Eph. 1:4–5; 1 Tim. 1:9–10; Tit. 1:2–3).

The more striking indication that Christ is the revelatory key which makes sense of all God's mighty acts, from the beginning, is given in the identification of Christ with divine Wisdom. As we have seen, the Jewish wisdom tradition solved the problem of the hiddenness of divine wisdom by identifying it with the Torah. The first Christians took the still bolder step of seeing this wisdom most clearly expressed in Christ. The claim is most strikingly made in 1 Corinthians, where the wisdom of the world and the wisdom of fine rhetoric is contrasted with the foolish wisdom of God displayed in the cross (1 Cor. 1:18–31). The foolishness of the cross is both revelation and revolution: it turns upside down the normal standards of success and status; it becomes a wholly different measure of value.

And Paul does not hesitate to press the point in referring to Christ the place and role in creation usually assigned to Wisdom in the wisdom writers (Prov. 8:22–31; Ecclus. 24:1–22). The one God created all things 'through' Christ (1 Cor. 8:6);

> 'he is the image of the invisible God, the firstborn of creation; for in him all things in heaven and on earth were created . . . all things have been created through him and for him' (Col. 1:15–16).

For those who understood that Wisdom was a way of speaking of the character of creation, the claim was far-reaching. Christ now spoke the message of the created world still more clearly; he now embodied most fully that image of the Creator which had been so obscured by the creature's disobedience; salvation could now be seen as the fulfilment of, not as escape from, the created world. Even more, for those who understood well enough that the figure of divine Wisdom was a way of speaking of God's self-manifestation, the claim was spectacular. Christ was now to be seen as the fullest expression of God's self-revelation; he could be recognised as 'the human face of God'; he showed as no one and nothing had previously done what God was like; he made visible the invisible God.

It was evidently also important for the first Christians to affirm that both 'comings' or 'appearings' of Christ have revelatory significance. This is part of an answer to the problem of the prophecies unfulfilled by Christ. The point is that the full revelation/revelatory significance of Christ for history and for human existence will only become clear in the end and from the perspective of the end. The unclarity which remains regarding his first coming, not least in what it means for Israel, will only be finally resolved by his coming again (Rom. 11:25–7). In this connection it is worthy of note that while the terminology of 'revelation' proper (*apokalupto, apokalypsis*) is used in reference to the initial impact of Christ (Gal. 1:12, 16; 3:23), its most common use in the New Testament is of the final 'revelation of Christ' (particularly Luke 17:30; 1 Cor. 1:7; 2 Thes. 1:7; 1 Pet. 1:7, 13). In the same spirit it is Christ who is identified as the central figure in the Apocalypse of John – the 'one like a son of man' (Rev. 1:12–18), 'the lamb slaughtered from the foundation of the world' (13:8), 'the Alpha and Omega, the first and the last, the beginning and the end' (22:13). The revelatory significance of Christ at the mid-point of history spans the full stretch of time from beginning to end.

Of all the New Testament writings it is John's Gospel which brings out most fully and clearly the force of Jesus as the revelation of God (though the claim is foreshadowed in the Johannine-like Matt. 11:27/ Luke 10:22). It is sometimes said that all that the Jesus of John reveals is that he is the revealer. But such a claim is inaccurate: what the Johannine Jesus reveals is *God*. As the Logos (Word), like Wisdom, he reveals the mind of God in creation (John 1:1–4). As the descending Son of Man he reveals the secrets of heaven (3:11–13). In his healing and teaching he shows what the Father's works are (5:19–21; 10:32). As the Son sent from heaven he reveals the Father (6:46; 14:9). As the first Paraclete he sends the other Paraclete who will guide into all the truth (16:13). As the summoner of disciples he makes known God's name (17:6). As the 'I am' in repeated self-affirmations he expresses the character of God. Thematic for the whole Gospel is the climax to the prologue: 'No one has ever seen God. It is God the only Son, who is close to the Father's heart, who has expounded him' (1:18).

The Biblical Concept of Revelation

We can therefore speak of biblical concepts of revelation which run across both Testaments, or perhaps better, across both Bibles. Apart from the last section, the above outline applies equally to Tanak (Old Testament) as to New Testament. The traditional Jewish/Israelite conception of revelation is the same as the Christian conception. The Christian conception arises out of and remains thoroughly rooted in the ancient Hebrew conceptions. Jew and Christian alike, on the basis of their common scriptures, will want to recognise revelation of God in creation, in providence, in the moral law within, in the wisdom of tradition, in the law and the prophets. But also, and still more clearly, but always in positive interaction with the preceding revelation, in the wisdom that comes from above, in inspired prophecy, in the revelation of what had previously been hidden.

For Christians, however, more or less by definition, there will always be the still clearer, more definitive and normative revelation of Christ. Here too what is of particular interest is the degree to which this revelation partly dovetailed with and partly went beyond or superseded what had previously been recognised to have revelatory force. Presumably if the revelation of Christ had been wholly and solely in line with previous expectation it would not have required any break between the movement which took Christ's name and its Jewish heritage. And if, alternatively, the revelation of Christ had broken completely with that heritage there would have been no question of Christianity even retaining the Jewish scriptures (the Old Testament) as its own. What is so fascinating about the very concept of a biblical revelation of which Christ is a prominent (supreme?) part is precisely the reality and degree of the continuity and discontinuity between the two parts of the (Christian) Bible. At the very least, Jesus (the event of Christ) functions for Christians as the revelatory key to scripture, the illumination in whose light all earlier (and subsequent claims to) revelation are read; it is 'in Christ' that the veil is removed from the eyes of the one who reads the earlier revelation (2 Cor. 3:14).

And if the New Testament writers are correct, the revelatory significance of Christ is still the greater. For he not only unveils the meaning of the earlier scriptures. He also unveils the character of God's creation and God's purpose and God's future. Most significant of all, he makes visible the invisible God; he makes God known. In him the greatest mystery of all is revealed.

For Further Reading

Anderson, B.W., (ed.), *Creation in the Old Testament*, London, 1984.

Ashton, J., *Understanding the Fourth Gospel*, Oxford, Clarendon, 1991.

Aune, D., *Prophecy in Early Christianity and the Ancient Mediterranean World*, Grand Rapids, Eerdmans, 1983.

Barr, J., 'Revelation in History', *Interpreter's Dictionary of the Bible*, supplementary volume, Nashville, Abingdon, 1976, pp.746–9

Bockmuehl, M.N.A., *Revelation and Mystery in Ancient Judaism and Pauline Christianity*, WUNT 2.36, Tübingen, Mohr-Siebeck, 1990.

Brown, R.E., *The Semitic Background of the Term 'Mystery' in the New Testament*, Philadelphia, Fortress Facet Book, 1968.

Bultmann, R., 'The Concept of Revelation in the New Testament' (1929), *Existence and Faith*, London, Collins Fontana, 1964, pp.67–106.

Childs, B.S., *Old Testament Theology in a Canonical Context*, London, SCM, 1985, chs.3–4.

Dentan, R.C., *The Knowledge of God in Ancient Israel*, New York, 1968.

Downing, F.G., *Has Christianity a Revelation?*, London, SCM, 1964.

Dunn, J.D.G., *Christology in the Making: An Inquiry into the Origins of the Doctrine of the Incarnation*, London, SCM, 1980, ²1989.

Gärtner, B., *The Areopagus Speech and Natural Revelation*, Uppsala, Almqvist & Wiksells, 1955.

Gruenwald, I., *Apocalyptic and Merkavah Mysticism*, Leiden, Brill, 1980.

Harrington, W., (ed.), *Witness to the Spirit: Essays on Revelation, Spirit, Redemption*, Irish Biblical Association, Koinonia, 1978, including essays on Revelation in the OT (J.R. Bartlett) and NT (S. Freyne).

Hill, D., *New Testament Prophecy*, London, Marshall, Morgan & Scott, 1979.

Pannenberg, W., (ed.), *Revelation as History*, New York, 1968.

Rahner, K., 'Revelation', *Sacramentum Mundi: An Encyclopedia of Theology*, vol.5, New York, 1969.

Robinson, H.W., *Inspiration and Revelation in the Old Testament*, Oxford, Clarendon, 1946.

Rowland, C., *The Open Heaven: A Study of Apocalyptic in Judaism and Early Christianity*, London, SPCK, 1982.

Rowley, H.H., *The Faith of Israel*, London, SCM, 1956, ch.1.

Rylaarsdam, J.C., *Revelation in Jewish Wisdom Literature*, University of Chicago, 1946.

Scott, E.F., *The New Testament Idea of Revelation*, London, Ivor Nicholson & Watson, 1935.

Wright, G.E., *God Who Acts*, London, SCM, 1952.

2

Revelation in the Theology of the Roman Catholic Church

Gabriel Daly

'For Scholasticism, whether in its original form or as modified by teachers of our own time, the concept of Revelation as the supernatural and infallible communication of propositional truths is indispensable'.[1] Thus wrote John Martin Creed, observing Roman Catholic theology in 1938. Few Roman Catholic apologists – and it was an age of combative apologetics – would have quarrelled with Creed's description of revelation as it was understood in mainline Roman Catholic theology in the period between the two Vatican councils. Not only was the theology of revelation propositional and deductive, it formed a basic segment of fundamental theology, which was then constructed along strongly apologetical lines. Only thirty years later another external observer could write, 'Roman Catholic theology today is catching up with Protestant theology; it is no longer sure of what it means by revelation'.[2] The startling divergence between these two estimations can be explained mainly by the fact that the second Vatican council had met in the interim.

Assessments of the decisive character of the council range from enthusiastic approval to Marcel Lefebvre's sour verdict on it as 'the worst tragedy that the Church has ever experienced'. No one denies its radical effect, for good or ill, on Roman Catholic life and theology. The second Vatican council is central to the theme of this essay, not merely because it issued an important document on revelation, but mainly because it constitutes an historical axis for any treatment of Roman Catholic attitudes. The council marks a decisive break with an imposed theology which was uniform and monolithic and which was deployed within a system that has been appositely called 'integralist', in that it was presented and defended as a composite dogmatic system of which no part could be altered without danger to the whole. The principal reason for the change from theological uniformity to pluriformity is not decentralisation of Church government (conciliar teaching on collegiality remains largely a dead letter), but the abandonment of neo-Scholasticism as an explicit criterion of orthodoxy. The rise and fall of mandatory Thomism is central to our theme.[3]

The Middle Ages

Revelation was not a prominent category in medieval theology. When it was used, the word 'revelation' tended to convey the Augustinian idea of illumination. The emphasis was on what happens to the person who receives the illumination. St Augustine's Platonism disposed him to appreciate and dilate upon the Johannine christological predicates: way, truth, life, and light. Christ the light of the world enables the believer to live in faithful pilgrimage on the way to the glory of eternity. St Bonaventure carried on this tradition of revelation as illumination of the mind. For concrete instances, he looked to the prophets who were illumined by God so that they might reveal the divine will to others. External instruction, however, always needs an inner illumination if it is to be truly revelatory. In a sense, Bonaventure sees external things as occasions for the work of revelation. The same is true of the sciences and philosophy: they minister extrinsically to theology but do not share in its activities. Alexander of Hales, Bonaventure's teacher, while conceding that theology is a science, was careful to add 'but not in Aristotle's sense'. Theology, Alexander wrote, 'is not a rational or demonstrative science, but one which is affective, moral, experimental, and religious'.[4]

Where Bonaventure had been taught to regard Aristotle as the source and master of error, Thomas Aquinas learned from his teacher, Albert, to see Aristotle as 'the Philosopher'. Aristotelianism enabled Aquinas to recognise the autonomy of the natural world. There are, according to Aquinas, truths about God and God's dealings with creation which are in principle open to discovery by the exercise of natural reason. However, fallen human nature, if left to its own devices, would in practice find it virtually impossible to arrive at a true and salvific knowledge of God. Revelation for Aquinas is the gratuitous act of a God who makes available to men and women whatever truths are necessary for salvation, including not only truths, such as the Trinity, which transcend the power of human intelligence to discover them, but also truths, such as the omnipotence or goodness of God, which are in principle open to natural enquiry. The instruments of this divine instruction are the prophets, the apostles, and of course principally Jesus Christ. Thomism therefore makes a very firm distinction between the revelation given to the prophets and apostles and its mediated transmission to the rest of humankind. The mediators of revelation have to establish their credentials by the working of miracles, which Aquinas likens to the royal seal that establishes the king's letters as authentic. Although Aquinas has a clear doctrine of divine light as a prerequisite to faith, he does not use the word 'revelation' to describe the illumination. The model of teacher and pupil is prominent in Thomas's conception of revelation. The educative process, as manifested in history, is gradual and progressive until it culminates in Jesus Christ who is the perfection of all that has gone before. After Christ there is no more to be added to what God has revealed.

Augustinian and Aristotelian Approaches

Paul Tillich saw in the debate between the Augustinians and the Aristotelians an important instance of the 'eternal conversation' of Plato and Aristotle and a rehearsal of 'almost all the problems of our present-day philosophy of religion'.[5] Ironically, in the period between the two Vatican councils it was Aristotelianism which represented the conservative position, while Augustinianism was always potentially suspect. Thus in 1930 Maurice Blondel could write, 'The revival of Thomism makes the revival of Augustinianism still more desirable, less dangerous, and more beneficent.[6] Blondel's choice of the word 'dangerous' is a reminder of the anti-Modernist climate with which Roman Catholic theology still had to contend two decades after the condemnation of Modernism.

In the light of what happens later, it may help if we single out the salient, though generalised, differences between the two schools of thought as they affect the theology of revelation. First, Augustine's epistemology does not allow of a sharp distinction between natural and supernatural knowledge, and this epistemology remains generally true of Augustinianism. Thomas Aquinas, on the other hand, favoured the autonomy of reason, and consequently of philosophy, thus separating philosophy from theology in a way which struck the Augustinians as constituting a dangerous break with tradition. Second, Augustinianism refused to make an explicit distinction between rationally derived and revealed truths; whereas Thomism sees revelation partly as a supplement to the functional defects of an autonomous reason. Third, Augustinianism values the will and the affections – in short, the heart – over the speculative intellect; whereas Thomism sees in the intellect the highest human faculty. Finally, the Augustinian predisposition to regard revelation as illumination favours attention to revelation as a continuing process; whereas Thomism lends itself to the objectivisation of revealed truths. The medieval Augustinians felt that Aristotelian analysis, rooted as it was in abstraction, removed the contemplative element from knowledge. Later theologians would react in a similar fashion against the 'bloodless abstractions' of neo-Scholasticism.

The Enlightenment

The characteristic concerns of the Reformation did not produce a crisis for the Roman Catholic doctrine of revelation. Luther's emphasis on faith as trust and his polemic against the influence of Aristotle ('that rancid philosopher') on Scholastic theology produced a relatively mild reaction at the Council of Trent, where faith was described as a free assent to truth. Trent was more concerned to reply to the Protestant doctrine of *sola Scriptura* (i.e., that the word of God is to be found in Scripture alone and not in the teachings of councils or popes). Both Protestant and Roman Catholic theology soon entered a period of scholastic rationalism which intellectualised the content of revelation and located it in the propositions of Scripture (alone, in the case of Protestantism) or (in the case of Roman Catholicism) in the propositions of both Scripture and tradition.

The real crisis for the Christian theology of revelation, both Protestant and Catholic, came with the Enlightenment. Descartes had prepared the way with his methodical doubt and his emphasis on clear and distinct ideas. Hume's radical empiricism awoke Immanuel Kant from his dogmatic slumbers. The result was Kant's 'Copernican revolution', with its turn to the subject and its conception of religion as limited by the bounds of human reason. By allowing moral experience to provide a tenuous link between humanity and God, Kant, in Karl Barth's phrase, offered 'terms for peace' to Christian theology. A significant section of Protestant theology accepted the terms and did what it could to salvage Christian faith from the ruins brought about by the Kantian critique. With very few exceptions, Roman Catholic theologians set their face resolutely against Kantianism and carried on as if the Kantian revolution had never happened.

It took time for Roman theology to formulate its post-Enlightenment position on revelation, faith, and reason. A series of individual

26

condemnations put down markers for the definitive statement of the first Vatican council. As the nineteenth century progressed, the major concerns of the Roman teaching authority became increasingly clear. These concerns turned on first, the competence and second, the limitations of reason in the process leading up to and following from the act of faith demanded of the Christian. Fideism was adjudged to be unorthodox because it seriously underrated the competence of reason, while rationalism was adjudged to be unorthodox for failing to recognise the limitations of reason in matters of faith. The prescribed cure for both conditions was fidelity to the Scholastic heritage of Catholic theology and philosophy. After 1879 that heritage was specifically identified with Thomism.

Traditionalism

Early nineteenth century Catholicism in both France and Germany was influenced by the romanticist reaction against the Enlightenment obsession with Reason. There was already the precedent of Pascal, who had been execrated by Voltaire precisely for those characteristics which romanticism valued. The romanticists would have approved heartily of such reflections as: 'We know the truth not only through our reason but also through our heart. It is through the latter that we know first principles, and reason, which has nothing to do with it, tries in vain to refute them'.[7] Traditionalists such as Joseph de Maistre, Louis de Bonald, and Félicité de Lamennais held that unaided human reason was simply incompetent in religious and moral matters. Whence, then, human religious and moral convictions? The Traditionalists answered 'revelation'. The revelation that they had in mind was given by God at the dawn of history and transmitted to succeeding generations by tradition. De Maistre appealed to innate ideas in the individual mind. De Bonald refined the individualism of this by finding the innate ideas not in the individual but in society. Among the ideas revealed from the start, and not discovered by the use of reason, is the existence of God.

The most philosophically competent of the Traditionalists was Louis Bautain. With the other Traditionalists, he dismissed Scholasticism as just another form of rationalism. His knowledge of German philosophy enabled him to deploy and place his own interpretation on Jacobi's distinction between *Verstand* (discursive reason) and *Vernunft* (intuitive reason). Bautain denied that discursive reason has any competence in matters of transcendence such as the existence of God or divine revelation to men and women. Only intuition of God can be the source of any salvific knowledge. Bautain thus returned to a full-blooded version of Augustinian illumination-theory, expressed now in the language of Kantian philosophy.

Bautain's views stirred up fierce controversy especially in Strasbourg, where there was a strong Scholastic presence and where the bishop expressed grave concern about Bautain's disparagement of reason as an instrument in matters of religion, metaphysics, and morality. Bautain was forced to sign a declaration which stated, among other things, that reason precedes faith and that, although weakened by original sin, it can nevertheless arrive at a knowledge of God's existence.

In Germany the Catholic faculty of theology at Tübingen pursued ideas which had some similarity to those of Bautain. The Tübingen theologians set the theology of revelation within the context of tradition, Church, and doctrinal development. Revelation unfolds gradually within tradition. It is given by God as a living thing and is sustained in the Church by the Holy Spirit. Tradition is much more than an historical phenomenon, the content of which is contained in the sacred texts. Tradition is the life of the Church and as such is revelatory. The thought of the Tübingen school has much in common with that of J.H. Newman in its personalism and its Augustinian concern with revelation as continuing process. The Scholastic hegemony which obtained from the middle of the nineteenth century to the middle of the twentieth century effectively displaced the insights and characteristic concerns of Pascal, Newman, and the Tübingen school in mainline Catholic theology. Their hour was to come at the second Vatican council.

Semi-Rationalism

The French Traditionalists and the Tübingen theologians were deemed by Rome to have erred, in varying degrees, on the side of faith. Rome's judgement was much more severe on the 'Semi-rationalists', who were condemned for erring on the side of reason. Although Kant had influenced Traditionalists like Bautain and the Tübingen theologians his influence on the 'Semi-rationalists', Georg Hermes and Anton Günther, was more profound and dramatic. Hermes, when a student at Münster, found his faith seriously shaken by the philosophy of Kant and Fichte. He was driven to ask himself Lessing's famous question: 'How can the contingent events of history serve as sources for the necessary truths of reason?' Hermes employed Kant's distinction between pure and practical reason in order to answer Lessing's question. Pure reason cannot make contact with the transcendent through historical events; but practical reason can, and indeed must, postulate historical facts as true if the categorical imperative is to be complied with. Hermes rejected the Scholastic authentication of revelation by miracles. The Kantian critique had invalidated that kind of apologetics. It was Hermes' adoption of the Kantian idea of faith which, more than any other feature of his thought, provoked Scholastic opposition and finally posthumous condemnation by Gregory XVI in 1835.

Anton Günther, an Austrian priest and scholar, shared many of Hermes' convictions about the relationship between faith and reason and, like him, took the view that theology is philosophy of revelation. Günther, like Hermes and Bautain, held that only intuitive reason (*Vernunft*) is competent in matters of metaphysics and revealed truth. Aristotle's philosophy operated through discursive reason (*Verstand*) and was therefore, according to Günther, incompetent in metaphysical and revelational questions. Günther went further than Hermes in claiming that intuitive reason enjoyed real if limited access to mysteries such as the Trinity. He was condemned by Pius IX in 1857.[8]

Pius IX

It had become very clear that Pius IX, whose pontificate lasted from 1846 to 1878, was intent on dealing firmly with what he saw as the errors facing the Church in the modern world. Although the pope was by no means unwilling to express his negative views on the contemporary world, his most severe comments were reserved for members of his own Church who were deemed to be guilty of even mild forms of the modern world's errors. He believed that a semi-rationalist inside the Church was far more dangerous than a host of fully fledged rationalists outside it.

The centralising of government in the Catholic Church which occurred in the long pontificate of Pius IX and which culminated in the definition of papal infallibility in 1870 went hand in hand with Roman teaching on revelation, faith, and reason. Under Leo XIII it was to find in the Thomistic renaissance of the nineteenth century an invaluable ideological instrument. At the beginning of the nineteenth century Scholasticism appeared to be a spent force. By the end of the same century it had, in the form of neo-Thomism, supplanted every other theology and philosophy in the Roman Catholic church and was supplying the criteria for theological orthodoxy. It was the methodological

29

coherence of Thomism, together with its thrust towards objectification, which fitted it to be the principal instrument of what was to become Roman Catholicism's command theology. Rome saw it precisely as a defence against Kantianism.

German Catholic theologians, philosophers, and historians were the first victims of this re-established Scholasticism. A congress of scholars met at Munich in 1863 under the presidency of the Church historian Ignaz von Döllinger.[9] Von Döllinger proclaimed the death of Scholasticism and the urgent need for a critical theology, i.e., one which would take account of what had been happening in both history and philosophy (described by von Döllinger as 'the two eyes of theology'). The Roman response to this manifesto was immediate and sharp. Pius IX, in a letter, *Tuas libenter*, to the archbishop of Munich-Freising, condemned the opposition of some moderns to the wisdom of the 'old school' and its doctors.

The growth of papal power in the Church found ideological support in a refurbished Scholasticism. Each fed the other in a remarkable manifestation of institutional symbiosis. Scholastic essentialism provided the Vatican with a language well-suited to the articulation of its immobilist position on doctrine, while the Vatican in turn used its authority to make neo-Scholasticism the exclusive language of its conception of orthodoxy. It is no coincidence that *Tuas libenter* not merely commended the 'old theology' over the new but also employed the term 'ordinary magisterium' for the first time in an official Roman document.[10] Not long afterwards the pope announced that he was thinking of calling a general council of the Church. It was clear that, among the topics to be dealt with by the council, revelation would be prominent.

The First Vatican Council

The council assembled on 8 December 1869 and was suspended *sine die* on 20 October 1870. Its definition of papal infallibility tends to overshadow its teaching on revelation in the Dogmatic Constitution, *Dei Filius*, which stated that God's existence, together with certain divine attributes, could be known with certainty by the natural light of reason.[11] Revelation is necessary, not because of the deficiencies of reason, but because God has raised man to a supernatural level. At this level God reveals himself and the eternal decrees of his will to mankind. Faith is a supernatural virtue whereby 'we believe that the things which he has revealed are true, not because of their intrinsic truth, but because of the authority of God who reveals them'. Nevertheless, so that faith may be in harmony with reason, 'God willed that to the interior helps of the Holy Spirit there should be joined exterior proofs of his revelation, to wit, divine facts, especially miracles and prophecies.'

The Constitution then turns, in a celebrated and much quoted passage, to the competence and limitations of reason in matters of supernatural revelation: Reason enlightened by faith, when it is properly used, can achieve 'some understanding – indeed a most fruitful understanding – of mysteries, both by analogy with those things which it knows naturally, and from the connection the mysteries have with one another and with man's last end.'

Although the council did not refer explicitly to the need for Catholics to adhere to the Scholastic tradition and methodology, its language was plainly Scholastic and its draftsmen were Scholastics who took as their brief the need to chart a course between Traditionalism and Semi-rationalism. They made a radical distinction between the natural and the supernatural and they regarded revelation as the communication of supernatural knowledge. In spite of the fact that the council spoke of God's revealing 'himself and the eternal decrees of his will', its teaching was generally taken in a propositional and impersonal sense.

Aeterni Patris

Almost a decade later Pius IX's successor, Leo XIII, gave further authentication to the Aristotelian character of Rome's understanding of revelation, faith, and reason by imposing Thomism on the Church at large. Leo's encyclical letter, *Aeterni Patris* (1879), was an extraordinary, indeed unprecedented, document.[12] It broke with a long-established convention that the Roman teaching body does not interfere in disputes between the various Catholic schools of theology and philosophy. Leo wrote to the General of the Franciscans informing him that the Order was not free to follow St Bonaventure and Scotus, if it meant departing from the mind of St Thomas.[13] The Franciscans and other followers of the Augustinian tradition were thrown into disarray. Non-Thomists found themselves frowned on by the Vatican. Leo's encyclical presented Thomistic philosophy as the structuring agent of a theology within which the data of revelation were to be arranged. The pope almost certainly underestimated the differences between Thomism and Augustinianism. (One effect of Leo's programme was the stimulus it gave to scientific study of medieval thought within the Church.) Bishops were instructed to have their seminary teachers trained in Thomism.

We need to note that neo-Thomism differed significantly from the authentic teaching of Aquinas. For one thing, the methodology was different. Aquinas dealt in *questiones*, whereas neo-Thomism dealt in *theses* which were apodictic pronouncements. Again, Aquinas treated Scripture as a central authority, whereas neo-Thomism promoted official church teaching as the controlling authority and raided Scripture for supporting proof-texts.[14] Neo-Thomism

> reacted against modern philosophy and the Enlightenment, and yet it was as much a child of modernity as it was a foe of modernity. This Neo-Thomism sharply separated nature and grace; it expanded the preamble of faith into a full-blown natural theology; and it developed a fundamental theology and apologetics in distinction from systematic theology. These developments were deeply indebted to the very modernity that Neo-Thomism opposed.[15]

Promulgated by the manuals, or textbooks, and effecting a remarkable uniformity across cultures, neo-Thomism became a command theology throughout the Church. It allowed for little variation or dissent.

Manual Theology

The manuals treated revelation under the heading of 'fundamental theology' which, in the period between the two Vatican councils, was strongly apologetical in character. Fundamental theology was seen as the link between philosophy and dogmatic theology. The philosophy of God undertook to study the divine existence and aspects of the divine nature, allegedly from the standpoint of natural reason alone. In practice, officially sanctioned philosophy of God was radically shaped by the theology for which it was designated as a preparation. The manual theology of revelation was divided into two parts, and the argument was deployed in strict logical sequence. Revelation was first proved to be possible (i.e., that there is no valid rational argument against the notion that God is able to communicate with human creatures). Then the question was raised, again at a purely theoretical level and in a radically *a priori* manner: if God were to communicate with creatures, how would the divine origin of the communication be known without error? The answer to this question was unambiguous: miracles and fulfilled

32

prophecies would offer clear testimony to the divine origin of whatever a prophet might put before his listeners as coming from God. Miracles were then in a similarly *a priori* manner proved to be possible: God can suspend the laws which God himself has given to nature. The argument then moves from possibility to actuality. Jesus Christ claimed to be speaking in the name of God. He vindicated his claim as divine legate by working many miracles of which the greatest was his resurrection from the dead. The fact that the resurrection was treated in fundamental rather than in dogmatic theology is characteristic of neo-Scholasticism. One effect of this preoccupation with the apologetical character of Christ's resurrection was the virtual absence of New Testament resurrection theology from the textbooks. The mere act of relocating the resurrection in systematic rather than fundamental theology would cast it in a new light. In the 1960s, during and after the second Vatican council, there was, in mainline Catholic theology and catechetics, a euphoric rediscovery of Pauline teaching on the resurrection, largely due to the biblical renaissance launched by the council.

In manual theology, analysis of the act of faith followed the same clinical pattern. The would-be Christian believer considers the evidence in favour of belief in Jesus Christ. In the 'preambulatory' stage the only aim is to remove any reasons for 'prudent doubt'. Having satisfied oneself that revelation is possible; that Jesus Christ claimed to be speaking in God's name; and that he supported his claim by working miracles, one is ready to make one's submission of faith to what God has revealed – not because of any intrinsic reasons (which would be rationalism) but because it is God who reveals it, and God cannot deceive.

Paradoxically the neo-Scholastic system was both rationalist and positivist. Its rationalism, which was more methodological than substantive, resulted from its propositional view of revelation and its deductive method of argument. It neglected and, after the condemnation of Modernism in 1907, repudiated, any experiential, affective, or intuitive mode of thought. It was positivist in that its approach to Scripture was innocent of any hermeneutical awareness of the literary character of the text. History was what really happened, and the documents which bore witness to these happenings shared in their objective givenness.

Modernism

The case against this presentation of revelation was put most trenchantly by a group of Catholic scholars, labelled 'Modernists' by Rome, who were writing at the end of the nineteenth and the beginning of the twentieth centuries. They had diverse interests and never formed the coherent and organised movement which their Roman enemies represented them to be. They did, however, share a strong dislike of Scholasticism. Alfred Loisy, who is generally seen as their principal, remarked that since the Catholic Church had freely bound itself to the Middle Ages, it could equally freely cast off these bonds. Maurice Blondel and George Tyrrell, each in his own way, led the Modernist assault on the neo-Scholastic conception of revelation.

Blondel coined the word 'extrinsicism' to describe the structure and methodology of neo-Scholastic fundamental theology. (His basic argument is not unlike Coleridge's case against Paley nearly a century earlier.) The neo-Scholastics, following the first Vatican council, regarded 'external facts' (i.e., miracles) as authenticating a supernatural message delivered by a divinely commissioned representative. Since in the Scholastic argument miracles can be seen and registered by anyone with eyes to see, Blondel in effect accused his Scholastic opponents of sheer positivism. They had nothing to say about the interior dispositions necessary for hearing the word of God. Blondel was very conscious of being a philosopher rather than a theologian. Hence he gave it as his aim to show that while philosophy has no competence in the sphere of revelation, nor any power to produce faith, it can, nevertheless, by analysing the interior dynamic of human willing demonstrate the human need for God's revelation and 'determine the mental dispositions which prepare for the understanding of facts and for the practical discrimination of truths the provenance of which is to be found elsewhere'.[16] Miracles play no part in Blondel's scheme of things, since they have meaning 'only for those who are already prepared to recognise the divine action in the most usual events'.[17]

Lucien Laberthonnière, Blondel's friend and collaborator, disliked neo-Thomism intensely and condemned it not merely for its extrincism but also for its 'intellectualism', which he saw as robbing revelation and faith of their moral and personal dimension. 'With the liberal Protestants it was faith without belief: here [with neo-Scholasticism] it is belief without faith', was Laberthonnière's verdict.[18] If Blondel was disposed to see the Thomistic revival as a valuable check on Augustinianism, Laberthonnière saw Augustinian concern with desire, will, and the affections as breathing moral and religious life into a system which seemed to him to reduce revelation to the status of external communication and faith to the purely mental acceptance of that communication.

Though Blondel was never formally condemned, as Laberthonnière was, his devastating case against Scholastic apologetics was either ignored or rejected by the manualists, who continued, with Rome's full support, to practise 'extrinsicism' until fundamental theology was radically overhauled in the light of the teaching of the second Vatican council. Blondel's 'method of immanence' bore fruit, however, in the work of the Transcendental Thomists who, though they had reservations about Blondel's Augustinian voluntarism, fully accepted his method of immanence. From a Blondelian standpoint, Karl Rahner and Bernard Lonergan are intellectualists who have been purged of their Aristotelianism by having been obliged to reckon with the Kantian revolution.

George Tyrrell shared Blondel's estimate of neo–Scholastic extrinsicism but was less interested in its apologetical implications. Tyrrell set out to counter the neo–Scholastic concept of revelation as theological statement. Revelation for Tyrrell is prophetic experience which, when analysed, and not before, becomes theology. In a lecture given shortly before he died Tyrrell said, 'Experience is revelational. It reveals God as every cause is revealed in and with its effects; it reveals Him not in a statement but in the moral and religious impulse that proceeds from Him'.[19]

The Modernists in their attempt to free themselves from the notion of 'an immobile church in possession of an immutable dogma' (the phrase is Archbishop Mignot's), appealed to a pre–linguistic substratum of truth which they saw as the primary source of revelation and of which historically controlled formulas were the symbolic and variable expressions. By definition, as pre–linguistic, this substratum would be beyond church control, which is why Rome fought so relentlessly to make formally expressed doctrine the criterion of truth and orthodoxy and condemned as 'agnostic' any appeal away from it to a deeper pre–dogmatic level of revealed truth.[20] Today, pre–linguistic theories of experience are vulnerable to post–modern critiques such as that of George Lindbeck, which claim that 'it is necessary to have the means for expressing an experience in order to have it'.[21] However, Friedrich von Hügel's locating of revelation in 'dim experience' (which, following Leibniz, he contrasts with 'reflex knowledge') may escape this critique of experience as pre–linguistic.[22]

The Modernists were condemned in a series of documents issued by Rome between 1907 and 1910. In September 1910 an oath was prescribed to be taken by all clergy and office–holders in the Church. It remains a useful historical index to the doctrinal position on revelation struck by the Roman authorities in response to the Modernist challenge. The oath was not repealed until 1967. On revelation and faith it prescribed the following:

> I accept and willingly recognize . . . the external proofs of revelation, that is, the divine facts, in the first instance miracles and prophecies, as most certain signs of the divine origin of the Christian religion, and I hold that they are valid in the highest degree for the intelligences of all in every age, including the present time. . . I hold as certain and sincerely profess that faith is not a blind religious sense welling up from the recesses of the subconscious under the impulse of the heart and at the bidding of a morally informed will, but a genuine assent of the intellect to a truth received extrinsically by hearing, by an assent, that is to say, based on the authority of an all-truthful God, and given to a truth that has been revealed and attested by a personal God, our Creator and Lord'.[23]

The effect of the condemnation of Modernism was a reinforcement of the very elements which the Modernists had tried to reform or modify: supernaturalism; heavy emphasis on divine transcendence at the expense of immanence; neo-Thomism as a criterion of orthodoxy; virtual exclusion of experience as a significant theological datum; predominantly propositional presentation of revelation; and an almost exclusively deductive method in theology, coupled with an uncritical use of the Bible in support of previously decided theses.

Although the Scholastic system predominated in teaching institutions throughout the Church, there were pockets of innovating scholarship, like the Dominican house of studies at Le Saulchoir and the Jesuit house of studies at Fourvière. Theologians from these and similar centres, some of whom were condemned as 'innovators' by Pius XII in 1950, went on to become the mentors of the second Vatican council.

The Second Vatican Council

The council achieved in four years what reforming Catholics had tried to bring about – or at least had hoped for – at various times during the previous hundred years. No conciliar document set out explicitly to dismantle the Scholastic structure within which Roman Catholic orthodoxy had been so rigidly defined. On the contrary, the council expressed its continuing esteem for Thomism. What it did do, however, was to introduce other theologies and theological methods, thus in effect destroying Leo XIII's vision of a command theology which served as a criterion of Catholic orthodoxy.

The council issued a Dogmatic Constitution, *Dei Verbum*, on revelation.[24] It is a relatively short document and was the product of five drafts which witness to extensive and important changes brought about during the debates. To appreciate the extent and significance of these changes one has only to compare the first draft, produced by theologians from the Roman pontifical institutions, with the fifth draft, produced during the council under the influence of the 'new theologians'. The first draft was entitled 'On the Sources of Revelation', and it retailed the Scholastic doctrine that revelation is contained partly in Scripture and partly in Tradition. The final document presents revelation as the self-disclosure of God through word and event, culminating in God's definitive self-manifestation in Jesus Christ. The first draft incorporated the Scholastic theory of the verbal inspiration of Scripture and the 'absolute immunity of the entire sacred Scripture from error'. It claimed that the gospels reproduce the historical acts and words of Jesus. The final document gives a broad interpretation of biblical inspiration and accepts the presence of errors in the Bible. It gives full recognition to the rights of scientific exegesis and points out that in order to appreciate what God wants to communicate, the reader must 'carefully search out the meaning which the sacred writers really had in mind' and attend to the literary forms of the various biblical writings.

Dei Verbum pointedly refrains from re-stating the traditional dictum that revelation was 'closed with the death of the last apostle'. This phrase was commonly invoked in support of a static, essentialist view of revelation. The Second Vatican Council in effect revived the Augustinian/Franciscan understanding of revelation as illumination, thus promoting the idea of revelation as a dynamic ongoing influence. This mode of presentation emphasises the divine action at work in the Church at any moment in its history. The privileged status of the Bible as mediator of divine revelation was safeguarded by *Dei Verbum*'s tacit, though immensely significant, abandoning of the two-source theory ('revelation is contained *partly* in Scripture and *partly* in Tradition'). Instead it teaches that 'Tradition and scripture make up a single sacred deposit of the word of God, which is entrusted to the church'.[25]

In addition to *Dei Verbum*, other documents of the council have implications for the theology of revelation. For example, *Gaudium et Spes*, the Pastoral Constitution on the Church in the Modern World, with its emphasis on the need for the Church to open itself to, and involve itself with, the world, implies a concept of revelation which is dynamic and illuminative in the Augustinian sense. *Gaudium et Spes*, following Pope John XXIII, speaks of the need to listen to the 'signs of the time' and to judge them in the light of the Gospel.[26]

Developments after the Second Vatican Council

The relentless extrinsicism which had been reinforced in fundamental theology by the anti-Modernist campaign collapsed as soon as neo-Scholasticism ceased to carry out the function of a command theology. The turn to the subject which had long since taken place in liberal Protestantism became perhaps the most prominent feature in post-conciliar Roman Catholic theology. Experience, hitherto rigidly excluded from the textbooks as an unstable and untrustworthy theological datum, was now accorded all the attention due to a new and exciting area for exploration.

The theologian who arguably made the most significant contribution to the transition from neo-Scholastic uniformity to post-conciliar pluralism was Karl Rahner. He had been appointed consultor to the commission working on *Dei Verbum* and he quickly achieved magisterial status in the Church, not least for his contribution to the theology of revelation. Rahner was ideally placed to be a bridge between the old and the new. He was a theologian who never cut himself adrift from his Thomistic beginnings but who nevertheless had come to terms with the turn to the subject and was open to the insights of Heideggerian existentialism. He is commonly described as a Transcendental Thomist, because he devoted much attention to the conditions which make it possible for any human being to recognise and respond to divine revelation. He thus set himself the task of relating the universal transcendental features of human openness and response to God's revelation, on the one hand, to the categorical and particularised revelation embodied in Jesus Christ, on the other.

The Scholastics had dealt with this task, as J.M. Creed had noted in the 1930s, by classifying all non-Christian religion as 'natural'. Rahner refuses this convenient strategem. For him all human beings without exception are offered a universal supernatural revelation precisely because God wills all human beings to be saved. For many men and women such a revelation remains purely transcendental and never becomes categorical, in that they are never confronted with the historical revelation embodied in Jesus Christ. Yet for Rahner universal transcendental revelation has its history too. Indeed Rahner understands history, i.e., universal, secular history, as the event and record of human trans-cendence.[27] The real problem (which Rahner never finally solves) is how to relate universal to particular revelation. Both have histories, but Christianity as a categorical answer to the transcendental question appears to make a claim which excludes the non-Christian categorical and particular experience. Rahner attempts to meet this problem with his controversial theory of the 'anonymous Christian', thus trying to be faithful to the uniqueness of the person and work of Jesus Christ while recognising the presence of God's saving and revelatory power in other faiths.

Hans Küng dismisses the theory of anonymous Christianity as a 'pseudo-solution' to the problem of christocentricity and one, moreover, which insults non-Christians. Küng claims that Rahner is in effect trying to give some kind of ecumenical reference to the dictum 'outside the Church there is no salvation', while purifying it of its triumphalism.[28]

Revelation and Praxis

Rahner's transcendental theology was challenged by J.B. Metz's Political Theology, which aimed both to reckon with the Marxist critique of bourgeois liberalism and to escape the charge of false consciousness. Metz had been a disciple of Rahner but he came to the conclusion that once neo-Scholasticism had been defeated, transcendental theology lost much of its point and underwent a crisis of identity.[29] Metz outlines a fundamental theology which is rooted in praxis, that is, a theology which begins from socio-political involvement and thus attempts to break free from the false consciousness of a purely speculative theology. Salvation is related to suffering; to solidarity with victims, past as well as present; and to the 'dangerous memory' of the life and death of Jesus Christ.

The Second Vatican Council had, as we have seen, exhorted the Church to listen to the signs of the time. Latin-American bishops and theologians, meeting at Medellín in Colombia in 1968, found themselves compelled to examine the nature of those signs in a culture where the poor are systematically exploited and persecuted by the rich and powerful. At Medellín the word 'liberation', in it contemporary socio-political sense, appeared for the first time in an official document of the Roman Catholic church. Liberation theology shares with political theology a controlling concern with praxis. Revelation takes place not only in transcendental experience and in the person, life, and work of Jesus Christ, but also in practical involvement in the plight of the poor and oppressed. 'The poor man, the other, reveals the totally Other to us'.[30] We have here a return, in suitably politicised form, to the Augustinian understanding of revelation as illumination rather than as objectified content. Indeed Hugo Assmann actually regards the present situation as the primary source of revelation. The Bible and church teachings become revelation only when they are related to the signs of the time in which we live.

The Roman response to liberation theology has been largely negative. In a document issued in 1984, the Congregation for the Doctrine of Faith expressed a dislike of what it saw as the Marxist orientation of liberation theology's methodology and preoccupations. It also took issue with the concept of praxis, which it saw as subverting the concept of truth. Joseph Ratzinger, the Bavarian theologian who is now Prefect of the Congregation, sees liberation theology as exploiting the concepts of praxis and history in an anti-metaphysical and this-worldly direction. Praxis substitutes action for reality; while 'the concept of history swallows up the concepts of God and of Revelation'.[31]

Conclusion

Many Roman Catholic theologians who were initially trained under the *ancien régime* of mandatory neo-Scholasticism laced with a strong dose of anti-Modernism, experienced the Second Vatican Council as an enormously liberating force. This was less perhaps because of what the individual documents had to say than because the council broke down so many barriers which had been erected to shelter Catholics from the sharp blasts of modernity. One emerged into this brave new world with initial euphoria but continued on one's journey with the alarming realisation that a heavy price had to be paid for the newly achieved authenticity. One now had the opportunity of being as cognitively miserable (to use Peter Berger's nice phrase) as any post-Enlightenment Protestant theologian. In addition, the new post-conciliar pluralism has made it less appropriate to speak of specifically Roman Catholic theology of revelation, at least in the univocal sense of the period before the Second Vatican Council.

As Hans Küng has frequently observed, the Second Vatican Council was the instrument, not of one, but of two paradigm shifts. Catholic theological sensibilities had to take on board both Reformation and Enlightenment values at the same time, and to do so in the growing realisation that these values were in crisis themselves A new sensitivity to history and to historical modes of thinking was an influential feature at and after the council. It helped to free Roman Catholic theology both from its non-historical conception of orthodoxy and from its Hellenistic disposition to view immutability as an ideal and change as an imperfection, if not indeed as a hazard. The conciliar renaissance occurred just in time to allow Roman Catholic theologians to take some part in the debate on whether revelation was to be found in word or event.

The New Quest of the historical Jesus had begun a decade earlier; but since the original Quest had not really affected mainline Catholic theology, the New Quest did not have the same frame of reference for Roman Catholics as it did for Protestants and Anglicans. The Second Vatican Council opted for the view that revelation is expressed in both word and event, each relating to the other in a unified way and in response to God's plan.

> The pattern of this revelation unfolds through deeds and words which are intrinsically connected: the works performed by God in the history of salvation show forth and confirm the doctrine and realities signified by the words; the words, for their part, proclaim the works, and bring to light the mystery they contain.[32]

Far more significant than the word-versus-event debate was the increasing recognition that although history provides a stimulating alternative to essentialist metaphysics, it is vulnerable to hermeneutical objections. The biblical renaissance together with the new pluralism in Catholic theology has inevitably raised the problem of interpretation.

The location of revelation in any kind of inner experience, mystical or transcendental, is even more exposed to hermeneutical question than its location in history, especially if, as with the Modernists, it is located in pre-linguistic experience. For Edward Schillebeeckx, 'there can be no revelation without experience'.[33] Experience, however, is always interpreted experience. 'We experience in the act of interpreting, without being able to draw a neat distinction between the element of experience and the element of interpretation'.[34] The hermeneutical character of all theology, including the theology of revelation, is widely accepted today by Roman Catholic theologians.

This acceptance also implies recognition of the distortion, personal and systemic, which can occur in the recording and transmission of the revelatory experience through tradition. Thus David Tracy can write, 'To interpret well must now mean that we attend to and use the hermeneutics of both retrieval and suspicion'.[35] The feminist critique of

41

patriarchy has serious implications for all Christian theologians, Catholic and Protestant, who are aware that divine revelation has been mediated through sources which have been clearly affected by androcentrism. Biblical androcentrism poses problems for the canonicity of Scripture.

Ecological concern is re-focusing attention on the theology of creation and on the 'general revelation' that is mediated by nature. During and following the Second Vatican Council, Roman Catholic theology turned with enthusiasm from mandatory essentialism to history, personalism, and existentialism. This turn did nothing for either the theology of creation or the notion of cosmic revelation. The need to respond theologically to the ecological crisis, coupled with the desire for dialogue with science, is giving a fresh impetus to the theology of cosmic revelation. John F. Haught has observed that

> If we are to move toward an environmentally wholesome theology of nature, we must also reshape our inherited ways of understanding revelation. We must look at it not simply as a set of historical events, but even more fundamentally as a *cosmic* phenomenon.[36]

It remains to be seen if this direction will be taken by a significant number of theologians. Catholics may find it easier to do so than Protestants who may have a stronger inclination to distrust nature as fallen and therefore not a fit source for mediating divine revelation.

Mainline Roman Catholicism postponed its engagement with modernity (in the sense of post-Enlightenment thought) until the 1960s, just when modernity was itself in serious trouble. The experience, though exhilarating, has been not unlike joining a ship in keen anticipation of an exciting voyage only to discover that the ship has been quietly corroding below the waterline and that much of the voyage will have to be spent operating the pumps. If Carl Braaten is right that Roman Catholic theology is no longer sure what revelation is, this may be thought to be no bad thing when one remembers that only a few years ago it was excessively sure what revelation is. As Maurice Blondel remarked at the height of the Modernist crisis, it is possible to see things too clearly to see them properly.

Notes

1. J.M. Creed, *The Divinity of Jesus Christ: A Study in the History of Christian Doctrine since Kant*, London, 1964, pp.114–15; first published, Cambridge, CUP, 1938.
2. C.E. Braaten, *History and Hermeneutics*, London 1968, p.116.
3. See G. Daly, 'Catholicism and Modernity' in *Journal of the American Academy of Religion*, LIII/3; reprinted in R.L. Hart (ed.), *Trajectories in the Study of Religion: Addresses at the Seventy Fifth Anniversary of the American Academy of Religion*, Atlanta, Scholars Press, 1987, pp.229–52.
4. Y. Congar, *A History of Theology*, New York, 1968, p.11.
5. P. Tillich, *A History of Christian Thought*, London, 1968, p.141.
6. *A Monument to St Augustine*, London, 1945, p.342.
7. A.J. Krailsheimer (ed.), *Pascal: Pensées*, Harmondsworth, Penguin Books, 1966, p.58.
8. On Traditionalism and Semi-rationalism see G. McCool, *Catholic Theology in the Nineteenth Century: The Quest for a Unitary Method*, New York, 1977.
9. T.F. O'Meara, *Church and Culture: German Catholic Theology, 1860–1914*, London, 1991, pp.26–9.
10. See J.P. Boyle, 'The "Ordinary Magisterium": History of the Concept', parts 1 and 2, *The Heythrop Journal*, 20 (Oct., 1979), pp.380–98; 21 (Jan., 1980), pp.14–29.
11. Latin text in H. Denzinger and A. Schönmetzer (eds), *Enchiridion symbolorum definitionum et declarationum de rebus fidei et morum*, Barcelona, 1967, pp.586–95.
12. *Dei Filius* and *Aeterni Patris* are discussed in McCool, op. cit., pp.216–40.
13. L.F. Barmann, *Baron Friedrich von Hügel and the Modernist Crisis in England*, Cambridge, 1972, p.140n. According to von Hügel, a similar letter went to the Jesuit General (*ibid.*).
14. See F. Schüssler Fiorenza, "Systematic Theology: Tasks and Methods" in F. Schüssler Fiorenza and J.P. Galvin (eds.), *Systematic Theology: Roman Catholic Perspectives*, Dublin, 1992, pp.30–32.
15. Ibid., p.36.
16. *Les premiers écrits de Maurice Blondel*, vol.2, Paris, 1956, p.14.
17. *Ibid.*
18. L. Laberthonnière, 'Dogme et théologie' in *Annales de philosophie chrétienne*, 5 (1908), p.511.
19. T.M. Loome (ed.), ' "Revelation as Experience": An Unpublished Lecture of George Tyrrell', *The Heythrop Journal*, 12 (1971), p.144.
20. Already in 1899 Leo XIII had written to the French bishops to express his alarm at the 'doctrinal scepticism' which had, he claimed, become so evident in France (J. Bellamy, *La théologie catholique au XIXe siècle*, Paris, 1904, p.150.)

21. G. Lindbeck, *The Nature of Doctrine: Religion and Theology in a Postliberal Age*, London, 1984, p.37.
22. See F. Von Hügel, 'Experience and Transcendence', in *The Dublin Review*, 138 (1906), p.358.
23. Latin text in Denzinger-Schönmetzer, *Enchiridion*, nos.3539 and 3542, pp.688–9.
24. The text can be found in A. Flannery (ed.), *Vatican Council II: Constitutions, Decrees, Declarations*, Dublin 1996, pp.97–115. For a history of the constitution see H. Vorgrimler (ed.), *Commentary on the Documents of Vatican II*, Vol. 3, London, 1968, pp.155–272.
25. *Dei Verbum*, art.11, Flannery, p.103.
26. *Gaudium et spes*, art.4, Flannery, p.165.
27. K. Rahner, *Foundations of Christian Faith: An Introduction to the Idea of Christianity*, London, 1978, pp.138–75.
28. H. Küng, *On Being a Christian*, London, 1977, pp.97–8.
29. J.B. Metz, *Faith in History and Society: Towards a Practical Fundamental Theology*, London, 1980, p.13n.
30. H. Assmann, *Practical Theology of Liberation*, London, 1975, p.13.
31. J. Ratzinger and V. Messori, *The Ratzinger Report: An Exclusive Interview on the State of the Church*, Leominster, 1985, p.182.
32. *Dei Verbum*, art.2; Flannery, p.98.
33. E. Schillebeeckx, *Christ: The Christian Experience in the Modern World*, London, 1980, p.45.
34. *Ibid.*, p.33.
35. D. Tracy, *Plurality and Ambiguity: Hermeneutics, Religion, Hope*, San Francisco, 1987, p.77.
36. J.F. Haught, *Mystery and Promise: A Theology of Revelation* , Minnesota, 1993, p.164.

3

Divine Revelation in Modern Protestant Theology

Paul Avis

Protestant Theology in the Shadow of the Enlightenment

At the Reformation, the Protestant cause stood or fell with a particular view of revelation. The Reformers claimed, against the Roman Catholic synthesis of scripture and tradition, that the Bible contained all that was required for salvation, while the stricter Calvinists and Puritans went further and held that the Bible legislated, by precept or precedent, for all matters of faith, morals, worship and church order. But the reality of revelation was not in question, nor its inerrant inscription in the Bible, nor its unquestionable authority. The question of divine revelation became problematic in Protestant theology as a result of the Enlightenment and the Romantic reaction. The Enlightenment subverted all claims to unchallengeable authority and subjected all traditions, including those of Scripture, to critical scrutiny in the light of objective universal canons of human rationality.

Lessing and Kant rejected the notion of particular revelations in history, for truth must conform to the universal norms of reason which are freely embraced by the autonomous intellect. Lessing argued that ideas which had previously been attributed to revelation should be drawn within the sphere of reason. He famously asserted that 'accidental truths of history can never be the proof of necessary truths of reason'. Fichte insisted that only the metaphysical can save, never the historical. Kant claimed that historical facts can serve only for illustration, not for demonstration. Kant added, crucially, that ultimate reality was unknowable by our finite minds, thus undermining the possibility of an informative (cognitive) revelation that would be true to the very nature of God and making any knowledge of God merely a regulative construct (Lessing, 1956, p.53; Kant, 1934; ibid., 1960, pp.98f, 105).

The Romantic reaction to the Enlightenment, both in the arts and philosophy, turned away from the ideals of objectivity and universality and sought its criteria in subjective experience and the particular moment. Kant and Hegel, the two greatest philosophical influences on modern Protestant theology, mediate between the Enlightenment and Romanticism. Kant reinforced the 'turn to the subject' in philosophy that perhaps began with Descartes and also fatally wounded the power of speculative reason. The synthesis of Enlightenment and Romanticism is seen in Hegel's combination of rationalism and subjectivism. In Hegel's philosophical system the individual mind is a manifestation of ultimate reason and what is true for reason is true of reality (Hegel, 1931). For both Enlightenment rationalism and Romantic idealism, truth imposed from without was alien and threatening – a heteronomous authority. Between them, these two formative movements of modern western culture challenged any notion of a divine revelation confronting humanity from without and bearing the insignia of unchallengeable authority. But the Enlightenment is the decisive watershed: however profoundly they may be influenced by Romantic sensibility (as in the case of Schleiermacher), modern Protestant theologians are children of the Enlightenment – as are we all.

This means that revelation cannot be taken for granted in modern theology: it has to be justified and shown to be rational and coherent (even Barth does this, albeit after affirming its actuality and givenness). The connections between revelation and history and between revelation and natural reason become highly contestable. The agenda is set by Descartes' method of systematic doubt; Locke's appeal to experience; Hume's destructive scepticism; Butler's abandonment of certitude for probability; Bayle's skilful deflating of ancient authorities; Voltaire's lampooning of ecclesiastical tradition; and a whole army of biblical scholars bringing to light the human, fallible and culture-bound aspects of the biblical texts. The response to the agenda varies and we shall look at a small selection of distinctive approaches. (Notable general discussions of the question of revelation, from a Protestant perspective, are found in Baillie, 1956; H.R. Niebuhr, 1960; Abraham, 1982; Thiemann, 1985; Gunton, 1995. In spite of its title, Farmer's *Revelation and Religion* (1954) only gives a few sentences to revelation as such, though it has a useful discussion of natural theology. Modern Anglican writing on the question of revelation is extensive and, regrettably, cannot be treated here.)

Schleiermacher: Revelation grounded in Experience

F.D.E. Schleiermacher (1768–1834) presupposes the Enlightenment but reacts against it and in so doing launches Protestant theology into its modern form. (For a detailed discussion of Schleiermacher's theological method, see Avis, 1986, ch.1.) He accepts that, after the Enlightenment, all theological assertions must be empirically grounded. For Schleiermacher, that empirical grounding is found in religious experience. He acknowledges, with Kant, that ultimate reality is unknowable and that theological statements about the nature of God will be merely regulative, heuristic statements. In Schleiermacher's dogmatics, these statements are derived from expressions of religious feeling. He believes, with the Romantics, that intense aesthetic experience, rather than the realm of either cognition or action, is the locus of human perception of the truth of reality. He brings these three presuppositions together by locating divine revelation in the distinctive religious experience of the Christian community – normatively in the apostolic Church, derivatively in the Church of his time and place, the united Protestant Church of early nineteenth-century Prussia.

By his early twenties, Schleiermacher had expressed in his *Soliloquies* a philosophy of life directed to fully realising one's humanity and individuality. The development of one's unique expression of human nature was the highest ethical goal. He asserted the metaphysical primacy of the unconditioned spiritual self. The distinctive emphasis on religious feeling appears ten years later in the *Speeches to the Cultured Despisers of Religion* (1799) where refined aesthetic experience is interpreted as an encounter with the divine. Schleiermacher's later work in dogmatics spells out the theological implications of this identification.

His radical reinterpretation of Christian doctrine is set out in his *Brief Outline of the Study of Theology* (1811, 1830) where dogmatics is subsumed under historical theology as a descriptive discipline and (in the second edition) its data are located in the realm of feeling or immediate self-consciousness. In his greatest work *The Christian Faith* (1821–2, 1830) Schleiermacher attempts a systematic account of Christian beliefs as the critical articulation of the aesthetic consciousness of his Church. He defines dogmatics as 'the science which systematises the doctrine prevalent in a Christian Church at a given time' and defines that doctrine as an account of 'the Christian religious affections set forth in speech'. Schleiermacher's intention, in this the crown of his life's work, was to make Christian doctrine (dogmatics) a descriptive, empirical

47

discipline, employing the historical method and founded on the scientific study of the phenomena of Christian self-consciousness.

For Schleiermacher, God is known immediately (that is, intuitively) in religious experience. There is a universal human sense of being completely dependent on God for our existence. In Christianity, this sense of absolute dependence receives a Christological form, being shaped by the person and work of Jesus Christ and experienced only through the community that derives from him, the Church. Revelation is received in this realm of immediate experience. In the *Speeches* Schleiermacher had already claimed that 'every original and new communication of the universe to man is a revelation. . . Every intuition and every original feeling proceeds from revelation' (pp.88f). In *The Christian Faith* he points out that the word 'revealed' is never applied either to what is discovered by one person and handed on to others or to what one person works out for themselves and passes on to others. It presupposes a divine communication. Therefore, 'the idea of revelation signifies the originality of the fact which lies at the foundation of religious communion' and which cannot be explained by its historical antecedents. This revelation, communicated by God, is not propositional, but experiential, for doctrines are deduced from communal experience (pp.49f).

'Originality' is a word that evidently suits Schleiermacher's descriptive, almost phenomenological method. He is not primarily concerned with making value judgements (which would transgress Kant's veto on knowledge of ultimate reality, *noumena*) but with evoking what is given in the religious experience of the Christian community. Schleiermacher's method is highly contentious: in this case it leads him to a patently inadequate definition of revelation. Schleiermacher is not deeply concerned about revelation and gives it cursory treatment in *The Christian Faith* (pp.47ff, 62ff). It is not a first-order theological question for him, but merely an inference from experience.

Even if, for the sake of argument, we go along with Schleiermacher's method, there is a serious flaw in his approach that has been picked up by many critics, concerning Schleiermacher's identification of religious feeling or intuition with immediate experience of God. Thiemann has recently written (and he can speak for many): 'That an experience of absolute dependence is an experience of God is a judgement which must be warranted. Appeals to perceived uniqueness or degree of intensity are insufficient to establish the veridical character of the claim.' Thiemann concludes: 'his defence of revelation founders on the incoherence of the notion of intuition or immediate self-consciousness. . . Schleiermacher's attempt to ground revelation in universal immediate experience is thwarted by his inability to demonstrate that the experience stems from a divine origin' (Thiemann, 1985, p.31).

Barth: Revelation as Transcendent Word of God

Karl Barth (1886–1968) attempted to reverse Schleiermacher's theological innovation, to turn him on his head, and thus to undermine the whole Liberal Protestant synthesis of Christianity and modern culture. (For a detailed discussion of Barth's theological method, see Avis, 1986, ch.3.) Barth saw his own theological approach as the antithesis to Schleiermacher's and as its antidote (Barth, 1982).

In the first place, he denies that there is a universal religious experience, such as the sense of absolute dependence, on which Christian theology can build its specific claims. Such a religious *a priori* would be an example of the natural theology that is anathema to Barth. Human subjectivity provides no firm basis for theological construction, being fallen, corrupt and prone to idolatry. The only sound basis for theology is the word of God which is given, objective and coherent.

Second, he rejects Schleiermacher's assumption that doctrine is to be deduced from the corporate feeling or piety of the Church. For Barth, doctrine is not the creature of the Church, but judges and masters it. Doctrine is the exposition of the word of God, the word that creates the Church and brings it into being.

Third, he completely disagrees with Schleiermacher's criterion of immediate self-consciousness as the measure of theological relevance. It was this criterion that led Schleiermacher to consider the doctrine of the Trinity as a speculative inference from other doctrines and to relegate it to a postscript to his dogmatics. Barth, by contrast, begins with the trinitarian framework and it informs all his work. For Barth, we do not ourselves decide what counts as revelation; we merely humbly accept revelation in its totality and submit ourselves to it in the obedience of faith.

Above all, Barth insists on the absolute priority of a prevenient act of divine revelation before all other theological business. The golden thread of his theological method is the principle that God can only be known through God. Barth thus makes revelation a first-order theological doctrine, not a derivative, second-order deduction. He effectively put the question of revelation at the top of the theological agenda for twentieth-century theologians.

In his early commentary on the Epistle to the Romans (1919), Barth developed a revolutionary, dialectical concept of revelation which, with some change of emphasis, he continued to expound through his various dogmatics (McCormack, 1995, stresses the continuity), and which found definitive expression in the many volumes of his *Church Dogmatics* (1932–67), but particularly in the first. Barth defined revelation as one of the three forms of the word of God, the other two (derivative) forms being the proclaimed word and the scriptural word (Barth, 1956, pp.98ff [*CD* I,1,4]). This concept of revelation has a number of features:

• Revelation is a sovereign act of the triune God. God acts in revelation at his good pleasure and no human actions can induce or facilitate the granting of revelation. The revelation of God intersects the world vertically from above, asserts Barth in *Romans*.

• Revelation can never be domesticated in human thoughts or words. It remains solely under divine control. There cannot, for example, be any synthesis of divine revelation and human philosophy. Revelation occurs only in the event – a sort of revelatory 'occasionalism'. There is at all times an infinite qualitative distinction between divine revelation and human insight. The word of God is never irrevocably committed into human hands.

• Revelation creates its own vehicle in human speech. Ordinary language is inadequate to convey revelation: analogies taken from the world and human life are inept and fall short. Instead, divine revelation adopts certain privileged human speech forms and endows them with the capacity to mediate revelation in a reversal of normal theological ideas of analogy.

• Revelation is essentially dialectical, an unveiling that is at the same time a veiling, and vice versa. It is, says Barth in the *Church Dogmatics*, 'both the *unveiling* of God in his veiling as well as the *veiling* of God in his unveiling' (McCormack, p.465). No particular statement can be affirmed unequivocally to be the revelation of God. It both is and is not revelation.

• Revelation is mediated. Revelation is not experienced nakedly, but comes to us from God 'clothed in the garments of creaturely reality'. The divine content of revelation requires a secular, 'this-worldly' form in order to become available. This is Barth's notion of the 'secondary objectivity' of God. Barth stated in the *Church Dogmatics*:

'the secular form without the divine content is not the Word of God and the divine content without the secular form is also not the Word of God' (McCormack, 1995, p.465). Both must be acknowledged in their irreducible integrity and to attempt a synthesis of the two would be worst of all.

- Revelation is an unjustifiable given. Barth insists on the actuality of revelation before he discusses its possibility. God has spoken: that is the fact with which we must reckon. It is inappropriate and ultimately blasphemous for us to attempt to show, through apologetics, natural theology or philosophy, that it is credible that there should be a revelation. Barth asserted in the (earlier) Göttingen dogmatics: 'The problem of the possibility of revelation can only be seriously raised and treated where its *reality* is known. The possibility of revelation can, as a matter of principle, only be constructed *a posteriori*. All reflection on how God can reveal himself, is really only a thinking-after of the fact that God *has* revealed himself' (McCormack, p.359).

- Revelation is the self-revelation of God. What is given in revelation is not a set of doctrinal truths in propositional form, for divine revelation must always transcend any particular expression or embodiment. Nor is it a series of actions brought about by God in history by remote control, for that would be less than a personal self-communication of God. It is a true personal disclosure of God's being and nature. There is no ultimate disjunction between the economic Trinity (God at work in the world) and the essential or immanent Trinity (the life of God within himself). Revelation is nothing less than divine presence, action and speech.

- Revelation is conveyed through the witness of holy Scripture. The Bible is not identical with the word of God but attests it. The prophets and apostles testify to the revelation of the word of God but cannot possess it. The word of God transcends the text of Scripture but cannot be heard apart from Scripture. Barth's theological method actually centres on the exposition of Scripture, but Scripture only points to the word of God.

- Revelation is given only in Jesus Christ. As the anti-Nazi Barmen Declaration of the Confessing Church affirmed under Barth's guidance in 1934, Jesus Christ is the one and only Word of God that

51

we must hear and obey. He is God's full and final word to humanity. But, for Barth, Jesus Christ is not reduced to the historical figure of Jesus of Nazareth or simply identified with his words and deeds inscribed in the text of scripture. Barth is interested in neither the historico–critical method of biblical interpretation nor the quest for the historical Jesus. 'Jesus Christ' is defined elliptically and elusively in Barth, postulated by faith and known through the free and sovereign Word of God.

- Revelation is not confined to Jesus Christ but can only be known through Jesus Christ. Barth acknowledges a natural or general revelation, imprinted by God on his works of creation. But that cannot be known apart from the definitive revelation in Jesus Christ which opens our eyes and sheds light on the structures of the world (see Barth in Baillie, ed., 1937, pp.50f). Natural revelation cannot, therefore, be the subject of a natural theology – theology constructed without reference to Jesus Christ – which Barth regards as a snare of Satan and gross idolatry, or form a point of contact for the Christian gospel (see Barth and Brunner, 1946). But the fact of natural revelation means that the Christian is free to enjoy God's gifts in the natural world and the artistic creations of human culture. Barth himself did both to a pre-eminent degree.

Barth's contemporary Emil Brunner (1889–1966) stands for a significant variation on the neo–orthodox, dialectical view of revelation and represents an important criticism of Barth. He stands with Barth in his insistence that 'through God alone can God be known' (Brunner, 1934, p.21), but departs from Barth in holding that there is a real natural knowledge of God which forms a point of contact, a bridge, for special revelation. It is only on the basis of this general revelation that humankind can be held accountable to God. 'It is impossible to believe in a Christian way in the unique revelation, in the Mediator, without believing also in a universal revelation of God in creation, in history, and especially in the human conscience' (ibid., p.32; see also Barth and Brunner, 1946). For Brunner, divine revelation is not identified with the Bible but transends it. He deplores the 'fatal equation of revelation with the inspiration of the scriptures' (Brunner, 1947, p.7). Revelation is not even propositional, it is personal – 'not a book or a doctrine . . . [but] God himself in his self-revelation within history' (ibid., p.8).

Tillich: Revelation through Symbol

Paul Tillich (1886–196) is the twentieth-century Schleiermacher. Like that 'prince of Protestant theologians', Tillich constructs his theology in dialogue with philosophy and culture: he sets it within the framework of secular disciplines; he gives full weight to religious experience; and his work culminates in a highly formalised systematic theology, as remarkable for its architectonic power as for its adventurous thinking. (For a full study of Tillich's theological method see Avis, 1986, ch.8.) Where Tillich markedly departs from Schleiermacher is that, early in his career, he made it clear that he would not be content with a purely historical, descriptive or phenomenological method, but that he was committed to making theological value judgements. Thus his systematic theology (Tillich, [ST], 1968), the crowning achievement of his life, consists largely, not of interpretations of phenomena (as does Schleiermacher's) but of theological assertions, judgements and principles that claim objective validity. Schleiermacher went wrong, Tillich believes, in making experience the source of theological statements; it is, rather, the unavoidable medium of theological reflection.

Tillich's rejection of Schleiermacher's phenomenological method does not mean that he was sympathetic to Barth's alternative. Tillich has harsh words to say of Barth's approach, as the following summary of his critique indicates.

* Theology is not merely the orderly presentation and exposition of the deliverances of divine revelation. Though real, revelation is not susceptible to that treatment because it is given, not in propositions – however dialectical – but in symbols. Revelation can only take place in conditions of human receptivity, as the answer to existential questioning. Tillich endorses Bonhoeffer's memorable criticism of Barth: that in his theology revelation is lobbed like a stone from God to humankind.

* Theology cannot take God as its direct object. In contrast to Barth's naive realism in epistemology, Tillich embraces a highly symbolic realism. Theology must approach the unconditional reality of God through the study of human apprehension of the divine. Theology cannot be undertaken in isolation from the study of religion; it is the concrete and normative science of religion.

- Tillich is scornful of neo-orthodox 'dialectical theology' that is for ever equivocating about revelation and will not come to rest in a final affirmation. For Tillich, who cut his philosophical teeth on the idealist dialectic of Schelling, true dialectic presupposes a unitary worldview. The counterplay of 'Yes' and 'No' must eventuate in an ultimate 'Yes'.

- There remains a need for an appropriate natural theology by means of which revealed theology can engage with contemporary social and political concerns (such as Nazism and the Cold War). Barth's methodological avoidance of the questions raised by human dilemmas is, in Tillich's view, self-deception. So is his use of metaphysical symbols and philosophical terms which originate in the autonomous spiritual process. Tillich acknowledges the reality of revelation through aesthetic, artistic experience and gives it a theological interpretation.

- Philosophy and theology are integrally related since they both deal, in their various ways, with the ultimate questions of existence. Philosophy of religion reflects on the totality of significant human experience. Theology engages with the conclusions of philosophy of religion on the basis of divine revelation mediated through Scripture and clarified by the historic confessions of the Christian churches.

However, Tillich does reveal important common ground with Barth in that he upholds the principle that God can only be known through God, and that there can be no knowledge of God without God's gracious goodpleasure. Tillich makes two major contributions to modern Protestant thinking about revelation: his method of correlation and his insistence that revelation is given through symbols.

Throughout his career Tillich attempted some kind of correlation between human thought and experience, on the one hand, and theological statements, derived from revelation, on the other. The 'method of correlation' forms the controlling method of his *Systematic Theology*. Theology addresses the issues that emerge from 'the totality of man's creative self-interpretation', found in philosophical, scientific, artistic, economic, political, psychotherapeutic and ethical forms. This self-interpretation is intrinsically problematic: 'Man is the question he asks about himself.' To start from human experience, however, seems to invite all over again the damning criticisms which Barth and others brought against the liberal Protestant theology that stemmed from

Schleiermacher. Tillich responds to this challenge in four ways (Tillich, 1968, [ST] 1, pp.65ff; 2, pp.14ff).

First, he acknowledges that the method of correlation does indeed, in a sense, make God dependent upon humanity. This is not theologically objectionable because it reflects the condescension or accommodation of God to humankind disclosed in the Christian revelation. Second, he avoids reductionism by insisting that the answers are not contained in the questions or derived from them. They are given from beyond the situation in the revelatory events that have given rise to Christian beliefs. Third, the revealed answers contain the power to modify and correct the questions. It is as though the questions are evoked under the impact of the revealed answers. Revelation has theological priority and divine prevenience is safeguarded.

Finally, Tillich states that it is one of the tasks of theology itself to formulate the questions within 'the theological circle': 'Theology formulates the questions implied in human existence, and theology formulates the answers implied in divine self-manifestation under the guidance of the questions implied in human existence.' Tillich defends his method as self-evident and unavoidable when he insists that 'Man cannot receive answers to questions he has never asked.'

If God is defined as the unconditioned reality, it follows that God cannot be the direct object of knowledge but can become known only as mediated through created forms in divine self-disclosure. This is not controversial: even Barth insists that God is revealed 'clothed in the garments of creaturely reality', Tillich's contribution at this point is twofold. First, he is clear that there remains a God above or beyond the God who is known in revelation. That means that Tillich's is also a dialectical theology, an apophatic theology, in which the ultimate mystery of the Godhead remains cloaked in darkness. And second, Tillich has more to say than any other Protestant theologian about symbols as the mediating forms of revelation.

Tillich's final position was that all we can say about God is symbolic, for even one non-symbolic (i.e., literal) statement about God would infringe God's 'ecstatic transcendent character'. Revelation is 'the self-manifestation of ultimate reality in ecstatic experiences, expressed in symbols'. Revelation takes place in divine–human encounter which is apprehended as 'miracle' and received in 'ecstasy'. In revelation, the ground of our being shines out and claims us completely. Revelation is confined to what concerns us ultimately. 'The mystery which is revealed is of ultimate concern to us because it is the ground of our being.' It follows that no revelation can take place where there is no one to receive it as their ultimate concern (Tillich, [ST] 1968, I, p.123).

For Tillich, original revelation generates dependent revelation where the original symbol is incorporated into a tradition and retains revelatory power. The supreme and definitive revelation is (as Tillich puts it) the appearance in history of the New Being in Jesus as the Christ as our ultimate concern. Revelation conveys the possibility of salvation. 'Revelation is not information about divine things; it is the ecstatic manifestation of the Ground of Being in events, persons and things. Such manifestations have shaking, transforming and healing power' (Tillich, [ST] 1968, II, p.192). Revelatory symbols are irreducible and cannot be 'cashed in' for some purely empirical (such as historical) value. Tillich insists on the ultimate historical earthing of revelation, but is somewhat cavalier about the implementation of this. Finally, symbols have an integral power; they cannot be devised at will and should be respected. Symbols require to be systematised, explained and criticised.

Tillich is out of fashion in this postmodern age that cannot believe that knowledge can be unified or that theology can be brought together into a system. Even though he believed that Christian theology must pass through the fires of Marxist and Freudian critique, Tillich's systematics are hardly chastened and tentative. A grandiose idealist conception is dominant. But Tillich's theology – and in particular his treatment of revelation – has not been overthrown. His method of correlation stands for the vital principle of engagement with the created order, which is for us the order of experience. His insights into the role of sacred symbols have a hitherto untapped potential and ought to commend themselves to the postmodern mentality which takes images to be central to our construal of the world and of God.

Pannenberg: Revelation in History

Wolfhart Pannenberg (b.1928) has evolved a distinctive third way in modern Protestant theology. (For an introduction to Pannenberg's theological method, see Avis, 1986, ch.4.) Having studied under Barth, he retains the thrust of the biblical witness at the centre of his theology. But, having rapidly rejected Barth's approach, Pannenberg operates a theological method that is distinguished by its open boundary to all sources of information and insight that may shed light on that crucial biblical revelation and which will also bring it to full effect. With Barth, Pannenberg insists that there is no revelation without the Bible. But with Schleiermacher and the liberal Protestant tradition he also asserts that the biblical revelation can neither be vindicated nor understood until it is set in the light of all our knowledge – and this, of course, can only be done by means of non-theological disciplines. Like Schleiermacher, Pannenberg takes religious experience seriously; unlike Schleiermacher, he does not confine his theological data to experience. Like Barth, Pannenberg believes in the objectivity of divine revelation; unlike Barth, he does not confine revelation to the event of Jesus Christ.

Early in his career, Pannenberg defined the task of theology as 'to understand all reality in relation to God' (Pannenberg, 1970, [*BQT* I], pp.1f). But as his theological method matured, it became apparent that he believes that this can only be done by seeking to understand God in relation to all of reality. Pannenberg upholds the traditional scope of theology as the science of God, but it can only be this by being first the science of religion and specifically of the Christian religion.

Revelation in History (1969), which signalled Pannenberg's arrival on the scene as a major force in modern theology, contains an important programmatic statement on his view of revelation. First Pannenberg rejects the approaches of Barth and Schleiermacher respectively. Then he announces the orientation of his theology to the totality of meaning which is anticipated in history and will become manifest at the *eschaton*. Finally, he espouses the method of historical and critical investigation of claims of revelation. In a key statement of his position, Pannenberg writes:

> Revelation is no longer understood in terms of a supernatural disclosure or of a peculiarly religious experience and religious subjectivity, but in terms of the comprehensive whole of reality which, however, is not simply given, but is a temporal process of a history that is not yet completed, but open to a future which is anticipated in the teaching and personal history of Jesus and is open to rational discussion and investigation. (Pannenberg, 1969, p.ix).

The contrast with Barth is striking: the latter would turn in his grave at the thought of divine revelation being subject to rational and critical investigation. Clearly Pannenberg, unlike Barth, is no enemy of the Enlightenment. He believes that the Enlightenment cannot be revoked and that all authoritative claims, such as those of the Christian revelation, require justification through research, criticism and argument. In fact, Pannenberg violently objects to Barth's view of revelation and the theological method that it entails. He is brutally dismissive of Barth's

position, calling it an 'unfounded postulate of the theological consciousness'; that is, a groundless subjective assertion on the part of Barth
himself. Pannenberg does not believe that the *kerygma* – the revealed
Christian gospel – is sacrosanct. That presupposes that we know what
it is and where it is to be found. In fact, Pannenberg does less than
justice to Barth's proper insistence on the givenness, the actuality, of
revelation.

Pannenberg's theological destination, then, is the revelation of God
in Christ, but to get there he considers it necessary to start with humanity
and the world. His method is to work from below, with particular
facts and their interpretation, even though his aim is universal truth
and the totality of meaning. Since God is, by definition, the all–determining reality, God is implicated in all reality and so is also to some
extent reflected by it. God cannot be said to determine reality without
being involved in it. This is the ultimate mandate for scanning all
significant human experience, especially that of a religious kind, for
intimations of revelation.

Pannenberg has always insisted that revelation is not to be identified
immediately with religious experience *à la* Schleiermacher, though
religious experience is relevant to revelation. Religious experience is not
self-evidently experience of revelation. Its claims must be assessed by
means of all we know. We cannot isolate revelation, hold it up and
compare religious experience of various kinds with it. It is integral to
experience and cannot be disentangled from it. Therefore claims to have
received revelation, such as those of the Hebrew prophets and the New
Testament writers, must be subjected to critical evaluation. In his early
work, Pannenberg emphasised the historical *locus* of revelation and the
need for historical research to verify it. At the same time, he affirmed
the importance of philosophical analysis. In his middle period, he borrowed from the philosophy of the natural sciences, seeing the claims of
religious doctrines as hypotheses to be tested. Then Pannenberg moved
on to consider the implications of the social sciences and strengthened
the theological anthropology that had always been part of his repertoire.

In the first volume of his *Systematic Theology* (German 1988, ET
1991) Pannenberg includes a substantial discussion of revelation. Indeed
the theme of revelation pervades the work. Pannenberg insists that
doctrinal theology cannot be subjected to any particular philosophical
position, for 'the first task of philosophical theology is to fix its intellectual point of departure in the historical revelation of God' (p.ix). His
further premise, that God is the only source of the knowledge of God
(p.2), indicates continuity with Barth. The task of dogmatics is defined

as an enquiry into the truth of dogma (p.16) and Pannenberg notes that the testing of truth claims is repressed in Schleiermacher. In contrast to Barth, who deplored any form of apologetics as lack of faith, Pannenberg maintains that apologetics and dogmatics should be integrated. We test the truth of doctrine by bringing its content to light, expounding its meaning, in the context of our knowledge of the world and of human nature. To give doctrines the status of hypotheses is not to trivialise them, but to take their cognitive truth claims seriously (pp.56ff). We are compelled to adopt this approach, for though God is the one subject of theology (p.5), we cannot begin directly with God: we have to build up our ground by means of fundamental theology (p.61).

In his later work, Pannenberg has more to say about the role of metaphysics (as opposed to historical research or the natural and social sciences) in theological construction. Since he is committed to pursuing the totality of meaning, metaphysics is inescapable. Following Kant and Rahner, Pannenberg insists that the concept of God is indispensable in speaking of totality (pp.69ff). 'Talk about God has the totality of the world as its theme as well as God's own existence' (p.253). At this point, Pannenberg rescues the term 'natural theology' from the obloquy to which Ritschl and Barth had committed it (pp.95ff). There is a natural knowledge of God and natural theology is the reflective and critical expression of that natural knowledge, but only in the light of the gospel can we see that a knowledge of the God of the gospel is possible through reflection on natural phenomena (pp.107ff).

As far as religious experience is concerned, Pannenberg argues that experience must yield common, objective meanings, otherwise we would be reduced to radical subjectivism – solipsism. Therefore 'there are implications of meaning in the actual contents of experience' and those meanings are articulated in statements of a religious nature (pp.164ff; here Pannenberg makes a connection with Schleiermacher's *Speeches on Religion*). It is these statements, or assertions, that are subjected to critical scrutiny in theology: 'the gods of the religions must show in our experience of the world that they are the powers which they claim to be' (p.167). Theology enquires whether religious traditions, including those of Christianity, can justifiably claim to be based on revelation. The history of religion can be read as the history of 'the manifestation of divine reality and the process of criticism of inadequate human views of this reality. . . The manifestation of divine reality even within the unresolved conflicts of religious and ideological truth claims is called revelation' (p.171).

Pannenberg has said this much, and a good deal more, before he gets on to the chapter (ch.4) devoted to the problem of revelation. Now he expounds the multiplicity of biblical ideas of revelation (pp.198ff) and questions the assumption (made by Schleiermacher and Barth) that revelation must refer to the origination of new knowledge of God. In fact it presupposes a prior, ongoing relationship with God. Revelation must include all self-communication of God to humanity (pp.194f). The primary witness to this self-communication is the biblical narrative. Since it was given to ancient Israel to grasp that God's revelation was primarily in history, theological research must tackle the question of the historicity of those narratives in order to address Christian truth claims (p.232). But this is no detached analysis; it must be conducted in intimate connection with the substance of Christian belief. The 'theological testing and verification of the truth claims of Christian revelation will take place in the form of a systematic reconstruction of Christian doctrine' and its truth will be confirmed to believers by its power to illuminate their experience (p.257). When by this process revelation is attested, it establishes the 'deity' of God, so inviting the response of faith.

The strength of Pannenberg's approach to the question of revelation is its seriousness about the manifold forms of reality and its engagement with the various disciplines that shed light on them. This he does on theological grounds – because God is by definition the reality that determines all created reality. The tough critical stance stems from the ethos of the Enlightenment and the location of revelation in history is also an Enlightenment (or perhaps post-Enlightenment) theme. Unlike Schleiermacher or Barth, Pannenberg does not attempt to short-circuit the process of theological enquiry by postulating some self-authenticating, foundationalist, *terminus a quo* for theological construction, whether in the immediacy of religious experience or the self-validating actuality of revelation. It is a great merit of Pannenberg's approach that his theological method is worked out in rigorous dialogue with historical method, the philosophy of the natural and social sciences, and metaphysics. There is no loss of theological nerve in Pannenberg: he meets the challenge of secular thought and the reductionist critique of religion head-on and faces it down. Not for him any retreat into postmodernist fideism or narrative worlds. He aims to articulate a Christian theological worldview, to sum up the totality of meaning in Christ.

And yet the quest for totality of meaning through engagement with the disciplines that bring reality to light in its manifold forms is also the Achilles' heel of Pannenberg's theology. In spite of his profound engagement with modern philosophy of science, and that of Karl Popper in particular, his method remains impossibly inductive. Pannenberg's theology gives the impression of an uncontrolled diffuseness of method. You cannot scan the whole range of significant reality for intimations of revelation unless you know what you are looking for. How do we evaluate the innumerable doctrinal hypotheses (as Pannenberg regards them) of the world's religions, without some key criterion of interpretation? What is Pannenberg's instrument of interrogation? Pannenberg seems to need something like a concept of the essence of Christianity (such as Schleiermacher has, though an inadequate one) as a guiding thread to lead him through the labyrinth of religions and their claims. If Pannenberg had not been quite so dismissive of Barth's emphasis on the givenness of revelation and its decisive embodiment in Jesus Christ, he might have found it easier to do this.

Moltmann: Revelation as Eschatology and Experience

Jurgen Moltmann is not a theologian whose work has been dominated by the problem of divine revelation. Unlike Barth, he does not make it a first-order theological issue. Whole volumes of his work proceed blithely without so much as mentioning revelation. Moltmann's method is like Barth's in that it entirely takes for granted the world of biblical revelation – its reality, integrity and validity – without attempting to justify it or to question it. Moltmann speaks from faith to faith. Through powerful rhetoric he creates a world of biblical faith which is inspiring to those who accept the premise. He uses biblical and theological material eclectically in his exposition of a series of theological themes.

Moltmann discusses revelation from two aspects: its eschatological validation and its manifestation in experience. In his view of the former, the theme of revelation as eschatology, he shares a point with Pannenberg, whose early thought stressed that revelation is anticipated, proleptically, in history but fulfilled and verified in the last time. In discussing the latter, the manifestation of revelation in experience, he has something in common with Schleiermacher, but without the latter's notion of immediate self-consciousness which is coterminous with the sense of absolute dependence on God. Let us look at these two matters more closely.

Regarding revelation as eschatology, Moltmann insists in *Theology of Hope* (1964) that the only starting-point of Christian theology is the biblical history of revelation. Theology begins with these particular, unique revelatory events which culminate in Jesus Christ, and then it attempts to demonstrate their general significance for all people at all times. Like Barth, Moltmann insists that the biblical revelation must not be subjected to some external framework of enquiry, but must be elucidated purely on its own terms. If allowed to do so, by an appropriate theological method, biblical revelation will itself question down to its fundamentals any external framework with which it is brought into contact (Bauckham, 1987, pp.25f). There is nothing in this that departs from Barth, but Moltmann does actually intend to offer an alternative to Barth – and moreover to Bultmann and Pannenberg.

The distinctiveness of Moltmann's approach lies in his emphasis on the historicity of revelation – a historicity that can be predicated of the God who reveals. Moltmann believes that Barth construes revelation as a window into the eternity of God and that he does this because he is under the influence of the Greek notion of the *Logos* as the outworking of the rationality immanent in the godhead, which corresponds to Gentile religions of divine epiphany – the shining out of what is eternally true and real (probably an unduly harsh and one-sided interpretation of Barth). In the Hebrew Bible, by contrast, revelation is not an epiphany of the eternal present but the performative utterance of God's promise that contains the power to change the course of events. It is one thing to ask: where and when does an epiphany of the divine, eternal, immutable and primordial take place in the realm of the human, temporal and transient? And it is another thing to ask: where and when does the God of the promise reveal his faithfulness and in it himself and his presence? (Moltmann, 1967, p.43)

Moltmann acknowledges that there is no guarantee that God's revealed promise to act in history will be fulfilled as it stands. It depends on human collaboration and adapts to changing circumstances. The promises to ancient Israel were continually reinterpreted and in a wider sense. 'In an "expanding history of promise" each fulfilment left an overplus of promise pointing to further fulfilment, since a reality wholly corresponding to the God who gave the promise was never reached,' until the history of promise arrived at the explicit monotheism of the lordship of Yahweh over all the nations, the belief in resurrection of the dead and the apocalyptic hope of the renewal of the entire cosmos (Bauckham, 1987, p.30).

By thus putting all his revelatory eggs in the basket of divine promise, Moltmann is inviting the comment that he has substituted a history of mere promise for a history of divine action. – We cried out for divine intervention on the basis of the promise and what we got was another instalment of ever more grandiose promises! So Moltmann's scheme of revelation as promise has set up the question of theodicy, of how the justice of God can be maintained in the light of evil and suffering. Moltmann addresses this crucial theological problem in his next major work *The Crucified God* (ET 1974), where God is most fully and finally revealed in the darkness and despair of Golgotha. In turn, it raises the question of whether Moltmann sees a proper transition from his theology of hope, with its notion of revelation as promise in the field of historical events, to this new paradigm. The continuity and consistency is not self-evident.

Moltmann is constrained to admit that the four New Testament words for revelation, which denote unveiling, disclosing, making known or unconcealing, derive from the mystery religions of epiphany. However, he is confident that they have broken free from their Gentile setting and have been adapted to the eschatological framework which is dominant in the New Testament (Moltmann, 1967, pp.44f). At this juncture, Moltmann is perhaps open to the very charge of tendentiousness and one-sidedness that he applies to Barth. In other respects it seems that Moltmann is still under the spell of Barth, particularly when he insists that revelation cannot be objectively explained but only experienced in the dark, defenceless depths of non-objectifiable subjectivity. Revelation is unfathomable and (as Protestant theology has been inclined to say, following Melanchthon) is known only in its effects (Moltmann, 1967, p.52). However, this sounds more like mystical encounter with a hidden reality than receiving a promise of God's action in history.

Regarding revelation in experience, also in *Theology of Hope*, Moltmann had already challenged the antithesis of revelation and reason which was standard in Protestant orthodoxy and had been intensified into a dualism by Barth and Brunner. It had the effect, Moltmann argued, of making theological talk of revelation increasingly irrelevant to our knowledge of reality and our life in this world. Revelation had been backed into a *cul de sac*, cut off from the busy thoroughfare of life. 'The result of this unhappy story,' Moltmann concluded, 'is that our task is to set the subject of divine revelation no longer in antithesis to man's momentary understanding of the world and of himself, but to take this very under-standing of self and world up into, and open its eyes for, the eschatological outlook in which revelation is seen as promise of the truth' (Moltmann, 1967, p.44). In other words, revelation as eschatological promise must be brought into living contact with human experience.

Moltmann takes up the relation between revelation and experience in

The Spirit of Life. Addressing the issue in a section significantly headed 'Overcoming the False Alternative between Divine Revelation and Human Experience of the Holy Spirit', he sets aside the dualism of the dialectical theology of Barth, Brunner and Bultmann as 'unfruitful'. If revelation remains external – 'wholly other' – to the human spirit, it remains 'inexperienceable and hidden', producing a 'permanent discontinuity between God's Spirit and the spirit of human beings'. The dialectical theologians introduced a double bind for theology: either revelation remains wholly other, in which case it is ineffective; or it correlates with human religious aspirations, in which case it seems less than revelation. We end up with either revelation that cannot be experienced or experience devoid of revelation (Moltmann, 1992, pp.5ff).

Moltmann believes that this is a false dichotomy. God's revelation is by definition a 'making–itself–experienceable' by human beings. Barth has merely replaced divine immanence, as in Schleiermacher and Liberal Protestantism, by divine transcendence. But, says Moltmann cryptically, there is an immanence of God in human beings and a transcendence of human beings in God. 'Because God's Spirit is present in human beings, the human spirit is self-transcendently aligned towards God. Human experience functions within the context of anticipation – not that God will lift the veil of his eternal being, but that God will act in history according to his promise. 'The Holy Spirit is not simply the subjective side of God's revelation of himself, and faith is not merely the echo of the Word of God in the human heart.' The Spirit is the power to raise the dead and faith is the beginning of rebirth to new life (Moltmann, 1992, pp.5ff).

Is God an object of possible experience? Modern philosophy since Kant has answered with a decisive negative. God is not an object. The limits of human reason make it intrinsically impossible for God to reveal himself to humans. But in modern thought, God can be postulated as an inferred corollary of moral experience (Kant) or contingent experience (Schleiermacher). Moltmann believes that experience has been too narrowly defined in modern epistemology. Experience is socially constructed and always embodied. Transcendence can be discovered in every kind of experience, once the narrow concentration on self-consciousness has been overcome. 'The experience of God's Spirit is not limited to the human subject's experience of the self. It is also a constitutive element in the experience of the "Thou", in the experience of sociality, and in the experience of nature. . . It is therefore possible to experience God *in, with and beneath* each everyday experience of the world.' This is grounded theologically in the truth that God is in all things through his

Spirit and all things are in God by virtue of creation, so that we can even say that God himself experiences all things in his own way (Moltmann, 1992, pp.31ff).

With regard to the form of experience of revelation, Moltmann seems to side with Schleiermacher: experience of God is given with experience of the world – of the community and of nature – for those who are open to it. With regard to the content of experience of revelation, Moltmann has a distinctive contribution to make: revelation is not a momentary glimpse into the eternal life of God, but the performative promise of God's involvement in the sufferings of the world. The outstanding question is whether form and content here are fully compatible.

Bibliography

Abraham, W.J., *Divine Revelation and the Limits of Historical Criticism*, Oxford, OUP, 1982.

Avis, P., *The Methods of Modern Theology*, Basingstoke, Marshall Pickering, 1986.

Baillie, J., (ed.), *Revelation*, London, 1937.

———, *The Idea of Revelation in Recent Thought*, London, OUP; New York, Columbia University Press, 1956.

Barth, K., *The Epistle to the Romans*, trans. E. Hoskyns, Oxford, OUP, 1968.

———, *Church Dogmatics*, ed. T.F. Torrance and G.W. Bromiley, Edinburgh, T. & T. Clark, 1956.

———, *The Theology of Schleiermacher*, ed. D. Ritschl, Edinburgh, T. & T. Clark. 1982.

Barth, K., & Brunner, E., *Natural Theology*, trans. P. Fraenkel, London, 1946.

Bauckham, R., *Moltmann: Messianic Theology in the Making*, Basingstoke, Marshall Pickering, 1987.

Brunner, E., *The Mediator*, trans. O. Wyon, London, Lutterworth Press, 1934.

———, *Revelation and Reason*, trans. O. Wyon, London, SCM, 1947.

Gunton, C.E., *A Brief Theology of Revelation*, Edinburgh, T. & T. Clark, 1995.

Farmer, H.H., *Revelation and Religion*, London, Nisbet, 1954.

Hegel, G.W.F., *The Phenomenology of Mind*, trans. J.B. Baillie, 2nd edn, London, Allen and Unwin, 1931.

Kant, I., *Critique of Pure Reason*, London, Dent (Everyman), 1934.

———, *Religion Within the Limits of Reason Alone*, New York, Harper Torchbooks, 1960.

Lessing, G.E., *Theological Writings*, ed. H. Chadwick, London, A. & C. Black, 1956.

MacCormack, B., *Karl Barth's Critically Realistic Dialectical Theology: Its Genesis and Development 1909–1936*, Oxford, Clarendon Press, 1995.

Moltmann, J., *Theology of Hope*, London, SCM, 1967.

——, *The Crucified God*, London, SCM, 1974.

——, *The Spirit of Life*, London, SCM, 1992.

Niebuhr, H.R., *The Meaning of Revelation*, New York, Macmillan, 1960 [1941].

Pannenberg, W., (ed.), *Revelation as History*, London, Sheed and Ward, 1969.

——, *Basic Questions in Theology I*, London, SCM, 1970.

——, *Theology and the Philosophy of Science*, London, Darton, Longman & Todd, 1978.

——, *Systematic Theology I*, Edinburgh, T. & T. Clark; Grand Rapids, Eerdmans, 1991.

Schleiermacher, F.D.E., *Soliloquies*, trans. H.O. Friess, Chicago, 1926.

——, *The Christian Faith*, trans. H.R. Mackintosh and J.S. Stewart, Edinburgh, T. & T. Clark, 1928.

——, *On Religion: Speeches to its Cultured Despisers*, trans. J. Oman, New York, 1958.

——, *Brief Outline on the Study of Theology*, trans. T.N. Tice, Richmond VA, John Knox, 1966.

Thiemann, R., *Revelation and Theology: The Gospel as Narrated Promise*, Notre Dame IN, University of Notre Dame Press, 1985.

Tillich, P., *Systematic Theology*, 3 vols in 1, Welwyn, Nisbet, 1968.

4

Revelation and Philosophy

Terence Penelhum

Those philosophers in modern times who have considered revelation have been concerned with deciding how rational it is to believe in it. Throughout the seventeenth and eighteenth Centuries, debate on this issue was based on a particular understanding of what revelation (if it is a reality) is, and of how it is offered for our acceptance. For want of a better title, I shall refer to this understanding as the traditional view of revelation. It is essentially that found in the system of St Thomas Aquinas. Because of the severe criticisms of it that contributed to Enlightenment scepticism, many Christian thinkers (particularly Protestant thinkers) have seen its abandonment as a means of answering that scepticism. I shall argue that, in spite of its limitations, the main epistemological contentions associated with the traditional view still merit acceptance by Christian apologists. To this end, I shall concentrate exclusively on philosophical debates, even though their theological ramifications will be obvious.

The Traditional View of Revelation

The view of the nature of revelation that we find in Aquinas was taken as normative for several centuries after him, both by those who accepted that revelation is a reality and those who did not.[1] It was designed to resolve a long debate about the proper place of secular philosophy and science in a culture assumed to be Christian.[2] In the modern era, when philosophers have been debating how far a culture increasingly determined by secular science can still remain Christian, it has come under increasing strain.

On this understanding, revelation provides us with a body of truths about God, our nature, and our salvation. These truths are made available to us in verbal form, through the Scriptures and the doctrinal pronouncements of the Church, in particular the creeds. The faith that the Christian proclaims in reciting the creeds is primarily a matter of accepting these truths. Such acceptance inevitably entails no more than a very dim and partial understanding of the realities of which these doctrines tell us, for they transcend the powers of our finite intellects. Nevertheless, it is not irrational to accede to them and very good reasons can be given for so doing.

The first reason is that some of the doctrines revealed to us can be demonstrated independently by our own, unaided reason. These include the existence of God, his unity and perfection, and his providential governance of the world. So philosophical reasoning and revelatory pronouncement overlap substantially in their subject matter. There are good theological reasons why this should be so: why, that is, some truths are included in revelation when the human intellect can discover them for itself. To prove them requires more time and training than most people have; and it would be contrary to the loving nature of God that he should confine awareness of truths necessary for salvation to those who can construct, or follow, metaphysical arguments. On the other hand, if none of the truths of revelation could be proved by reason, one might well ask why one should believe them; and if some of them can be proved, this question can be given a plausible answer. The authorities who tell us these truths can be seen to have good credentials if some of the things that they tell us can be established independently; and if we learn some religious truths through reason, it is wise to look favourably on the others, even if they cannot be established independently. Further, even though the majority of believers believe without the aid of philosophy, it is clearly more reasonable for them to believe when those with philosophical competence can perform the demonstrations. It is always more reasonable to accept what is told us when it can be vouched for by an independent expert.

A second reason for accepting what the Scriptures and the Church reveal is that even those revealed items that cannot be proved have strong supporting evidence in their favour. Those who proclaim them to us can point to many remarkable events that reinforce their claims: there are prophecies fulfilled, miracles performed, and the astonishing growth of the Christian community itself. These evidences show that those who have been used by God to make the truths of revelation available to us are persons whose authority it is foolish to question.

Although acceptance is so reasonable, and rejection so foolish, acceptance of revelation is something we give freely. Faith is a freely adopted state, involving the will as well as the intellect, even though it is also due to an infusion of grace. This makes it clear why reason can only demonstrate some of the saving truths. For if something is proved to us, it becomes a matter of knowledge for us, and we cannot say 'No' to it; and if all the savings truths were like that, there would be some for whom salvation would be the result of changes that did not involve the will. Our freedom and responsibility before God, and the voluntariness of faith, are thus providentially preserved by the fact that some revealed truths, however reasonable, are not demonstrable but entirely revealed. Strictly speaking, it is only these that are properly called articles of faith, since faith and knowledge are exclusive.

Those truths that are demonstrable by reason, yet also form part of the subject matter of revelation, are the propositions composing what came to be known as natural theology. Those learned only through revelation, however good their support by evidences, form the content of revealed theology.

Some Implications of the Traditional View

The view which St Thomas formulated perfectly fitted the era in which he formulated it. The Church insisted that there was no way to salvation outside the acceptance of its creeds, and participation in its sacraments. The doctrines of the creed must be accepted in their entirety. Indeed, Thomas holds that the inner act of acceptance must be reflected in the outer act of confession, which he clearly equates with the sincere recitation of the creed;[3] it is only the heretic who presumes to pick and choose among the Church's proclamations.[4] The Church that maintained this was no longer a small body of underprivileged poor on the fringes of an alien culture, but a vast and ubiquitous institution that unified a high civilisation. What it claimed, therefore, had to be integrated with the sciences and philosophy of that civilisation, and there had to be clear marks of its right to speak for God to the citizens of that civilisation. For a rational and informed hearer to recognise these marks, the reality of God had to be established independently.

These requirements led to some important features of the traditional view, that were tacitly assumed and only questioned later. The most obvious is the assumption that revelation is propositional, that it consists of truths about God and about our salvation. Hence the right response to it – faith – is itself primarily a propositional act, of belief and confession.

Another implication is that revelation is represented as having a necessary indirectness. There is, in the first place, the fact that revelation is about God, and that we come to faith in Him through learning about Him. (This is both shown and hidden in Thomas' doctrine that God is the First Truth.[5]) In the second place, both the proofs and the evidences depend on arguing from facts that are known independently of faith. The proofs, such as Thomas' own 'five ways', are arguments from created things, and depend for their cogency on the certainty that they start from facts we can know without conceding that God exists. The evidences depend upon historical knowledge: although the alleged events are for the most part miraculous, they only attest to the Church's authority because they are known to have taken place in the same way we know about non-miraculous past events, namely through records and testimony. So the recognition of the Church's teaching authority is indirect, or mediate, and the knowledge of God presupposed in that recognition is also mediate.

Early Modern Criticism of the Traditional View

Those early modern philosophers who began the attack on the reality of revelation did so by arguing that natural theology did not support it, but undermined it. The most important arguments of this form were those of Spinoza[6] and those of the deists.[7] Both believed that we could learn of God's reality through reason, but then maintained that what reason shows us of his nature is at odds with the traditional claims for revelation. Spinoza held that reason showed God to be eternal, infinite, and immutable, and that he was not separate from his creation but immanent in it. This is inconsistent with the anthropomorphic stories of the Hebrew Scriptures, where God is represented as passionate, inconsistent, and meddlesome. So although they contain some useful sources of personal piety for the untutored, the scriptural documents have to be assessed naturalistically as a single nation's record of its own history, not a revelation for all mankind. The deists accepted that natural theology, which was dominated in Newton's era by the 'argument from design', proved that our world was created by a God who governs its daily course. But the law-abidingness of nature and the phenomena of adaptation, which show us these things, also demonstrate the rationality of the deity, who would not indulge in miraculous interventions and who would have no need of such interventions to teach us, when he has endowed us all with consciences and has not confined his moral instruction to a single ancient people. All that is of pedagogical value in the Scriptures is a myth-ridden restatement of moral truths we can learn independently.

The most enduring results of arguments like these have been in biblical criticism, which is not our present theme. The most telling response to the deists was Joseph Butler's *Analogy of Religion*. Butler argued that the knowledge of God which the deists said they possessed was not extensive enough to justify their confidence about what God would not do. There might indeed be miraculous phenomena that violated natural laws but still made rational sense in the context of *super*natural divine plans.[8]

The most far-reaching criticisms of the traditional view, however, were those of Hume, who attacked both the claims of natural theology and those of special revelation as well. For tactical reasons, the attacks appear in separate parts of his work, but their full import is only clear when they are combined. The most notorious essay is the section 'Of Miracles' in his *Enquiry Concerning Human Understanding*.[9] The essence of his argument is that the testimony we have for the miracles of the Christian tradition can never suffice to establish that they occurred, because the very miraculousness of an alleged event, which entails it has never been encountered before, is itself a reason for disbelieving the witness who reports it to us – however honourable or expert that witness may be. In fact the witnesses who have told us of the Christian miracles have never been of high quality, but were for the most part ignorant and barbarous.

This argument, whatever its merits, tells us that the records of the Scriptural miracles must be rejected when assessed by the standards we would use to judge secular historical writings. The strongest of the many attempts to answer it was offered by Paley. In the 'Preparatory Considerations' that open his *Evidences of Christianity*,[10] he said that there is good reason not to approach the Scriptures in exactly the same way as secular histories, even though he maintains they can survive scrutiny if we do. For we must surely concede, Paley holds, that there are good philosophical reasons to think there is a God who might wish to reveal himself to us; and if there are, they prevent us from dismissing miracles *a priori*, as Hume does.

Paley's answer, which attempted to restore the traditional connection between natural and revealed theology, ignored the fact that Hume had also attacked natural theology itself, in the section immediately following the essay on miracles[11], and in the *Dialogues concerning Natural Religion*.[12] The main burden of this work is that the design argument for God is a very weak one, if it is judged by the scientific standards its users claimed to be observing. In this Hume was followed by Kant, who also joined him in noticing that the wide acceptance of such a weak argument demands special independent explanation.[13] Since Hume and Kant it has been commonplace for philosophers to say that demonstrating truths about God is beyond the powers of the human intellect. If this judgement is combined with doubts about the historical credentials of the Christian Scriptures, acceptance of revelation, as traditionally understood, no longer seems rational.

Believers can respond to this conclusion in two ways. One is to try to rehabilitate all or part of the traditional view by defending natural theology and the integrity of the Scriptures. The other is to make a virtue of the perceived necessity and maintain that the attempt to provide intellectual foundations for the faith is a mistake. On the latter view, Hume and Kant did theology an unintended favour, and Hume was more correct than he realised when he made the ironical remark that 'to be a philosophical sceptic is . . . the first and most essential step towards being a sound, believing Christian.'[14]

The Post-Enlightenment Defence

This second response outlined above is to be found mainly in the writings of Protestant theologians, and is common in the twentieth century. Yet it involves a major conceptual shift in the understanding of what revelation is, and is therefore in essence a philosophical position. It is due in large measure to the influence of the most clearly philosophical writings of Kierkegaard, especially the *Philosophical Fragments* and the *Concluding Unscientific Postscript*.[15] The nature of the conceptual shift involved is brought out clearly in the following summation by John Hick:

> The locus of revelation is not propositions but events, and its content is not a body of truths about God, but 'the living God' revealing himself in his actions toward man.[16]

The most perspicuous way of indicating the nature of this change, however, is in terms of a schema invented by George Mavrodes, and utilised to great effect in his book, *Revelation in Religious Belief*.[17] Mavrodes claims (correctly, in my view) that the four elements this schema

72

contains are all necessary conceptually for it to be correct to say that revelation has occurred. The schema is as follows:

(S) *m* reveals α to *n* by means of (through, etc.) *k*.

The traditional understanding of revelation is then to be expressed by saying that for *m* we must substitute 'God'; for α we must substitute a truth, or a body of truths, about God and his dealings with us; and the substitutions for *k* will be sayings of the prophets, or teachings of Jesus, or proclamations of the Church, the first two of these three, at least, being in the language of the Scriptures. The only ambiguity lies in the choice of substitution for *n*: the choice is between those who hear or read the sayings and proclamations, and those who actually accept them. The issue here, which I leave aside for the present, is whether faith must follow for revelation to have taken place.

The post-Enlightenment Protestant view can be expressed by saying that although *m* once more, is God, so is α. God reveals himself, not propositions about himself.[18] In Mavrodes' language, the model for revelation is that of manifestation, rather than (verbal) communication: God reveals himself, on this view, not (or not primarily) through utterances, (and this in spite of the centrality of preaching in the Protestant tradition) but through events. These are most centrally the 'saving' events in the history of Israel, the life of Christ, and the early history of the Church.

This appears to evade many difficulties posed by Enlightenment scepticism. Believers are no longer required to insist on the detailed truth of scriptural accounts of the events in which God chose to reveal himself, because these accounts are not themselves the content of revelation. They are merely responses to the revelatory events made by individuals present at them or informed of them, and can therefore be erroneous in detail. Later believers can differ in the way they interpret the events from those reporting them, who may have misunderstood their full significance. In other words, those who hold this 'saving event' view of revelation can be receptive to historical criticism, and need not resist it. It also seems to open up the possibility that those who learn of the saving events can encounter God individually through doing so, without having first to be assured of God's reality through indirect argument, thus evading the offensive suggestion that the rationality of faith depends on the prior sanction of philosophy.

But there are some natural objections from those holding the traditional view, or someone made into a sceptic by its apparent failure.

One objection is to say that in the absence of natural theology there is no epistemological justification for reading the Scriptures, or listening to a preacher, with any expectation that God will be encountered if we do so, or even that there really is a God. Another objection is to suggest that the revised understanding of revelation makes us more, not less, dependent on accurate accounts of the supposedly saving events; if these are (or were) indeed the locus of revelation, we need more than ever to be sure of what happened, and any misinterpretations of them by the witnesses are obstacles to the assurance we need. The more vital the events are theologically, the greater the obstacles to the reception of revelation for those who can only learn of them from reports, and were not actually there. The saga of the quest of the historical Jesus is only the most obvious example of how hard it is to remove these obstacles.

In Kierkegaard we find the classic attempt to refute these objections. The sixteenth-century reformers had attacked the traditional assumption that revelation needed the support of philosophical argument, because it suggested we could attain to knowledge of God without the need of grace and repentance. Kierkegaard argues the same way, but with unique penetration and philosophical skill. He uses the tools of philosophy itself to show the absurdity of suggesting that philosophy can supply either necessary or sufficient conditions for faith. The most philosophy can do is show why faith cannot make philosophical sense at all.[19]

Philosophy is the quest for knowledge of eternal truths. Its paradigm teacher, Socrates, recognises that his role is merely that of enabling the intellect of the learner to attain such knowledge on his own account – which implies that he is intrinsically capable of doing so, and is only hindered by circumstances and mental confusions. Salvation, however, requires a change in the hearer, who is prevented by his own corrupt will from even acknowledging his real needs. So if God seeks to teach us, He has to change us in order to enable us to recognise the way to Him. But the change he has to make in us has to be a change that does not annihilate our identity. He cannot, therefore, reveal himself as Lord, for that would elicit responses of fear or selfish calculation, not of love. He has consequently to reveal Himself in a humble guise, as a servant. But this entails that his identity can be completely unrecognised by those to whom he appears; they can always complain that his historical reality does not measure up to his claims. For what he must claim from us is not assent to some truth that we can work out for ourselves: He must claim free submission and love – a surrender to His person, not a concession to an argument. To think otherwise is to approach Him by night, like Nicodemus who presumed to treat him as a professional equal. So any attempt to liken the response to God to the response to a philosophical teacher obscures the fact that the barrier to faith is not ignorance or confusion, but sinfulness. The demand for philosophical justification is merely an intellectualised form of this, and a refusal to recognise its true character.

In addition, the failure to see the divine Servant for what He is is not a failure that is confined to those who hear about his appearance at a later time. It is a failure that can occur as readily among his contemporaries, and does. So the demand for historical accuracy about divine interventions in history is as much of an evasion of God's claims upon us as the demand for philosophical demonstrations of His reality.

This argument, which is the forerunner of later theological attempts to sever the 'Jesus of history' from the 'Christ of faith,' expresses profound insight into the differences between the philosophical student and the Christian disciple, and between the role of the philosopher and that of a preacher of the Word. It is also a classic source of reflection on the theme of divine hiddenness. But it does not succeed in showing the epistemological supports of faith offered in the traditional view to be religiously undesirable. Nor does it circumvent the historical difficulties Kierkegaard addresses.

Kierkegaard adds two elements that I cannot hope to evaluate here: he argues against the possibility of theistic proofs on grounds derived from Sextus Empiricus and Hume; and he insists that the recognition of God in the historical servant is doubly paradoxical – in requiring the ultimate paradox of the God-man, and in requiring the recognition of God in the face of His disguise as a creature. Both arguments, however, would surely provide an unbeliever with rational excuses for rejection if they were true. If sinfulness prevents our yielding to God, then we could hide behind our intellectual incapacities in our attempt to escape Him. What proofs of his existence or perfection would do is help expose the real nature of our reluctance; they would not compel us to acknowledge His reality (although Kierkegaard appears to follow Aquinas in supposing that they would). For one of the most common forms of human corruption is our skill in evading the acknowledgement of unwelcome truths that are indeed proved to us (like the injuriousness of tobacco or the cruelty of the fur trade); and the determination of philosophers to find flaws in the proofs of God is itself a sign that flawless proofs would also meet rejection, if we had a mind to it. Kierkegaard is no doubt right that the undisguised appearance of God would overwhelm us and not leave us free to deny Him, as the incarnate God could be denied; but that does not show that a philosophical proof of God would overwhelm us in the same way. No doubt a demand for proof can be sinfully motivated, but this does not show that a search for a proof is always corrupt, any more than the evidence suggests that those who have offered such arguments have always done this for sinful reasons. They have not claimed that assent to a proof of God is itself faith, and it cries out for demonstration that it could never increase a hearer's openness to it.

Kierkegaard is right to stress that a comtemporary of the Servant can miss the point of his appearance as much as a later reader of accounts of it, and that many later readers have yielded. But this point must be made with care. The more complete a disguise, the more likely it is that an innocent person will fail to penetrate it. (This is a necessary truth.) Wilful rejection is rejection that can occur in the face of the obvious, not rejection that needs complete obscurity. This does not mean that revelation cannot take a form that changes the witnesses' expectations, but that the new understanding, like the mistaken expectation, needs a connection in logic with a previous awareness of God. That the servant is a proper object of devotion and submission, and that these should not be held in reserve for a warrior king, is something one can only accept while hoping for someone who will offer deliverance in the name of God. Someone who does not want the kingdom of God will not accept the servant, indeed; yet someone who does want the kingdom, but expects it in the wrong way, may be confused by the form of the divine intervention. And someone who must rely upon the records of the servant's appearance might well think the stories express what would satisfy his or her hopes, but be worried that they are fabricated just to please the reader, and that God may not have entered history at all.

These last two possibilities are real ones. This is shown by the anxiety that has visited many believers on their first encounter with the problems of biblical scholarship, and by the response of fundamentalists who try to close off debate on these matters in the name of scriptural inerrancy. Kiekegaard's argument is of no help in the face of such anxieties, for it merely impugns the motives of those who feel them. Tillich states the case wrongly when he says that 'Kierkegaard exaggerates when he says that it is sufficient for the Christian faith nakedly to assert that in the years 1–30 God sent his son.'[20] This is not an exaggeration; it is a dangerous falsehood. Even if it were correct, it would entail some element of reliance on the authenticity of the records. But its falsehood can be seen when we reflect that the records tell the story of the event in ways that, for all their variations, are consistent with the loving nature of God on which Kierkegaard's argument itself depends. It is hard to see how his argument could have been penned if the gospel stories told not of one who entered Jerusalem on an ass and was put to death on trumped-up charges of rebellion and did not resist, but of one who entered in a chariot and was executed for disobeying military orders and died fighting to the last.

Kierkegaard contrasts the Socratic teacher with the divine teacher; the contrast is so radical that the many ironies of the *Fragments* seem to impugn the very use of this title to speak of the God–man. But what makes it right to use it is the fact that Christians have always supposed that the incarnation was indeed an act of teaching as well as a saving act. The divine pedagogy would be very mysterious indeed if the words and actions of Jesus were substantially at variance with those of which we read in the records, or (and it is the same thing) if the records of them could not, in general, be trusted.

Failures in natural theology, and problems in the historical records, can both give rise to reasonable doubts. Only if there are answers to reasonable doubts could it be said with assurance (and without uncharitableness) that unbelief is wholly due to sin. The non-propositional view of revelation does not obviate the need for such answers, or show it would be anything other than a religious blessing to provide them. Such considerations do not show that revelation must be in propositional form. But they show that recognising that it need not be in this form leaves the case for epistemological support of revelation unaffected.

Revelation and Basic Beliefs

Let us now consider a group of more recent arguments against the traditional view.[21] Those who employ them are not concerned to deny the possibility of natural theology, and in fact some of them practise it; but they deny it has the role assigned to it in the traditional view. They attack two traditional assumptions: first, the assumption that unless the knowledge gained through natural theology is available, acceptance of the claims of revelation is irrational; and second, the assumption that the knowledge that ensures the rationality of faith is indirect, or mediate, knowledge.

These arguments derive their influence from recent work in the theory of knowledge. Much of this work has shown a deep disillusionment with what is often called 'classical foundationalism'. This name is usually applied to the theories of all those thinkers since Descartes who have felt it their duty to provide arguments in support of our common-sense beliefs in the reliability of sense–perception, the law-abidingness of nature, and the like, on pain of surrender to the form of scepticism invented by Descartes in the first of his *Meditations*. Such arguments have usually been attempts to show that the beliefs the Cartesian sceptic questions can be inferred from a specially privileged class of truths that are beyond reasonable doubt – such as self-evident propositions, or propositions about one's own sensory experiences. It is historically important to note that this epistemological programme is indeed one for which we can praise or blame Descartes, who changed philosophers' understanding of scepticism in order to impose it; so that it is one in which the primal figures of natural theology, such as St Thomas, took no part. Nevertheless, there is an obvious parallel between the suggestion that our common-sense secular beliefs about our world are only rational if they can be inferred from more privileged ones, and the traditional suggestion that our acceptance of the claims of revelation derives its rationality from the fact that some religious truths can be proved by reason, and others can be shown to be more probable because of this. Because of this obvious parallel, it is not surprising that we find some of our best philosophical apologists arguing that since the rationality of common-sense beliefs cannot acquire the support foundationalists have tried to provide for it, and does not need it, there is no epistemological case for demanding the parallel support for revelation that the traditional view takes to be necessary.

This apologetic has an ancestry that goes back to Pascal[22] and incorporates an insistence that there is no case for demanding that religious beliefs satisfy criteria of rationality that are more stringent than those we apply to other beliefs. This insistence, which I have dubbed the 'parity argument', is a powerful, though limited, apologetic tool; but it is not the whole of the position before us.

It is impossible here to explore the case against classical foundationalism. Suffice to mention Alvin Plantinga's argument that the assertion that beliefs are not rational unless they are self-evident or incorrigible or can be inferred from assertions that are, is itself not self-evident or incorrigible or inferred from assertions that are: hence foundationalism in its commonest form is self-refuting. He argues from this that a rational being will (indeed must) hold many beliefs that are not inferred from others; he calls such beliefs basic beliefs, and then claims that beliefs about God can well be included among them, unless their irrationality can be demonstrated independently. Religious beliefs are, he holds, 'properly basic' – they can be held without irrationality, even though they are not inferred from others. The traditional view does not, of course, deny that they are often held without being inferred from others; but it implies that their rationality depends in some manner on the fact that they can be so inferred. Plantinga does not deny that some of them can be inferred, but denies that their rationality depends upon this.

Plantinga is aware that this will appear to open the gates to almost any beliefs that are sincerely held and not clearly refuted. His response is to distinguish between a belief's being basic and its being groundless. The believer does not hold his or her beliefs without grounds, because they come in circumstances that ground them for him or her. The believer sees the heavens and says they declare the glory of God; or experiences an inner peace that impels the affirmation that God has forgiven him or her. The fact that these beliefs are occasioned by such experiences shows the beliefs are not groundless; but they are not inferred from the experiences. For similar reasons, William Alston has argued that it is proper to speak of 'perceiving God' on such occasions in a manner analogous to the common way we talk of perceiving objects in the world when we have sensory experiences; and in a similar way, Nicholas Wolterstorff has included the hearing of God's word through the reading of Scripture as a primary form of religious awareness.

It seems clear that we do not have here another form of the traditional 'Argument from Religious Experience.' The thesis is not that we can perform a successful piece of natural theology by inferring the reality of God from the fact that so many people have experiences in which they think they are encountering him. The thesis is rather that it is wholly rational for them to think that they are encountering him in those experiences, just as it is wholly rational for me to think my typewriter is in front of me because it looks and feels to me that I am now using it. While this is clear, there are questions that still arise. Most importantly, is it held that the theistic belief that is grounded by the experience is to be included within the experience that grounds it, or not? If I look at the heavens and think 'God made all this,' my belief is presumably a rational and not a fanciful one because of the experiential event that is its setting; but is that event the seeing of the heavens, or my seeing of them and my thinking God made all this?

Let us bypass this question for the present, however, for all its potential importance, because I do not wish to suggest that the apologetic move I have tried to outline depends for its cogency on giving one or other answer to it. Similar tangles arise when one tries to analyse the exact character of those sensory experiences that ground our beliefs in the world around us at the secular level, and most of us would not wish to make the rationality of our sensory beliefs depend on how we deal with them. For the moment, another implication of this apologetic is more important.

Let us recall Mavrodes' schema: (S) m reveals a to n by means of (through) k. Let us assume again that m is God. What do we substitute for k? The point made by the 'basic belief' apologists is that substitutes for k can be any types of experience God chooses to use, or any phenomena (such as the heavens at night) that we are aware of in such experiences, and they certainly do not have to be propositional in character. In consequence of this, some of them have revived what is sometimes called the doctrine of natural religion or natural revelation.[23] According to this doctrine, God has created us with a built-in (or innate) disposition to believe in him, which is activated by occasions that his providence brings before everyone, as well as by those special occasions available only to those who have heard the gospel. This doctrine is probably present in the first chapter of the Epistle to the Romans, and is certainly present in the opening chapters of Calvin's *Institutes*.[24] It enables those who hold it to follow Paul and Calvin in ascribing all rejection of God to sinfulness.

Although this doctrine is not entailed by the basic belief apologetic, it is readily suggested by the analogy drawn by that apologetic between beliefs about God and beliefs about the external world. This same analogy has the further implication that awareness of God is direct awareness, not merely in the negative sense where 'direct' means 'not inferred or mediate,' but in some positive sense comparable to that in which sensory awareness of the physical world around us is direct – whatever that sense is.

Revelation and Rationality

The apologetic strength of the position I have just outlined is easy to see. The history of modern philosophy is full of failed attempts to provide compelling inferences from sensory experiences to common-sense beliefs about the external world; but these failures do not make it irrational to hold those beliefs. It is similarly rational to come to hold those theistic beliefs that are occasioned in us by those experiences God chooses to use to arouse them. This analogy in my opinion holds. But it has other implications.

To return to my earlier example, although it is rational to believe that there is a typewriter before me now because it looks and feels as though there is, we can imagine circumstances in which rational convictions like this could be overturned. There could be good grounds for rejecting it. Plantinga calls grounds for rejecting otherwise rational beliefs 'defeaters'. There can clearly be defeaters for rational religious beliefs also. Alston expresses this point by saying that religious experiences give their associated theistic beliefs only *prima facie* justification, and do not justify them *simpliciter*. This obvious limitation has far-reaching consequences.

Opposing opinions are often both rational. If I believe something because I have a particular sort of experience, and am in some manner predisposed to form such beliefs on having such experiences, this alone would not make it irrational for someone else who had a similar experience not to believe what I have come to believe; or for someone without that experience to reject my interpretation of it, even whilst accepting my truthfulness in reporting it. Nor would it make it irrational for me, even though I am predisposed to adopt this belief, to refrain from yielding to this predisposition. These responses would only be irrational if the experience I had was not only a cause of the belief I had, but a proof of its truth; or if I had an independent proof, or at least very strong independent evidence, of its truth. In the absence of such guarantees, rejection in the face of the allegedly revelatory experience can still be rational, however unfortunate or mistaken.

This might be contested. If the analogy with sense–perception holds, someone may say that such rejection would be irrational if there are no good reasons for it. Only those corrupted by sceptical philosophy doubt the deliverances of their senses without special reasons; and the same must be true for doubts in the face of religious experience. In the absence of such special reasons, we have to turn to human sinfulness to explain our hesitations.

This may have been plausible once – perhaps up to the time of Calvin – but not any more. For it takes no account of the proliferation of rational alternatives to theism. There are, in the first place, those other religious traditions which Christian thinkers have either ignored or seen fit to treat as confused approximations to their own. There are also, in the second place, secular world-views of a similarly comprehensive and systematic character, such as Marxism, Freudianism, and Sociobiology. In both cases, the competitors have built-in explanations of the psychological forces that have predisposed so many to become Christians, and they have their own supposedly revelatory experiences to match those to which the Christians have appealed. The same can be said for the mind-set of those in our age who decline to reach for metaphysically ambitious world-views at all: they can explain the urge to system and completeness that such world-views satisfy, and can themselves be spurred to reject them by experiences of the supposed absurdity or meaninglessness of life, or of the sense of liberation that comes from throwing off the shackles of ideology. We live in an era of multiple religious ambiguity, in which there are many parallel, rational, experientially powered forms of life vying for our allegiance within one global culture.

In such a world, it may be true that all those who experience phenomena that Christians find revelatory are thereby inclined to accept the Christian interpretation of them, and only fail to yield through sinful obstinacy. Self-deception is a deeply pervasive feature of human nature. But there is every reason to think that it is not true; and it is dogmatic and uncharitable for Christians to insist that it is. In Europe and North America, particularly, the secularisation of our culture has turned Christianity into one of many possible religious options, each of which seems to many, throughout their lives, to be a purely voluntary and fanciful addition to self-sufficient desupernaturalised understandings of the human situation.

But what of the general revelatory signs that Paul and Calvin speak of – not to mention the special revelations of the Christian tradition? Are they not still there? No doubt they are: the heavens are still there – do they not still declare the glory of God? This leads us back to the difficult theme of those supposedly revelatory experiences that are rightly stressed in the 'basic belief' apologetic. As previously indicated, there is an interpretative difficulty: that of deciding whether the experience (such as the perception of the heavens) and the religious interpretation ('God made all this') are separable. It is not my intention to decide this question here, but to attempt to make a point about the contemporary status of revelation in a way that allows for both a positive and a negative answer.

Let us first suppose the experience and the interpretation are separable. On this assumption, I submit that there are many citizens of our culture who will have this experience, and judge it moving or wonderful; but they will not be inclined to interpret it theistically, because they think they know enough about how it all came to be without doing that. Alternatively, they may be inclined to interpret the experience theistically, and yet feel their knowledge of how it all came about to be enough reason to resist that inclination. They will then judge their own theistic

82

inclination to be a relic of a pre-scientific past. Let us now suppose that the experience and the interpretation are not separable; then the sceptic may be someone who simply does not have it, and merely has the distinct experience of seeing the heavens without thinking of God at all. Or, if we are inclined to agree with Paul and Calvin that everyone is theistically inclined by nature, we can say that sceptics are people who do incline to perceive the heavens as God's handiwork, but dismiss this phenomenon in their own mental life as a misleading relic of a superstitious past, because they think that they have better-founded explanations of nature ready to hand.

Let us now return to the Mavrodes schema: (S) m reveals α to n by means of (etc.) k. Who is n? If Paul and Calvin are right, there are at least some substitutions for α and for k which allow us to replace n by '*everyone*.' If the above argument has merit, in our era this can no longer be true, even if it was true once. At least, it appears that way. If, faced with some phenomenon, k, like the heavens at night, I have epistemically respectable reasons to be doubtful (even if it is also respectable to assent), does this not make it questionable whether God has revealed himself to me through that phenomenon? Surely he has only done this if I respond in faith and say 'Yes'?

Of course, Paul and Calvin would reject this. God may well reveal Himself and be rejected, for people are sinful. But the present difficulty is that rejection may not be sinful, but epistemically well-founded. If that happens, has God revealed Himself nevertheless? If we agree to this, we imply that there are at least some circumstances in which it is not blameworthy to fail to accept divine revelation. Some Christians accept this consequence, but many would not. It is an issue lying quite near the surface of the contemporary discussion of how Christians should view sincere adherents of other religions. But with Paul on Calvin's side here, those who accept this are at odds with a basic scriptural source.

Let us, for the sake of argument, adhere to the Pauline–Calvinian position, and insist that those who deny those phenomena or experiences which the Christian accepts are blameworthy for this. Why are they to be judged so harshly? As I read *Romans I*, it is because all who experience God's creation know very well that it is indeed God's creation. Can this be made to fit our situation today, or was it only true in Paul's time? Was it even true then?

What would show that sceptics in our own day know very well that some, or all, of the Christian claims are true, so that their rejection of revelation is without excuse? – Only, in my submission, one or both of the two things that the traditional understanding of revelation claimed are available: independent proofs of some of the Christian claims about God; and independent evidences that the scriptural or ecclesiastical authorities that claimed to pronounce the word of God do indeed have the authority claimed for them. Without one or both of these, there is nothing to break the religious ambiguity that clouds our vision, and nothing to justify the claim that it is only sinfulness that keeps so many from accepting what Christianity says to them. In the absence of either, it can be rational for many who accept Christian claims to do so, but it is no less rational for those who reject them to say 'No'.

Conclusions and Further Questions

In this essay I have attempted to argue that the post-Enlightenment view of revelation, although it does free us from the limitations of the traditional understanding of it – and in particular from the shackles of scriptural literalism – still leaves unanswered the epistemological problems of the rationality of faith. These are problems that the traditional view addresses, and that theologians are mistaken to ignore or to flaunt. I have also attempted to argue that the apologetic of basic beliefs, which does attempt to address these problems, succeeds only partially because it has nothing to say in the face of the parallel rationality of many alternative forms of life that entail rejection of Christian revelation. In being thus limited it fails to support the Pauline–Calvinian claim that unbelief is necessarily sinful. Faced with this limitation, an apologist can, of course, abandon the Pauline–Calvinian thesis and accept that non-culpable rejection is a fact (as indeed it seems to be). But if it is a fact, it is a puzzling and problematic one for the Christian, for even if he or she abandons the longstanding insistence on the exclusive status of the Christian faith as a road to salvation, it is bewildering that it should even have the status of *primus inter pares* if conscientious rejection of it is a fact.

To respond to this puzzle, or alternatively to reinstate the Pauline–Calvinian view, one would need to be able to show that some or all of the claims of the Christian revelation can be established independently, or at least shown to be more probable than their competitors. For if this could be shown, the case for saying that rejection is due to corruption would be far stronger – at least for those to whom these arguments had been made, and who persisted in unbelief. Faced with such arguments, those whose rejection was indeed conscientious would not persist in it.

The traditional view of revelation, therefore, may have been too restrictive in its understanding of the forms revelation has taken, but it was correct in its identification of the ways in which its epistemic credentials could be established. The Enlightenment sceptics maintained that these credentials cannot be established. It is dangerously wrong-headed for Christian apologists to be ready to follow them in this.

Notes

1. St Thomas' position is stated in the *Summa Contra Gentiles*, Book 1, chs.3–8, and Book IV, ch.1. See also the *Summa Theologiae*, 1, Q1.
2. For a brief account of this debate, see Etienne Gilson, *Reason and Revelation in the Middle Ages*, New York, Charles Scribner's Sons, 1938.
3. *Summa Theologiae*, 2a 2ae Q3.
4. *Summa Theologiae*, 2a 2ae Q11.
5. *Summa Theologiae*, 2a 2ae Q1, 1 and 2.
6. Spinoza, *Theologico-Political Treatise*, 1670. English translation by R.H.M. Elwes, New York, Dover, 1951.
7. See, for example, John Toland, *Christianity not Mysterious*, 1696, and Matthew Tindal, *Christianity as Old as the Creation*, 1730.
8. Joseph Butler, *The Analogy of Religion*, 1736, esp. part II, chs.2–4. The best edition is that of J.H. Bernard, London, Macmillan, 1900. See also Terence Penelhum, *Butler*, London, Routledge, 1985, ch.7.
9. *Enquiry concerning Human Understanding* (in *Hume's Enquiries*, ed. L.A. Selby-Bigge, rev. P.H. Nidditch, Oxford, Clarendon Press, 1975), section X.
10. *The Works of William Paley*, vol.II, London, Longman, 1838.
11. Hume, *Enquiry*, section XI.
12. *Dialogues concerning Natural Religion*, ed. N.K. Smith, Indianapolis, Bobbs-Merrill, 1980.
13. See *The Critique of Pure Reason*, A620–630, B649–658.
14. The remark is given to Philo at the close of the *Dialogues*. The majority view among scholars is that Philo most nearly represents Hume himself.
15. *Philosophical Fragments*, trans. H.V. and E.H. Hong, Princeton University Press, 1985; *Concluding Unscientific Postscript*, trans. D. Swenson and W. Lowrie, Princeton University Press, 1941.
16. John Hick, article 'Revelation,' in *Encyclopedia of Philosophy*, ed. Paul Edwards; New York, Macmillan and Free Press, 1967, vol.7, p.190. For an argument to the effect that the conceptual shift is not as radical as it might seem, see the Introduction to Richard Swinburne's *Revelation: From Metaphor to Analogy*, Oxford, Clarendon Press, 1992. Many of Swinburne's arguments show how the supposed advantages of a non-propositional view

of revelation (such as the release from biblical literalism) can coexist with a much more traditional understanding of what revelation is.

17. George Mavrodes, *Revelation in Religious Belief*, Philadelphia, Temple University Press, 1988. I am indebted to this illuminating study in many ways, not only because of the author's invention of this schema.

18. For a lengthier account of this position and its implications in twentieth-century theology, see John Baillie, *The Idea of Revelation in Recent Thought*, New York, Columbia University Press, 1956.

19. I have written more fully along the lines followed here in *God and Skepticism* (Dordrecht, Reidel, 1983) chs.4 and 5. See also Louis P. Pojman, *The Logic of Subjectivity*, University of Alabama Press, 1984, and Heywood J. Thomas, *Subjectivity and Paradox*, Oxford, Blackwell, 1957.

20. Paul Tillich, *Systematic Theology*, vol.II, University of Chicago Press, 1957, p.114.

21. The major brief sources here are the essays by Alvin Plantinga, William Alston, and Nicholas Wolterstorff in *Faith and Rationality*, ed. Plantinga and Wolterstorff, Notre Dame University Press, 1983; Plantinga, 'Rationality and Religious Belief' in *Contemporary Philosophy of Religion*, ed. S. Cahn and D. Shatz, New York, Oxford University Press, 1982; Alston, 'Perceiving God,' in *Journal of Philosophy*, 1986; Wolterstorff, 'Thomas Reid on Rationality' in H. Hart and J. van der Howen (eds) *Rationality in the Calvinian Tradition*, Boston, University Press of America, 1985. Plantinga's position is now being developed in a trilogy of which two volumes have at present been published: *Warrant: The Current Debate*, and *Warrant and Proper Function*, (New York, Oxford University Press, 1993). Alston's *Perceiving God* (Ithaca, Cornell University Press) appeared in 1991, and the valuable ancillary study *The Reliability of Sense Perception* (Cornell University Press) in 1993. I have myself tried to examine the important issues in religious epistemology that are raised in this apologetic tradition in *Reason and Religious Faith* (Boulder, Westview Press, 1995) esp. chs.5 and 6; for a briefer discussion, see 'The Idea of Reason' in *Companion Encyclopedia of Theology*, London, Routledge, 1995, 367–387.

22. Pascal, *Pensées*, trans. Krailsheimer; Harmondsworth, Penguin, 1966. See also Roger Hazelton, *Blaise Pascal: The Genius of His Thought*, Philadelphia, Westminster Press, 1974; A. Krailsheimer, *Pascal,*, Oxford University Press, 1980; and chs.4 and 5 of Penelhum, *God and Skepticism*.

23. See John Baillie, *Our Knowledge of God*, New York, Charles Scribner's Sons, 1959, and *The Sense of the Presence of God*, Oxford University Press, 1962, for an expression of this position.

24. John Calvin, *Institutes of the Christian Religion* (1559), Book I, chs.3–5; English translation by F.L. Battles, ed. J.T. McNeill, Philadelphia, Westminster Press, 1960. For an important examination of how far the doctrine of natural revelation is to be found in the Bible, see James Barr, *Biblical Faith and Natural Theology*, Oxford, Clarendon Press, 1993.

5

Revelation and Critical Theory

Charles Davis

What is Revelation?

There are a number of different accounts of revelation current in theology. A Catholic theologian, Avery Dulles, has recently grouped the differing views under five types or models of revelation.[1] My purpose here is not to enter into a detailed evaluation of the conflicting theologies of revelation, but to focus upon those elements that bring the problematic of revelation into relationship with the problematic of critical theory.

Let me begin by noting that revelation is considered as a distinguishing feature of the Western religions, namely Judaism, Christianity and Islam, all of Semitic or Near Eastern origin, in contrast to the Eastern or Asian religions. This means that revelation is linked to belief in a personal God. The God who reveals and is revealed is conceived as a personal agent who acts and who speaks. Revelation is thus a communication from a personal God to humans as persons, that is, as beings capable of an intelligent and free response to a divine communication.

I find it useful here to apply the distinction made by Gilbert Ryle between achievement verbs and task verbs.[2] Achievement verbs express success in attaining some goal; task verbs express the activities or process required to reach that goal. In the sentence 'The athlete won the race', 'win' is an achievement verb; in 'The athlete ran the race', 'run' is a task verb. We do not observe the distinction rigidly, often borrowing achievement verbs to express the process leading to the achievement; for example, we speak of a runner winning a race while still running. But it makes for clarity to be aware of the difference in logical behaviour between the two classes of verb. Now, 'reveal' is best understood as an achievement verb: it expresses the accomplishment of a communication between God and the recipient of the revelation. It affirms the completion of a communication, while allowing that the processes leading to the achieved communication may be many and various. These processes will be expressed by a variety of task verbs.

There are, therefore, two possible lines of reflection concerning revelation. The first examines the many means used by God to achieve a communication with human persons. These range from a providential ordering of events and images, so as to provoke new insights in a mind enlightened by grace, to paranormal phenomena, such as visions and miracles. The second line of reflection takes for granted the processes leading to revelation and seeks to analyse its constituent elements, asking questions about its permanence. Revelation should not be identified with the processes that bring it about, but should be understood as a relationship of communication in which God addresses human beings.

Some further qualifications are called for. Revelation as it concerns theology is public revelation, namely, revelation where the recipient is a community – even if the activities leading to revelation are the activities of representative individuals. Public revelation is achieved when an initial communication is embodied in a community and institutionalised, so that subsequent generations may join themselves to that communication, adding their response to the response of earlier generations. That means that revelation in its permanent reality is a particular kind of tradition. What distinguishes a revealed tradition as revealed?

Revelation, I have said, is an interpersonal communication between God conceived as a personal agent and human beings as free and responsible subjects. As such, revelation is characterised by contingency and positivity. It is the result of a free, gratuitous intervention on the part of God. As the result of free action, both on the part of God and on the part of human beings, revelation is a contingent state of affairs. It does not arise by natural necessity; it cannot be derived logically from universal principles. All finite beings and events are contingent, but revelation is not contingent merely in that sense. It is contingent because it cannot be claimed as a necessary feature of any finite order. It remains a free gift – unexpected, uncalled for, supererogatory. That is what is meant in speaking of it as a grace or, more technically, as supernatural, that is, as out of proportion to the inherent constituents of any created nature.

For that reason the authority claimed by revelation is in the last analysis always positive, that is, tied to a particular occurrence and not reducible to the universal claims of a general rationality. Consequently, for revelation to be achieved, it demands faith on the part of the recipient. Faith is the response of a person to the divine intervention of communication. Revelation as an achievement includes the faith by which it is received and, as a divine gift or initiative, it includes the enlightenment of the mind of the recipient to recognise the divine communication. Revelation is the coming together of a divinely controlled objective process and a divine illumination of the mind to interpret it aright. It is essentially historical, having its origin in a particular set of events and its permanence and continuity as a particular tradition.

What is revealed? What, in other words, is the content of revelation? Since revelation is conceived by an analogy with verbal communication, we may make use here of Roman Jakobson's distinction of the six constitutive factors in any verbal communication. An **addresser** sends a **message** to an **addressee**. To be operative the message must be in a **context** and expressed in a common **code**. Finally, there must be some connection or **contact** between the addresser and addressee, enabling them to enter and remain in communication. Notice that meaning is not limited to the message, but belongs to the totality of the verbal communication with its six constituent factors.[3]

Those who identify revelation as inner experience are highlighting the factor – contact – but at the expense of the other factors. Revelation always includes an experiential component, but it is not complete until the experience has been articulated in a message. What, then, is the message? Those who reject the propositional view of revelation, namely, the concept of revelation as a set of doctrines, formulated in propositions and transmitted as an unalterable deposit of truth, are so far right that revelation does not belong to the realm of theory. The message of revelation is a praxis, an ethical life, a way of being and acting. It may be partially articulate in propositions. It may stimulate theoretical reflection. But it is essentially the establishment of a practical way of life.

That concept of the message in revelation helps us to understand what can serve as a common code in a divine communication. The language used will not be the expression of univocal concepts. Both concepts and language will proceed by the use of analogy; in other words, by exploiting the resemblances between revealed content and the ordinary objects of human intelligence, while denying identity. Such analogical groping, with the figurative language that goes with it, does not provide a suitable basis for the erection of theoretical systems. The theoretical reflection to which it gives rise must remain tentative and very much a function of the secular intellectual context in which revelation is operative. The centre of reference which gives a revealed tradition its identity and continuity is the praxis it embodies. Revelation is basically a way of life. The word of God is not just a series of statements asserting propositional truths; it is a word of command, of promise, of forgiveness, of condemnation, of persuasion. There are certainly Christians who insist on understanding revelation as the transmission of a set of doctrines, and that doctrinisation of the Christian faith has led to a one-sided stress upon orthodoxy as the preservation of doctrinal purity. However, the emergence of the various liberation theologies has led to the recognition of the primacy of praxis in relation to religious faith, granted that praxis includes an intellectual component.

To sum up, public revelation is an achieved communication between God conceived as a personal agent and a community of human beings. Once achieved in the foundation of a community, the communication is rendered permanent in a tradition. What is communicated is a way of life, together with the insight it presupposes into the human condition and God's saving relationship with men and women. Because revelation, as understood by Christians, Jews and Muslims, is a contingent divine intervention and not explicable as a result of human intelligence and action, it invites human beings into mystery. In other words, it leads them into a mode of life, with an accompanying set of beliefs, disproportionate to what is implied in human agency and human intelligence. Hence, revelation is seen as a free gift of God, a grace supernaturally bestowed upon those whom God chooses.

What is Critical Theory?

The label 'critical theory' can be used in both a narrow and a wide sense. In the narrow sense it refers to a line of social theory belonging to western Marxism and originating in a group of thinkers associated with the Institut für Socialforschung at the University of Frankfurt. The leading figures of the group were Horkheimer, Adorno, Marcuse, Lowenthal and Pollock. Jürgen Habermas represents a second generation of critical theorists, but his prolific writings and the originality and range of his thought make it impossible to see him as a one of a group or school. In his own right he is a leading social theorist in Germany today. As represented in these thinkers, critical theory is the rejection of positivist social theory, which models all knowledge, including knowledge of social phenomena, upon natural science. In contrast to that scientism, critical theory insists upon the link between knowledge and human interests. As a form of social knowledge, critical theory understands itself as guided by the fundamental practical interest of emancipation. It is part of a self-reflective movement towards a more rational society.

In the wide sense, 'critical theory' refers to the practice of the unrestricted questioning of sacred and profane traditions and texts, which dates back to the Enlightenment, passes through the critical philosophy of Kant, Fichte and Hegel to the Marxist critique of ideology and remains active today in critical theory in the narrow sense.

At the outset in the seventeenth century, when criticism meant philological criticism of traditional documents, no antagonism was felt between religion and criticism. But this initial harmony was quickly lost. By the eighteenth century, when criticism had spread from philology to philosophy, history and politics, criticism assumed a negative attitude towards religion. Indeed, an opposition between critical reason and revelation was regarded as constitutive of criticism. Criticism was precisely the activity that supplanted revelation, with its positivity and its appeal to dogmatic authority by reason. Critical reason and revelation were not merely in conflict; they were essentially opposed activities.

But today the opposition is less clear-cut. One of the major contributions of critical theory in the narrow sense has been the acknowledgement of the limitations of the Enlightenment concept of reason and of the destructive consequences of its one-sidedness. The first generation of Frankfurt theorists, Horkheimer and Adorno, remained pessimistic about the possible rectification of the dominant paradigm of reason. But Habermas on his part has developed a wide-ranging theory of communicative rationality, designed to correct the one-sidedness of Enlightenment reason, so allowing us to bring the project of modernity to its completion.

Within that general context, let us follow two lines of thought where discussion among critical theorists has a bearing upon the understanding of revelation. The two themes are continuity and rationality.

Historical Continuity and Revelation

A revealed religion makes a strong claim to continuity. It does so because of the account of the past it must give and its vision of the future. The account of the past has to include a story of an initial communication from which its particular tradition arose and which remains as its permanent basis. Again, its vision of the future looks forward to a new state of affairs – individual, collective or both – which, as the final destiny of humankind, will alone replace the religious tradition in its present function.

Thus, the Christian religion claims immutability for itself as the final revelation. The revelation achieved in Jesus Christ is regarded as closed with the death of the last apostle; nothing further can be added. Hence the criterion of Christian truth given in these words of Vincent of Lérins: *quod ubique, quod semper, quod ab omnibus* ('what is taught everywhere, always and by all'). Novelty is heresy; yet the rise of historical scholarship has made it impossible to ignore the all-pervasiveness of change. So, since the nineteenth century, the question of the persisting identity in the midst of change of the Christian revelation has been a theological problem. Newman suggested 'development' as an alternative to immutability on the one hand, and to corruption or loss of identity on the other. But while Newman pointed to the fact of development, he did not have any theory of development to offer. He simply argued that in the midst of a development affecting all forms of Christianity the Roman Catholic Church was the least unlike the primitive Church.[4] Since Newman, theologians have not come up with a theory that in a satisfactory fashion explains the strict continuity or identity claimed by the Christian tradition. Let us, then, turn to the general discussion of the problem of historical continuity.

Baumgartner in his *Kontinuität und Geschichte*[5] argues that historical continuity is given with the narrative structure as one of its properties. It does not depict or reproduce a previously existing temporal duration of some subject. Historical continuity is not to be identified with temporal duration. It is an autonomous construction, not derived from a prior temporal structure, but the result of the form-giving constructivity, characteristic of historical consciousness. Historical consciousness, Baumgartner continues, is first constituted in the medium of a story. The idea of a story is a far better starting-point for reconstructing historical knowledge than *Verstehen* or hermeneutic understanding. The narrative structure of a story gathers together the three essential features of historical knowledge: retrospectivity, constructivity and practical interest. History is a retrospective construction, motivated by a need for communication and directed by a practical intent.

Here Baumgartner rejoins themes from Habermas. In his turn Habermas has commented briefly on Baumgartner's concept of historical continuity.[6] Before considering those comments, I want to record the extensive use both Habermas and Baumgartner make of Danto's analysis of historical knowledge. Though each has his own reservations concerning Danto's treatment, they both draw heavily upon Danto in setting forth the structure of historical knowledge. Here, first, are the points of agreement.

We cannot conceive of history without organisational schemes. The organisation schemes of history are always linked to particular human interests. History differs from science, not in using organisational schemes, but in the kind of scheme it uses. History organises events into stories.

History is all of a piece. There is no way in which we can distinguish pure description from interpretation or plain from significant narrative. To research history at all is to go beyond what is given. The production of a narrative organisation inevitably involves us in a subjective factor. There is, Danto remarks, an element of sheer arbitrariness in the narrative organisation of events, which is always done in relation to the topical interest of somebody.

The idea of a complete description of an event is logically impossible: to describe an event completely is to locate it in all the right stories. We can never do this because, to use the striking phrase of Danto, 'we are temporally provincial with regard to the future'.[7] A complete description of an event is impossible for the same reason as the speculative philosophy of history: we do not know the future and therefore we cannot relate events to it.

History is necessarily retrospective. Narrative statements can deal only with past events. Danto gives an analysis of the structure of narrative sentences, which is accepted by Habermas and Baumgartner. Narrative sentences are sentences that refer to at least two time-separated events, though they only describe the earliest event to which they refer. Thus, a narrative sentence describes an event E_1 in relation to an event E_2; E_2 is always later than E_1, although it is past for the historian. Even when the standpoint of the historian is his or her own contemporary situation, his or her description of E_1 must be related to the already determined features of that situation or, in other words, to the past present. To relate E_1 to a future event, an event not yet determined and in that sense past, is to write a futuristic novel – not history.

In brief, Baumgartner and Habermas agree with Danto that history is a retrospective narrative organisation of events, and so far the analysis of narrative has clarified the constructivity and retrospectivity of historical consciousness and knowledge. But, as previously mentioned, there is a third feature of historical consciousness: the practical interest or intent of the historian, guiding his or her choice of a frame of interpretation. On the latter point, Habermas objects to Danto's contention that the necessary function of the topical interest of the historian introduces an element of sheer arbitrariness. The procedure would be arbitrary only if we suppose a complete description is a meaningful historical ideal. It is not; it cannot be consistently formulated. Even a hypothetical last historian would view events from a standpoint not acquired from the events themselves, and as soon as the historian acts at all, he produces new relationships, which will combine into a new story from a fresh standpoint. Hence the previous 'complete description' ascribes to history a claim to a theoretical contemplation of historical reality, which is illegitimate and cannot be redeemed.

But that does not make history arbitrary. The historian does not organise his knowledge according to pure theory, but within the framework of his own life-practice. His choice of a frame of interpretation, guided by a practical interest, is dependent upon his expectations of future events. Thus, the historian does anticipate the future, but his anticipations are not part of the narrated history, but belong to the hermeneutic point of departure. History itself remains retrospective. The hermeneutic anticipations, rooted in a practical interest, are not arbitrary, because they hold good only if they bring reality within their grasp. The historian from the viewpoint of practice anticipates end-states, and thereby events in their multiplicity coalesce into action-orienting stories. History is not an imitation or duplication of the past, but a construction of past events in relation to practice and to the horizon of future expectations, which forms the context of practice.

Baumgartner for his part objects to Danto's understanding of continuity. Danto recognises the constructive function of narrative organisation in forming particular temporal structures out of the total happenings of a stretch of time. To that extent he conceives historical continuity as a product of narrative organisation. But Danto qualifies his view by arguing that change requires some continuous identity in the subject of change, and that it is an implicit reference to a continuous subject that gives unity to an historical narrative. Baumgartner does not agree. Historical continuity may presuppose or include a temporally enduring person, event or element, but such temporal duration of a subject or element offers the possibility, not the actuality, of history. The identity of an individual – say, Napoleon – through the temporal duration of his life belongs to the substratum of his history. It is not yet the historical continuity produced by the narrative construction of his biography. Further, the case of an individual subject is not a good analogy for understanding the historical continuity of such historical structures as the French Revolution or the Middle Ages. Baumgartner, therefore, insists that historical continuity is a property of narrative construction. History creates it; history does not reproduce a prior continuity of events.

Habermas, however, finds Baumgartner here guilty of an oversight in failing to consider 'that narratives not only organize the stories that the historian tells but also those that the historian presupposes as stories: the historian finds a pre-constituted, in fact narratively pre-constituted field of objects'.[8] Habermas admits that in a certain sense historical continuity is first constituted by the narrative of the historian. But this continuity is based 'on the unifying force of the vital contexts in which the events acquired their relevance for participants before the historian comes along'.[9] He finds the model for this pre-given unity in the identity of the self and the unity of its life-history kept through a series of narrative constructions. History is an objective life-context. It is not constructed 'theoretically' for the first time by the historian. The constructions of the historian follow upon and are added to the already formed traditional constructions.[10]

There is no denial, then, by Habermas that historical continuity is a matter of narrative construction. But he distinguishes two levels of narrative. There are the narratives produced by participants in the course of their life-practice, and there are the narratives produced subsequently by the historian, who chooses an interpretative frame, and thus decides on the beginning and end of a history and on which events are to be regarded as relevant.

What bearing has the discussion outlined above upon the concept of revelation? I suggest that it may well lead us to consider that revelation is best conceived as an historical narrative constructed from within a practical way of life. History, it has been argued, is a retrospective narrative organisation of events. Further, that construction of past events has been seen as effected in relation to practice and under a vision of the future. Two levels of narrative have been distinguished: narratives produced from within life-practice and narratives constructed subsequently by the historian. All that may be said of revelation: revelation is a narrative of past events, organised from within a way of life and understood as a divinely communicated pattern of events, serving to ground that way of life. Revelation itself is first-level narrative; theology offers a second-level narrative. In history as revelation, as distinct from profane history, the vision of the future has a more prominent function. Hope is central to a religious way of life. It is true that hope does not remove our ignorance of the future; it is not knowledge of future events. Hence future events are not incorporated into our narrative. Nevertheless, eschatological expectations form a symbolic epilogue to the revealed narrative, assuring us that despite the limited scope of the narratives we live by, there is final meaning.

The Rationality of Revealed Traditions

Revelation, history, tradition: all are marked by positivity, because the claim they make upon our assent is bound up with their particularity. But can a claim rooted in a particular history, a particular set of events, a particular tradition justify itself as rational? Is not reason essentially universal, so that an appeal to reason is an appeal to universal principles, to universal criteria and arguments? An appeal to a particular historical construction or to a particular tradition cannot be other, it would seem, than an appeal to authority. If that is in fact the case, then when confronted with the plurality of traditions we have no defence against the relativist contention that no issue between conflicting traditions is rationally decidable.

Alasdair MacIntyre[11] argues that the relativist challenge can be met by recognising the special kind of rationality proper to traditions. That rationality consists of an openness to development. Every tradition begins in a condition of pure historical contingency in which beliefs, institutions and practices constitute a given to be taken as authoritative without questioning. The fist unquestioning stage comes to an end when new situations giving rise to new questions lead to alternative and incompatible interpretations. The crisis is resolved by the construction of a new narrative. The new narrative allows the agent to understand both how he or she could have held his or her original beliefs and how he or she was misled by them, so as to come to need new formulations and new evaluations. The tradition avoids repudiation and remains worthy of rational assent as long as it can find within itself resources to meet new situations and questions, with sufficient inventiveness for the reformulation and re-evaluation of its authoritative texts and beliefs.

Tradition, then is constituted by a conflict of interpretations of the tradition itself. It embodies the narrative of an argument. Constantly threatened by the danger of lapsing into incoherence, it is rescued by an argumentative reconstruction of its narrative. At certain periods traditions need revolutionary reconstitution for their continuance. Far from excluding conflict, tradition presupposes the omnipresence of conflict, both within each tradition and between traditions, and the conflict itself has a history susceptible of rival interpretations. To belong to a tradition is to enter into an argument and to make the continuous argument intelligible by narrative.

The Continuity of the Christian Tradition

Nothing characterises the Christian tradition better than to describe it as a conflict of interpretations. Referring to the fact that from the beginning the Christian Church contained often contradictory movements within itself, the historian Frend remarks: 'It is difficult to point to any time after the Ascension when it was truly one'.[12] Down through the centuries the Church has been constituted by followers of Christ locked together in argument over their beliefs and practices. What the Christian tradition embodies is the narrative of an argument. It has constantly been threatened with dissolution and saved by the reconstruction of its narrative – a retelling that incorporates new insights or even revolutionary changes of interpretation. Orthodoxy may be conceived as the continuously reconstructed narrative. It is, however, the narrative of an argument. The attempt to make it a body of unchanging interpretations to be accepted without question is to block its transmission into new historical and cultural situations and eventually to kill it. All belong to the tradition who are willing to enter into the argument. Those who refuse the argument that continually reconstitutes the tradition put themselves outside the tradition, just as the flat-earthers have put themselves outside the scientific tradition. On the other hand, groups outside the mainstream who are still arguing represent elements that have not yet been adequately accounted for in the present narrative of the tradition and are rightly calling for a further reconstruction of the narrative and its argument.

The continuity of the Christian tradition is, therefore, achieved by narrative. But here I agree with Habermas against Baumgartner that what constitutes the basic continuity is not the narrative of the historian, but the narrative that originates in the life-world as its connatural expression. The Church lives as a community in the unity of its life by constantly retelling its story. All the same, while the narrative of the historian presupposes and expands the first-level participant narrative, historiography, however rigorous its methods, does retain an indispensable practical function in relation to the life of the community. Even the history of the historian has a particular perspective on the past, derived from the situation of the historian, and it has a practical mission in relation to the future. The practical function of the historian vis-à-vis

the community is especially evident at time of crisis – and crises punc-
tuate the ongoing life of any major tradition. The resources available to
the historian are called upon in the task of reconstructing the narrative,
so as to rescue continuity in the midst of revolutionary change. An
example is the rewriting of the history of the Reformation by Catholic
historians in recent decades. The gradual growth of the ecumenical
movement made unviable the previous account of Protestantism and it
became necessary to retell the story, in order to combine a positive
appreciation of the Protestant Reformation with a continued adherence
to Catholic values. The historian, then, remains tied to the life-world of
the community by his or her historico-hermeneutical situation and practical mission. That, however, does not exclude – indeed, would seem to
require – the historian making use of available theories in his or her
historical research. But it is through narrative that the unity and continuity of tradition is preserved in the context of an unavoidable conflict
of interpretations.

Notes

1. Avery Dulles, S.J., *Models of Revelation*, New York, Image Books, Doubleday, 1985.
2. Gilbert Ryle, *The Concept of Mind*, Harmondsworth, Middlesex, Penguin Books, 1988. First published 1949, pp.143–7. The application of the concept of achievement verbs to revelation was made by William J. Abraham, *Divine Revelation an the Limits of Historical Criticism*, Oxford, Oxford University Press, 1982, p.11.
3. For two texts from Jakobson's voluminous writings, see David Lodge, ed., *Modern Criticism and Theory: A Reader*, London and New York, Longman, 1988, pp.32–57.
4. Cf. Nicholas Lash, *Newman on Development: The Search for an Explanation in History*, Shepherdstown, Patmos, 1975, and his summary account in Alan Richardson and John Bowden, eds, *The Westminster Dictionary of Christian Theology*, Philadelphia, Westminster, 1983, s.v. Development, Doctrinal.
5. Hans Michael Baumgartner, *Kontinuität und Geschichte: Zur Kritik und Metakritik der historischen Vernunft*, Frankfurt am Main, Suhrkamp, 1972.
6. Cf. Baumgartner, *op. cit.*, pp.269–294; Habermas's comments upon Danto are given in two places. The first is *Zur Logik der Sozialwissenschaften*, Frankfurt am Main, Suhrkamp, 1970, pp.267–74; this section has been translated in Jürgen Habermas, 'A Review of Gadamer's *Truth and Method*

in Fred R. Dallmayr and Thomas A. McCarthy, eds, *Understanding and Social Inquiry*, Notre Dame, University of Notre Dame Press, 1977, pp.346–50. The second is 'Geschichte und Evolution' in Jürgen Habermas, *Zur Rekonstruktion des Historischen Materialismus*, Frankfurt am Main, Suhrkamp, 1976, pp.204–7; this essay has been translated as 'History and Evolution' in *Telos* 39, (1979), pp.5–44, the pages on Danto being 8–11.

7. Arthur C. Danto, *Analytical Philosophy of History*, Cambridge, Cambridge University Press, 1968, p.142.

8. 'History and Evolution', p.10, n.9.

9. *Ibid.*, pp.9–10.

10. Cf. *ibid.*, p.10, n.9.

11. Alasdair MacIntyre, *Whose Justice? Which Rationality?* Notre Dame, Indiana, University of Notre Dame Press, 1988, especially ch.XVIII 'The Rationality of Traditions'; cf. also his earlier essay, 'Epistemological Crises, Dramatic Narrative and the Philosophy of Science', *The Monist* 60 (1977), 453–71; reprinted in Gary Gutting, ed., *Paradigms and Revolutions: Appraisals and Applications of Thomas Kuhn's Philosophy of Science*, Notre Dame & London, University of Notre Dame Press, 1980, pp.54–74.

12. W.H.C. Frend, *The Early Church From the Beginnings to 461*, London, SCM Press Ltd, 1982, p.1.

6

Revelation and Divine Action

Maurice Wiles

Revelation and Apocalypse are alternative names for the last book of the Bible. That is hardly surprising, since they are the Latin and Greek forms of the same word. But move beyond the designation of that book, and the connotations of the two words begin to diverge. 'Apocalypse', or more commonly its adjectival form 'apocalyptic', suggests a very specific and detailed revelation of divine mysteries; moreover, the content of such revelations normally includes the promise of some dramatic form of divine intervention or self-revelation in the near future. 'Revelation', and its adjectival form 'revelatory', on the other hand, carry a much broader range of meaning; particularly when qualified by the word 'general', its range of reference can become virtually coterminous with the whole of human experience. Where revelation takes an apocalyptic form, divine action will be a prominent feature of both its formal and material aspects. But revelation in Christian thought has never been exclusively of an apocalyptic nature. Its relation to divine action is not necessarily, therefore, of the overt and dramatic kind that characterises 'apocalyptic'. How ought the broader concept of revelation to be seen in relation to divine action?

Meanings of the Word 'Revelation'

Let us start with some general reflections on the concept itself and on ways in which the word 'revelation' is used. Revelation is essentially a relational concept; it is the revealing of something by someone to someone else. We often speak of a particular thing, such as a newspaper article, as a 'revelation'. But it is not inherently a revelation in itself. It is so by virtue of the context in which it stands. It is the medium of an act of revelation by the journalist to his or her readers. It is that relational context that needs to be borne clearly in mind in our attempt to understand revelation in relation to divine action within the framework of a Christian theology. But before we turn to the explicitly theological use of the term, it is worth looking in a little more detail at some of the variety of ways in which it is used in ordinary speech.

The etymology of the word implies an unveiling, the removal of a cover, and we can begin with a physical example in which that underlying sense is still literally present. A VIP unveils a memorial plaque by pulling a string; the curtain is drawn back and the plaque is revealed – though only actually, rather than potentially, revealed, if a sighted audience has assembled for the occasion. In such a case, despite the needed presence of an audience to complete the act of revelation, the active role is exclusively that of the revealer. The same basic picture applies in the case of the journalist whose article is hailed as a revelation. The journalist's writing of the article is the essential action, though it will only be a revelation if the article is read, and if the information it contains was previously unknown to the readers. A more distinctive case of the same kind is one where the information provided by a speaker is not merely information that was in fact unknown to his or her hearers, but information that was logically unknowable by them in any other way, for example, when what the speaker relates is his or her dreams or feelings.

In all these cases the active role is that of the revealer; the role of the recipients of the revelation is largely passive. But that is not always true: we may reveal as much or more of ourselves unintentionally as we do by deliberate acts of self-disclosure. In such instances the more significant role in the revelatory process shifts from the revealer to the one who receives the revelation. – It is the sensitivity and interpretative skill of the observer which turns what was, for the one observed, no more than a commonplace remark or routine piece of behaviour, with no revelatory intent, into a moment of revelation. Sometimes the role of the revealer may recede even further into the background. A literary work or a work of art may be spoken of as having a revelatory power for those who pay attention to it: it can give rise to the disclosure of a world which the reader or viewer had never glimpsed before. The revealer is still there in the background, in the person of the author or the artist. But the case is significantly different from that of the journalist and the newspaper article, where what is revealed is the piece of information the journalist intended to provide. But, as literary and aesthetic critics are wont to insist, the work of art may reveal things to a reader or viewer that its original creator had never consciously envisaged or intended. The word 'revelation', indeed, can be used to refer to any

101

occasion where some new truth is grasped, not by a process of reasoned argument, but by way of some sudden and unexpected apprehension of it.

The primary purpose of this very incomplete sketch of the ways in which the idea of revelation is used in ordinary discourse is to remind us of how diverse is the analogical base which may serve to inform our theological use of the word. The word has certainly played a major role within theology, but in the light of our reflections so far we need to be alert to the wide range of signification it may carry there. Even at the human level, revelation is not always straightforwardly the action of a human revealer. We ought not to assume, therefore, that in the theological case it will necessarily bear a very straightforward relation to the idea of a divine agent.

Similar reflections could be pursued about the nature of human agency as the basic analogue for our understanding of divine agency. But such reflections have had wide currency in recent theological writing. They underlie much of my own discussion of divine agency in *God's Action in the World*.[1] I shall therefore refrain from repetition, but the variety of forms that human action can take is something that needs to be borne in mind as the argument develops.

The Complex Nature of Divine Revelation

One characteristic feature of the Christian view of revelation needs to be stressed at the outset, before we try to determine what model is most appropriate for its understanding. Revelation, as we have already emphasised, is essentially a relational concept. It necessarily involves not merely a revealer, but also a recipient of what is revealed. While the relationship may be a direct, face-to-face one, it may also be much more indirect, through some writing or artefact, such as a newspaper article or a painting. The strongly historical and corporate nature of Christian faith means that such media of indirect revelation will have a particularly important role to play. The scriptural record, for example, and subsequent written and pictorial reflections on the scriptural story may all be involved in any revelation to the contemporary Christian church or to a Christian individual today. Since the Christian wants also to insist on the immediacy of God's presence to the original scriptural writers and those who have handed on and interpreted the scriptural faith as it impinges on us now, as well as to the contemporary Christian church and to the individual within the church, the structure of any act of divine revelation has to be recognised as highly complex in character.

Moreover, there is clearly scope for the involvement of God's action in varied ways at different points within that revelatory process.

Revelation as the Impartation of Information

With this proviso in mind, let us ask whether any of the human analogues we have outlined offer a suitable model for relating revelation to divine action. The concept of a speaker imparting privileged information, otherwise inaccessible to the recipient, not only has a long history within Christian thought but also appears well suited to provide what Christians hope to receive from revelation for the proper grounding of their faith. Reflection on the more general experience of the natural world and human history, it may be argued, does not rule out the possibility of theistic faith, but cannot by itself take us beyond an open agnosticism. Certainly, such an argument will insist, it falls short of justifying faith in a compassionate and saving God. Some more direct self-disclosure on the part of God would seem to be necessary to warrant the affirmation and practice of faith in a God of love. Such a position has been adumbrated in recent times by Basil Mitchell as the conclusion of his *Justification of Religious Belief,*[2] and more fully developed by William Abraham in his *Divine Revelation and the Limits of Historical Criticism.*[3] An approach of this kind relates primarily to what I have described as the first stage in the complex structure of Christian revelation, in particular the inspiration of the scriptural writings. That is the natural focus for any understanding of revelation in terms of the model of the disclosure of information.

One difficulty in such an account, which is more acute today than in past ages, is our stronger sense of the variety and the lack of perspicuity in scriptural teaching. If what is envisaged is an actual, contemporary act of revelation and not merely the potential for it, some further divine act would seem to be called for in relation to the reader's understanding of scripture. This further divine revelation or *testimonium Sancti Spiritus*, whatever form it may be understood to take, will need to be more than a conviction that Scripture embodies divine revelation: it will need to provide an appropriate insight into the meaning of what will otherwise remain the highly ambiguous teaching of Scripture.

Although this difficulty is real, it is not the major problem that this account has to deal with, nor is it the major reason why so many theologians are unhappy with it. It is rather the difficulty of identifying and giving sense to the initial, purported act of revelation. It is there, as we have seen, that the main active role in the whole process is to be located. The question of how such an account of revelation is to be understood in terms of distinctive divine action is therefore one of crucial importance. Where is such action to be seen, and what form does it take? Prophetic inspiration may appear to offer a way of understanding it which would allow for the imparting of privileged information. But the inspiration of the false prophets by the lying spirits who lured Ahab to his death at Ramoth-Gilead is not distinguishable from the true inspiration of Micaiah – except *post eventum*.

If this is the essential mode of divine action in the process of revelation, there will always be grave difficulty in determining when and where it has taken place. But in any case most of the scriptural record, especially the gospels and the Pauline epistles, are of a very different nature. In whatever sense they may be said to embody revelation, the claim that revelation is at heart a matter of a divinely inspired imparting of otherwise inaccessible information about God seems so implausible that it ought not to be considered unless we have no other way of making religious sense of them. The more we explore the nature of their composition and of their contents, the less convincing any such account appears.

Reasons like these have led many scholars, particularly those associated with the biblical theology movement, to abandon a model of the divine imparting of information and to replace it with one where revelation is focused in the more public realm of the acts of God in history. But that move served only to aggravate rather than alleviate the difficulties. Most of the so-called 'acts of God in history' were actually a part of the public life of our common human history, to such an extent that it is as difficult to recognise any explicit divine action which would constitute them instances of directly intended divine revelation as it is in the case of the writing of the gospels.[4] Moreover, historical events do not convey meaning in the same relatively direct way that a written text can do, and so the acts of God in history cannot in themselves be the complete medium of divine revelation. Only those events appropriately interpreted could fulfil such a role. So it would require the contribution of a scriptural writer or some other privileged interpreter to declare their significance and thus enable them to achieve their revelatory purpose. Consequently, the difficulties already discussed of acknowledging a distinctive divine revelatory action in relation to the scriptural writers are not avoided. Instead there is the additional difficulty of acknowledging a distinctive divine revelatory action in the historical happening too.

The intensification of the difficulties inherent in the understanding of revelation, arising from a move which had held out hope of their amelioration, has meant, Ronald Thiemann suggests, that 'a sense of revelation-weariness has settled over the discipline'. He points out that many theologians, such as Gerald Downing, James Barr, David Kelsey and Gordon Kaufman have in effect advocated the abandonment of the category altogether.[5] He himself regards the difficulties as fatal only for a theology which sees God as extrinsically rather than intrinsically related to Christian belief.[6] And our own initial reflections about the very wide range of signification that the term can carry in ordinary discourse also suggest that it may only be certain understandings of the concept, rather than the concept itself, that have been shown to be unusable. The model with which we have been working so far is one in which an agent deliberately sets out by word or action (or a combination of both) to make some new disclosure to others. It may have seemed the most hopeful and potentially fruitful model to adopt; but it was not the only one on offer. And if it fails because we cannot make sense of the kind of divine action it implies, there are, as we have seen, other models in which the agency of the revealer does not play so crucial a role which may prove to have more to contribute to a coherent understanding of Christian faith.

Revelation and Human Insight

The main distinction between the various models of revelation we have adumbrated was between those where the intentional action of the revealer was paramount, and those where the interpretative insight of the recipient of revelation was of primary importance. Within the latter category of models we noted two main types. In the first, the medium of revelation was the ordinary words and acts of an agent, which become revelatory to an observer because of his or her perceptive insight. In the second, the medium of revelation was a poem or a work of art, considered as an entity in the world independent of its original author or creator; here, too, it was the creative response of the reader or viewer that is crucial to the occurrence of a moment of revelation. Can these models be of any help in providing an intelligible account of the relation between revelation and divine action?

The initial apparent attraction of the imparting of information model was that it seemed to promise a way of escape from the ambiguity of the more general experience of life in the world. But that promising way of escape has turned out to be an illusion. The moments of *prima*

105

facie unambiguous revelation, the scriptural writings and the acts of God in history, turned out to have their own inherent ambiguities. Even on that model there was no bypassing the crucial requirement of human interpretative insight. On the model now under consideration, that interpretative insight comes to the fore. The subject matter to be interpreted on this model will be the whole range of human experience. That does not, of course, exclude the scriptural writings or the historical happenings that have sometimes been dubbed 'acts of God'. Whatever else they may be, they are a part of ordinary human experience of the world. Nor is there any reason why they may not turn out to be of very particular significance for the interpreter. If everything in the world were equally and uniformly significant, there would be less call for discriminating insight.

How, then, does this second model serve to illuminate the relation of revelation to divine action? The two versions of the model with which we have been working correspond to two traditional paradigms for understanding God's relation to the world. One version envisages the ordinary words and actions of a person proving revelatory to the perceptive observer. In a theological context that version of the model suggests the idea of God's immanence. God is seen as immanently active within the structures of the physical and historical world of our everyday experience. The other version highlights the revelatory power of a work of art, produced by its creator but now existing in its own right. That places the stress on God's transcendence. It acknowledges God as the creator of the world, but stresses the relative independence of that world in view of the regularity of the physical laws which uphold its structure and also of the freedom with which men and women have been endowed. Both versions of the model are therefore needed, since Christian theology has always sought to insist on divine immanence and divine transcendence, despite the difficulty of holding them together within the confines of a single model. The divine action in revelation is therefore the same as the divine action involved in the creation and sustaining of the world. That continuing creative action, it is claimed on this model, conveys the potential of a revelation about God and the world, but it needs to be met by imaginative human response in order for the process of revelation to be complete. And that requirement is one that, as we have seen, remains in force, however we conceive the element of divine activity within the complex revelatory process as a whole.

Even if this second model offers a more plausible account of how revelation might be related to divine action, we have still to ask whether it is adequate to Christian faith. Will it do the job that Christian theology looks to the concept of revelation to do? If that job is conceived in terms of giving a knowledge of God and his purposes that is not otherwise available to us, and that is to be trusted because of its special and more direct emanation from God himself, then the answer has to be 'No'. If, on the other hand, the job is conceived as giving us grounds for believing that the world is such that in our response to it we can achieve an awareness of God which, however provisional and however tentative, is sufficient to warrant our reasoned allegiance, then the answer can be 'Yes'. The model does offer a way of understanding divine action in which revelation of that sort is possible.

A revised account of this nature admittedly involves a playing down of the type of claim that has often been made for revelation. A major reason for minimising the importance of such claims is precisely the difficulty of offering a convincing account of the kind of divine action that seems to be entailed in any strong form of revelatory claim. The supporting testimony of specific fulfilled prophecy or of attendant miracle, which have both played a major role at different times in the past, no longer carry conviction. Today the majority of scholars who still want to assert some form of special divine action as the basis of a strong doctrine of revelation – even one understood in terms of the imparting of information – also acknowledge the hiddenness of the divine action. However, there is something paradoxical about revelation effected by means of a hidden divine action, where, as Bultmann puts it, 'the word of the Revealer . . . at once reveals and conceals him'.[7] How is the recipient of revelation to know that it is divine revelation, except by way of that perceptive insight which is the essential feature of our second model? Such stress on the hiddenness of the divine action may indeed be necessary and right. But it means that sophisticated versions of the first model become virtually indistinguishable from the second. For them, too, the job that revelation can fulfil has to be toned down accordingly.

Revelation as Intrinsic to the Scriptural Narrative

There are other scholars who acknowledge the force of the problems that we have been raising but who believe that they can be met very differently, in a manner which will allow for the maintenance of revelation as a dominant theme in Christian theology. Ronald Thiemann, for example, believes that those difficulties are fatal only for a theology which sees God as extrinsically related to Christian belief – a category in which he would certainly want to place the position proposed in this essay. What, then, is meant by a theology for which God is intrinsically related to Christian belief? And does that offer a better answer to our difficulties? Thiemann insists that Christian belief in God is defined by the narrative logic of the scriptural story and not by broader forms of reasoning external to that narrative. On the basis of that approach God's self-revelation, and the divine activity in history through which it is given, are part of the underlying truth of Christian faith, and stand in no need of justification by arguments from outside that standpoint. It is impossible to discuss this alternative approach in full detail here, but in my opinion it does not represent an acceptable strategy that can get us out of our difficulty. In order to do so, it would not only require us to treat the scriptural story as a more unified coherent narrative than it appears in fact to be; but also, and more importantly, to assess it in isolation from our ways of understanding the rest of the world of which it is a part. The affirmation of God's self-revelation through a divine activity in history has to be evaluated and assessed in the light of all the other ways open to us for understanding the functioning of our world and the development of its history. And when we do that, the kind of modification of our understanding of the notion that I have been proposing seems inevitable.

Revelation and Inspiration

Two further points remain to be considered. In this account, the crucial role has been accorded to imaginative human insight. It is the creative vision of seer or prophet that recognises, and so actualises, the revelatory potential in God's created world and his sustaining presence in it. Is this to be understood, as the language used suggests, as a purely and exclusively human activity? Or is it related to divine agency in some way other than being a response to it? It is the old problem of the relation between divine grace and free human action. It is tempting to try to find room here for a more direct action of God, of the kind that it has proved so difficult to continue to assert in the physical world or in the public history of humankind, with the hope that the model we have adopted may prove more patient of a specifically divine active element in the revelatory process than at first appeared likely. But the temptation is to be resisted. We have already seen the difficulties of any comparable claim in relation to the inspiration of prophets or scriptural writers; those difficulties are no less present in the case of the recipient of revelation. In any straightforward form such an approach runs into serious moral difficulties in terms both of the apparent arbitrariness of God's election of those to whom such insight is given and also of the apparent manipulation of human freedom involved.[8]

Moreover, though individual insight is important, the occurrence of any such revelatory insight is dependent on a whole series of historical and social factors without which the preconditions for any revelatory occurrence would simply not be there. It is that whole process, rather than one particular part of it, that needs to be seen as carried on in conscious awareness of the presence of the creating and sustaining God whom it seeks to know. If it is in this broader sense that God 'inspires' those who recognise and communicate his truth, it is not one which enables us to point to any distinctive mode of divine action (beyond that in which God is more generally available to those who seek him) that effects or validates the reception of revelation.

Second, that same emphasis on imaginative human insight could also be challenged not only in relation to the penultimate word in the phrase but also in relation to the final one. Does not the stress on insight suggest too contemplative a mode of access towards the apprehension of Christian truth? That is a risk already introduced into the discussion by the posing of the problem in terms of revelation. As we saw at the outset, revelation is a word which tends to imply a passive role on the part of the human recipient. The stress on the need for human insight has been intended in part as a corrective to that natural implication. But the corrective could and should be taken a stage further. What is needed on the human side to bring an act of revelation to its completion will seldom, if ever, be a matter of pure reflection. 'Insight' is the most appropriate term as a correlative to 'revelation', but it is something that is unlikely to arise outside the context of a whole life of faith and practice. Genuine revelation does not simply inform its recipient; it also transforms.

Conclusions

Reflection on the relation between revelation and divine action should lead us to make comparatively modest claims about the proper place of revelation in Christian thought. Christian faith does not offer to provide its followers with otherwise unavailable truth about God, in the way that some mystery cults have promised to do for their initiates. What it does offer is a vision of the world that is based on the same public history and the same kinds of experience that are open to those who do not profess a Christian faith. There are many ways in which the world can be and is understood. The Christian claim is that the world is patient of being understood as the scene of God's purposive creation and presence. Revelation is a name for occasions in which that divine intention and divine presence are apprehended and responded to.

Of course, there are particular facets of human experience and particular features of human history that play a crucial role in communicating that apprehension, of which the life of Christ is the supreme exemplar. Furthermore, corporate celebration of and reflection on those crucial features is an important way of establishing and confirming such apprehension. But for revelation of this kind to take place, no appeal needs to be made to some exceptional form of divine action. The role of the revealer is fulfilled by God's continual creative presence in and to his world. In that sense God is even a part of the human response, whereby a genuine moment of revelation takes place. But his presence is what provides the potential of revelation, and we do not need to postulate a special form of that presence as the causal determinant of its actualisation.

Revelation, then, needs to occupy a less dominant place in Christian theological thought than has usually been accorded to it. It is part of the general background conditions which make Christian faith and Christian theology possible; the world is such that it can give rise to a trustworthy – but always highly provisional – knowledge of God. It can also be used to categorise those lives, events and writings which have proved and continue to prove fruitful occasions of such knowledge. But when it is so used, we need to be on our guard against two dangers. First, knowledge of God is not given by such a narrowly intellectual or information-giving process as the word 'revelation' might suggest. Second, we do not need to postulate any exceptional form of divine action to account for the occurrence of revelation in and through those central figures and events that have determined the distinctive shape of Christian faith and understanding.

Notes

1. See especially pp.27, 28 and 61.
2. See especially pp.155–6.

3. See especially the first chapter, significantly entitled 'Divine Revelation and Divine Speaking'.
4. For a discussion of some of these difficulties see my *God's Action in the World*, ch.5, 'Providence and Public History'.
5. Ronald Thiemann, *Revelation and Theology*, pp.1–2.
6. *Ibid.*, pp.81–2. For further elaboration and discussion of this claim, see pp.107–8.
7. R. Bultmann, *Gospel of St. John*, p.161, cited by A. Dulles, *Models of Revelation*, p.86.
8. See my *God's Action in the World*, ch.6, 'Providence and Personal Life'.

Bibliography

Abraham, W.J., *Divine Revelation and the Limits of Historical Criticism*, Oxford, OUP, 1982.

Dulles, A., *Models of Revelation*, London, Gill and Macmillan, 1983.

Mitchell, B., *The Justification of Religious Belief*, London, Macmillan, 1973.

Moran, G., *Theology of Revelation*, London, Burns and Oates, 1967.

Thiemann, R., *Revelation and Theology*, Notre Dame, Indiana, University of Notre Dame Press, 1985.

Wiles, M.F., *God's Action in the World*, London, SCM Press, 1986.

7

Revelation and World Religions

Gavin D'Costa

Introduction

Is there revelation within the world religions – other than Christianity? To many people today this would seem an obsolete question and they would prefer to ask: what does revelation teach us when we find it in Hinduism, Buddhism, Islam etc. – as well as in Christianity? Yet for other Christians, there would be difficulty in moving on to this second question as the first is far from resolved. And for some Christians the answer is so clearly, 'No, there cannot be revelation in the world religions other than Christianity', that the second question is rendered obsolete and even heretical! To negotiate the complex issues that face the Christian theologian reflecting on this problem, it is worth clarifying what are some of the right questions to ask and some of the presuppositions involved in posing the question. This involves making six brief points.

First, I should make it clear that this entire chapter is written with the presupposition that this is a Christian theological question and not one asked from the viewpoint of a historian of religion or some alleged neutral investigator into the issue (a chimera if there ever was one). Of course, Jews, Muslims and Hindus among others may pose an analogous question from their own viewpoint, but this is not the focus of my study.

Second, it will be part of my argument that the answer to the question of whether there is revelation outside Christianity will depend strongly on the understanding of revelation held when the theologian is dealing with the issue of revelation within Christianity. To put it simply: how we understand revelation within Christianity will heavily influence our view of its possibility outside Christianity. I am aware that some writers pose the question in reverse: in the light of our experience of revelation outside Christianity, should we revise our understanding of revelation in

Christ? I would suggest that, however sincerely asked, this is a pseudo question. – It is in part already answered in the very form that it is put for it suggests that we can speak of revelation apart from Christ and, in so doing, has answered the question in a particular manner – which I think unsatisfactory. Central to this study, then, will be the issue of how revelation is understood within Christianity and seeing the consequences of that answer upon the world religions.

Third, there is no clear rationale for limiting this question to the 'world religions'. When Avery Dulles turns to the question of whether revelation is present in the world religions in his very helpful book *Models of Revelation*, he problematically assumes that the world religions 'seem to be more likely bearers of revelation than philosophies such as neo-Platonism or ideologies such as Marxism.'[1] I cannot see any good reason for his assumption as 'religions' as much as philosophies and ideologies are historically a complex cluster of varying beliefs and practices with very different track records and our assessment of them will depend upon where we stand and at what precisely we look, chronologically and geographically.

Justin Martyr had more time for Greek philosophy than for the Greek mystery religions and Leonardo Boff has more time for Marxist analysis than for Latin American native religions. This leads to a further point: my suspicion of the term 'religion' because I do not know what on earth it refers to. There have been numerous attempts to define the term so that it includes Marxism and philosophical worldviews.[2] And there have been concerted efforts to deconstruct the term 'religion' so that we can see that it is a recent effort at labelling what was previously never generically grouped together (Wilfred Cantwell Smith), and to question the politics of power in this very act of labelling (Edward Said).[3] This debate cannot be prolonged here but whatever 'religion' may mean I shall assume, as an active working definition, that it must refer to the social structuring of power within which groups of people live and therefore refers to 'culture' in its broadest sense: the habitual structuring of performance and reflexivity. This allows us to recognise unmitigated plurality and difference even in our understanding of a single 'religion', be it 'Christianity', 'Judaism' or 'Maoism'. That said, for purposes of clarity and focus I shall concentrate on the four major religions of Judaism, Islam, Hinduism and Buddhism.

Fourth, it is very difficult in dealing with the question of revelation and world religions to know how one should classify Judaism. Is Judaism just another world religion or does it bear a *sui generis* relation to Christianity that thereby requires it to be placed in another category, theologically speaking? To justify an answer to this question will already push us to define 'revelation', so here I simply alert the reader to the profound difficulty of even organising materials to explore this question, for so often the organisation will itself reflect theological presuppositions. For example, Dulles, in the aforementioned study, dubiously extends this special relation to Judaism to say that 'the Christian can readily admit that Judaism and Islam, as "religions of the Book", contain revelation insofar as they accept sacred texts which Christians also recognize as Scripture.'[4] Underlying this view is a problematic assumption that 'revelation equals sacred texts', rather than a communal form of reading 'sacred texts' authorised in a particular manner. Given Dulles' formulation, logically, much of neo–Hinduism could then be included with Judaism and Islam by virtue of neo–Hindu use of the New Testament – for example, by Ramakrishna, Vivekananda, and Radhakrishnan – but this simply highlights the fact that what is at stake is not the question of 'sacred texts' *per se*, but their 'inspired' and communitarian context of interpretation.

Fifth, it should be clear in the light of the above that even in an alleged map–drawing exercise such as this, the cartographer's own positioning will affect the map. So I need to come clean! I write as a Roman Catholic theologian (who is not licensed by the church regarding my teaching status) within a western secular academic institution, and have varied intellectual and practical experience of Hinduism, Judaism, Buddhism and Islam – in that order. My own limited experience of these religions makes me realise that generalisations about them are well nigh impossible; and that within them I have met women and men, some of whom I have been fortunate enough to count as friends, who have shown me in their lives and practice that these theological questions require a response! My response has been in conversation with these friends, their texts and practices, and a response which is ongoing with real people and their lives refuses theoretical closure. This conversation has been steered by an attempt to theologically reflect within the parameters of the church's teachings on such issues.[5] I make no apology for the specificity of my own positioning and only request readers to recognise that they too come from a particular and specific location and that if they deny this, they are being dishonest.[6]

Finally, I have been asked to write with a non–specialist audience in mind. So I have tried to focus on issues as much as possible allowing for the fact that all my readings of various theologians will be contested and that readers should not take my word but read cited primary texts for themselves. These texts and others are cited in the endnotes. I have therefore cited the works which I draw on for painting a picture of a thinker and then summarised in my own words what I take to be their arguments and concerns. Many of the notes will permit readers to see other maps and cartographers at work and to find closer textual justifications of the readings offered here.

For those who want a map of the map: I shall first briefly outline some historical perspectives on the question so that the reader can get a wider context in focus. Then, I shall focus on the modern period and explore differing responses to the question: is there revelation outside of Christianity? In doing so, I shall be touching on many related issues such as hermeneutics, modernity, authority, trinity, Christology and the church; all of which I shall contend are central to understanding the meaning of revelation.

Historical Perspectives Prior to the Modern Period

There are two ways of mapping out the issues here. The first is the telling of a historical narrative and the second is in terms of isolating issues that arise out of this narrative, while recognising that the issues cannot be isolated from that narrative and cannot always be easily transposed into different contexts. The historical narrative could be painted with extremely broad brush strokes in the following manner. I shall insert the issues within this narrative context.

By the fourth century, with the emergence of a consolidating entity called 'Christianity' there was also the growth of an understanding of revelation within and without this tradition. Judaism was the main 'other' religion at hand and despite Christianity's fratricidal relationship with Judaism, the classic formula 'God is the author of both the Old and New Testaments' (taken from the *Statuta Ecclesiae Antiqua*) was required from newly consecrated bishops from the fifth century onwards. Marcion (second century) had rejected the Old Testament on the ground that the demiurge or creator god portrayed by the Jews was incompatible with the God of love revealed in Christ. This teaching was later deemed heretical, which meant that at the very least, Israel/Judaism up to the time of Christ was recognised as a tradition where divine revelation had taken place. Of course, this recognition did not have clear implications for post-Christian Judaism which still used the 'Old Testament'/Hebrew Bible as part of its revealed Scripture, for it was generally taught that Christianity was the legitimate fulfilment of the covenant: the New superseding the Old, the gospel of love fulfilling the law, and so on.

115

Hence Judaism had refused to recognise its own gift of revelation and in this sense many of the early fathers had no difficulty in condemning Judaism – with all the complex and tragic consequences of that action.[7] Hence, for most of the Christian tradition, the acknowledgement of revelation within Judaism was limited to its pre-Christian history.

In modern times, mainly due to the Shoah/Holocaust and Christian complicity and responsibility for participation in this tragic reality, some Christian theologians (many taking their cue from Paul in *Romans* 9–11) have reassessed the covenant with Judaism. They have done so in such a way that revelation is acknowledged within Judaism – by virtue of God's promise to Israel and by the Jewish adherence to the 'Old Testament'/Hebrew Bible – and then extended to the traditions generated out of such covenantal relation. What such theologians have put into question is the alleged underlying anti-Judaism present within certain understandings of revelation.[8] We will return to this modern perspective later.

The other main traditions in these early days were, of course, the Greek mystery religions and cults. On the whole there was a primarily negative assessment of these traditions as regards the question of whether any revelation was present there.[9] However, many of the fathers were deeply indebted to the Greek philosophical traditions in which they had been trained. So developed the *ratio seminalis* and *logos spermatikos* tradition whereby it was understood that the Wisdom and Word present in Jesus Christ had been positively foreshadowed by such philosophies – although only in part and then often very defectively. In this respect, the fathers were also responding to the question of revelation and salvation regarding those before the time of Christ.

As for those outside the Church, most of the early fathers concur in the following: there is the possibility of salvation for righteous Jews and Gentiles before the coming of Christ but only prior to the time of Christ. But here it must be noted – and this would be true until nearly the fourteenth century – there was the general assumption that the truth of the gospel was evident to everybody and non-acceptance therefore meant explicit sinfulness. This is most important because it cannot be rightly said, as so many modern writers do, that the Christian tradition has consigned to damnation those who, through no fault of their own, do not know Jesus Christ. This caricature has exercised a powerful and distracting influence in the modern debate as we shall see.

What is interesting is the way in which the pre-Christian Jews and pagans were said to be saved and here we find a reliance on the natural law and reason which are related to the Logos fully incarnate in Christ.

116

There is also the interesting tradition of the descent into the underworld and Christ's preaching to the dead (based on 1 *Peter* 3:19 and 4:6). All solutions insisted, however problematically, on the necessity of the revelation of Jesus Christ for salvation, even though speaking of people living chronologically before Jesus.

We see the patristic church giving much more affirmation to philosophical wisdom that pre-dated Christ than to the 'religions' *per se*; this relates to the third of my methodological points in the introduction. Although there is debate as to the status of this patristic affirmation, it can be argued that the positive view of Greek philosophy is more akin to the notion of 'natural' theology or 'natural' revelation than to 'special' revelation, more akin to the understanding of a preparation for the gospel than anything that amounts to the truth of the gospel. Hence, it would be difficult to find any strong sense of the term 'revelation' when applied to the non-Jewish traditions of the time. Needless to say, this story is narrated from the viewpoint of the victors, whereas various gnostic groups thought otherwise, though here I can do no more than acknowledge this fact.

A word on Augustine is pertinent here. On the one hand Augustine acknowledges the *ecclesia ab Abel* tradition (the presence of the church from the first children of Adam), while being unambiguous that there was no salvation for Jews and pagans after Christ. What is especially significant about Augustine is that he was aware of African tribes who had never heard the gospel, but his explanation of their situation must be similar to that given to Deogratias regarding gentiles who might have had no chance of coming to saving faith: no one lacked the opportunity of saving faith – if they did, it was because God foresaw that were it offered, that person would refuse it. In his later anti-Pelagian period, the guilt incurred through original sin was sufficient explanation of such a situation and adequate defence of God's justice. Again, there was no deviation from the necessity of the church for salvation, and the affirmation of revelation occurring only in the Judaeo-Christian tradition; there were just varied assessments of the sinfulness of those who did not belong. There is a popular mistake made by many in citing Augustine's distinction between those who are apparently 'outside' the church but are really 'inside' as evidence of his conceding that those outside may be saved while not being in the visible community of the church. Augustine's distinction is related to God's foreknowledge, with the assumption that these people would inevitably be joined to the Church before they died and therefore were saved by Christianity's explicit revelation – although only God knew who such persons were.[10]

The next major religious tradition with which Christianity comes into sustained contact – somewhat antagonistic socio–political contact at that – is Islam. As Edward Said and others have shown, this earliest contact was characterised by a fundamental questioning of Islam, for at least one simple yet complex reason: if Muhammad was right, then Jesus Christ (as Christians understood him) was wrong. After all, if Muhammad was the final prophet and if the Qur'an was revelation, then it would seem that Christians had misunderstood their own 'revelation' which was only properly understood within Islam. If this was a simple truth, it was also deeply complicated by many other factors. For example, the actual contact with 'Christianity' by emerging Islam (Watt suggests it was a heretical form of Christianity) may throw much light on some 'false' tensions between the traditions.[11] The socio–political rivalry between Christian and Muslim imperial powers also fuelled negative religious readings of each other which in turn not inconveniently bolstered some of the militaristic manoeuvers. Finally, there is evidence that for many Christians Islam was regarded as a Christian heresy rather than as an autonomous and independent religion.[12] However, it should be added that as with Judaism, there were many moments of real engagement and discussion in which the powerful monotheism of the three traditions brought them close together. But if Islamic monotheism had been admired, it was often due to the philosophical acumen of Islamic philosophers (and of course their use of Greek philosophy) rather than from a respect for the 'revelation' of the Qur'an *per se*. Hence, it has not been until the modern period that a positive account of revelation has been developed regarding Islam.

In the medieval period there was much 'debate' which would shape the modern period, but here I can only briefly mention St Thomas Aquinas.[13] Aquinas allows for the possibility of implicit faith in Christ to those before Christ (that is, those who were not granted private revelations) by means of their belief in God and his providence (arrived at through reason) and in their living an upright life (through the light of their conscience). However, for Aquinas, after Christ all had the chance to hear the gospel, and for those exceptions (like the child raised by wolves) God would provide special means, such as inner inspiration or by sending a preacher. Hence, it is clear that other than by natural theology, that is, the use of reason and conscience which could arrive at theism and correct moral acts, no supernatural revelation enlightened non-Christians. If it did, it was via private revelations or inner inspiration, although these could not run counter to the gospel. Natural knowledge of God was thought to be that knowledge which was derived from the intellect and reason reflecting upon reality and thereby arriving at the knowledge of God. Aristotle was the classic case – and he was also in this respect an important example of a non-Christian and a non-Jew who, by reason, arrived at the existence of God. But – and this should be made extremely clear – this knowledge was not salvific and could not fulfil all the aspirations of women and men in their search for God. It was a stepping stone by which reason prepared the mind for the full and saving illumination of the gospel: that which came in revealed knowledge. During the modern period this distinction was developed in all sorts of ways regarding the non-Christian figure.[14]

It is the case that the concept of implicit faith in Christ and implicit desire (*in votum*) for baptism and the eucharist when they could not be received in reality (*in re*), could and would be utilised by later theologians (like Rahner) to apply to non-Christians, despite Aquinas' intentions. So, too, would his teaching that justification is acquired through one's first moral decision in the remarks in *Summa Theologia* I–II, q.89, a.6.

It is worth noting at this juncture the development of the concept of 'general' and 'special' revelation, which has a relationship to the previous distinction between natural and revealed theology. General revelation referred to the revelation of God in creation and that attested to historically within the Bible (for instance, the Psalms and Paul), although there is considerable debate as to the significance of this revelation: enough for salvation? sufficient for condemnation? now obscured through sin and only accessible after special revelation? Special revelation was the salvific revelation of the triune God. The nineteenth-century notion of 'primitive revelation', which arose with ethnographical study of other religions, was closely related to the earlier notion of general revelation.[15]

The last of our two religious traditions, Hinduism and Buddhism, do not really enter the Christian picture in any sustained and serious manner until the European expansion into Asia – which takes us into the 'modern period'. During the eighteenth and nineteenth centuries the prevailing judgement in mainstream Christianity regarding revelation within these traditions is generally negative.[16] However, three important qualifications are in order. First, there were many Christians working in India who began to have a more positive view of revelation within Hinduism, such that it began to be viewed by some, with nuances and differences, as analogous to Judaism: a positive preparation for the gospel containing revelation.[17] Second, with the increasing secularism of Europe during this period, there were many who 'turned East' and found wisdom in Hinduism and Buddhism rather than in Christianity.[18] This of course prompted serious questioning within Christian circles. Third, with new indigenous churches developing, there would be serious voices of Asian theologians challenging the 'mainstream' Christian picture – as we shall see later on in this chapter. Their voices were joined by those of many white European Christians who were deeply suspicious of Christianity's complicity with European colonialism.

This brief historical narrative sketch gives an overall picture where it would be appropriate to say that for most of Christian history 'saving revelation' has only occurred within the Judaeo–Christian tradition. While other religions and philosophies may be elevated, inspired, and even contain glimpses of truth, their 'revelation', so to speak, is always short of being supernaturally salvific if it is seen as revelation at all.

Revelation and Other Religions in the Modern Period

The modern period, heralded by the European Enlightenment, marks a radically new perspective on our question. Beside the types of answer that we have seen above and sophisticated further developments, two new options emerge. First, with the growing scepticism about the very possibility of revelation (understood as interruption of natural causality) the question of God seemed increasingly obsolete, and equally the question of revelation in Christianity or in any other religion. Theologically this was expressed in the growth of deism, and culturally in the eventual secularism of the western mind.[19] Another option was an increasingly positive answer to the question of whether revelation existed outside Christianity. Today this is expressed in the work of Christian theologians who argue that all religions are revelatory and capable of being means to salvation, and this salvation is not causally or ontologically related to Jesus Christ. The very novelty of this solution requires special attention and I shall turn to it first.

Many Revelations Within the Many Religions

Kant can be seen as the ambiguous archetype of latter day 'pluralism', the term given to those who hold that all religions are revelatory and therefore capable of being means to salvation, and that this salvation is not causally, ontologically, or historically related to Jesus Christ.[20] This was not Kant's position as such, but was its logical outcome.[21] Kant insisted that 'revelation' was universally accessible via moral reason and not via particular historical events, such as the incarnation. To Kant, it was mistaken parochialism to claim that the truth about God and salvation was to be found solely in one particular historical stream within humanity, an assumption that shapes much of modernity. Rather, Christianity (in particular) exemplified the highest moral golden rule in the preaching of Jesus. Insomuch as Christians were ethically transformed by his teaching ('Do unto others as you would have others do unto you' – a definition singularly lacking any reference to God) they aligned themselves to the categorical imperative, the ethical 'ought' which necessarily for Kant presupposed God. With this ethical universalism in place, a sort of universal immanent 'revelation', it would be a short step to arranging all religions around an archimedian point that would implicitly entail a higher notion of 'revelation' than that claimed by individual religions.

A modern equivalent to Kant, both epistemologically and ethically, is John Hick whose position is extremely influential and well developed. Initially, Hick argued that the *solus Christus* assumption (that salvation is only through faith in the unique revelation of Christ) held in mainstream Christianity was incompatible with the Christian teaching of a God who desires to save all people. There are many millions who, through no fault of their own, have never heard of Christ, before and after the New Testament period. It is therefore unChristian to think that God would have 'ordained that men must be saved in such a way that only a small minority can in fact receive this salvation.'[22] Hick argued that it was God, and not Christianity or Christ, that counted as normative revelation and it is towards God that the religions were oriented and from whom they gain their salvific efficacy. Hick therefore proposed a theocentric notion of revelation, away from a Christocentric or ecclesiocentric focus which, he argued, had falsely dominated Christianity. But what then of Christ as the unique and singular self-revelation of God? Hick argued that the doctrine of the incarnation should be understood mythically – as an expression of devotion and commitment by Christians, not as an ontological claim that here in this particular place and in this particular man God has chosen to reveal himself uniquely and definitively.[23] Hick stressed the revelation of an all-loving God over that of the uniqueness of Christ.

An important later development in Hick's position came in response to the criticism that his theological revolution was still theocentric and thereby excluded non-theistic religions. Hick developed a Kantian-type distinction between a divine noumenal reality 'that exists independently and outside man's perception of it' which he calls the 'Eternal One' and the phenomenal world, 'which is that world as it appears to our human consciousness' – in effect, the various 'revelatory' human responses to the Eternal One.[24] These responses constitute the different revelations within the different traditions, both theistic and non-theistic (for example, God or Allah, Nirvana and Nirguna Brahman). In this fashion Hick tries to overcome his revelatory theocentricism.

The final Kantian move is Hick's emphasis on morality, or what he calls 'turning away from self-centredness to Reality-centredness', a characteristic of all authentic religious traditions.[25] He is clear that conflicting truth claims do exist on an historical, theological and philosophical level, but these can rarely be resolved, especially in the latter two spheres. But despite these differences, Hick argues that the different traditions still produce 'saints' and therefore the only definitive criterion for authenticity is the moral one.[26] Hence, we all have something to learn from each other's revelations and in this sense can act as correctives to each other's absolute interpretations. I want to suggest that while Hick's intentions are noble and serious, his project, like that of Kant's, finally divests all religions of any revelatory power and achieves precisely the opposite of its stated goal!

At the outset, let us be rid of the caricature that the *solus Christus* principle necessarily means that all non-Christians are damned. We have seen above that this is not 'necessary' in the logic of the tradition. But does Hick manage to extend our grasp of 'revelation' or does he, like Kant, finally reduce it to a moral postulate with an underlying agnosticism? There are reasons to suggest the latter. First, when Hick proposes to emphasise God rather than Christ, he is in danger of severing Christology from ontology and introducing a free-floating God divorced from any particular revelation. In fact Judaism, Christianity, and Islam have all tended to centre on revelatory paradigms for their discourse and practice. Hick's theocentricism pays little attention to the importance of historical particularity and cultic practice as the grounding of theistic discourse. (I would contend that there is no such thing as 'theistic discourse' in Christianity, rather 'trinitarian discourse', as Christianity is irredeemably Christocentric, theocentric and ecclesiocentric in its trinitarianism.) Actually, the very theological basis of his proposal (an all-loving God) is undermined if Hick cannot give normative ontological status to the revelatory events upon which this axiom is grounded; moreover, the revelatory shape of God is different in the three monotheistic traditions (without denying overlap and similarities, but always within the context of difference as well) and certainly is not to be found in Buddhism or Confucianism.

Modernity's escape from tradition-specific parochialism is doomed for there is no site of pure neutrality, except in the newly created tradition of modern liberalism, as Alasdair MacIntyre and others have argued.[27] And this new site is just one more tradition-specific location which has the misfortune of not recognising itself to be that which it castigates: tradition-specific reflection and practice. Hence, in Hick's desire to avoid Christian-revelatory parochialism, he replaces it with another: agnosticism. If 'God' lacks narrative specificity in Hick's theo-centrism, it seems further relativised in his recent work as the personal, loving, creator; 'God' is seen as one aspect of the 'Eternal One' that apparently can also be characterised by non-personal, non-creator, non-theistic predicates. As all such predicates are from the human side, Hick argues, they are thereby not properly applicable to the Eternal One. This argument has the effect of denying any ontological predication (even analogically) regarding the Eternal One, and is nothing short of agnosticism.[28] The Kantian *noumenon* encountered a similar problem in not providing for any correspondence between phenomena and things-in-themselves. Hick is left in the odd position of apparently accepting that all religions are revelatory, but is actually committed to then denying the revelatory claims as made by those religions. The exceptions, of course, are those that claim their revelation is myth and not ontologically definitive.

The only determinative 'revelation' that can be used to adjudicate authentic or inauthentic revelatory claims is that of Kant's golden-rule morality, what Hick calls 'turning away from self-centredness to Reality-centredness'. But such a non-narrative conception of morality is itself problematic. 'Self' and 'Real' are precisely what require narrative speci-fication, if Hick's golden rule is to have any significant meaning; and as soon as one begins specification, we find Hick retreating from such particularities. Hence, even the traditionless universal determinative 'rev-elation' of morality ends up, as it did with Kant, as no real revelation, except as a formal injunction. MacIntyre has shown that this is hardly surprising in terms of ethics within liberal modernity,[29] but what is sur-prising (I say this polemically) is to find a Christian theologian replicating this position within Christianity. One might say that the notion of 'revelation' is here dictated by extra-Christian considerations, such that Christian revelation is itself determined by categories other than itself. And this is to state one of the dilemmas of our debate: if one begins from Christian revelation, does this predetermine the analysis of the possibility of 'revelation' outside of Christianity? Can this be avoided? Hick shows one possible avenue for avoiding this – and I have argued that this is a cul-de-sac.

Keith Ward and Revelation

Instructive and pertinent to this debate is a recent book by Keith Ward, *Religion and Revelation: A Theology of Revelation in the World's Religions*, (Clarendon, Oxford, 1994) in which he tries to steer clear of the cul-de-sac, although it is not clear whether his navigation is finally successful. Ward sets out his agenda in Part I, 'Towards a Comparative Theology', and his basic argument is that the 'critical theologian' – who may or may not belong to any religious tradition – is required to decide what counts as revelation, not only from his or her own tradition but from all religious traditions. 'It is not enough to accept the canon of Scripture just as it stands as the starting-point of theology. For we will not know just what is authoritatively contained in Divine revelation until we have first decided what the character and authority of that revelation is' (p.36). Ward claims that he is not trying to construct an *a priori* model of revelation. Rather the comparative theologian must look at the 'phenomena of alleged revelation . . . asking what the best model of Divine revealing action seems to be, in the light of them' (p.90). However, implicit to this method is the presupposition that 'revelation' is a universal reality and that we must choose what counts as revelation, which somewhat begs the question of our being under the judgement of revelation. While comparative theology is Ward's stated methodological aim, he does not always appear to be consistent, especially when he comes to the final two parts dealing mainly with Christianity. However, at the beginning, while acknowledging that a comparative theologian may well be a Christian (as he himself is) he contrasts comparative theology with 'confessional theology': 'the exploration of a given revelation by one who wholly accepts that revelation and lives by it' (p.40). It is not clear why confessional theology cannot include comparative theology, except that Ward tends to assume that it will deny the claims to revelation found within the world religions (pp.15–21), although later he accepts that his model of comparative theology is done confessionally (p.108). These methodological difficulties are important, although they should not obscure the grand vision of the book.

In Part II Ward explores first the 'primal' religions. He concludes that they express, participate and mediate spiritual powers which cannot be clearly conceptualised. Ward draws three conclusions. Primitive traditions mediate God's power for the 'figures of the gods reveal what the inner nature of being is, its spiritual basis and purpose . . . they show how the goal of a true human life may be achieved' (p.78). Second, these revelations operate despite human sinfulness and error. Finally, revelation can at least be understood as 'persuasive influence' and 'co-operative causality, dependent for its success on human faithfulness' (pp.91–2). As can be seen from the first conclusion, Ward is inclined to generalise, as a result of which the intractable shape of the particulars of each religion is sometimes obscured.

Ward turns to Judaism, Hinduism, Buddhism and Islam in Part III. While not ignoring the profound differences between and within each of them, he is also deeply sensitive to various commonalities. The most important of the latter is allegedly their primary aim to 'overcome egoism and ignorance, and attain a supreme goal of intrinsic value' (p.191). For Ward, this common aim indicates the presence of 'revelation' in the world religions. Hence, the sometimes contradictory teachings in different religions are not necessarily final, but 'express different emphases and evaluations. Such differences can often be accounted for by noting their originative experiences and differing histories' (*ibid*). While this may be true to some extent, it certainly will not solve the conflicting truth claims that do exist. Also, one must question whether Ward's discovery of a common aim of overcoming egoism and ignorance and attaining a goal of supreme intrinsic value is historically falsifiable. The problem is that when one divests the particularities of each tradition, many such abstract commonalities can be found; but when one looks at the world from within the community of a particular tradition, such abstractions might seem so vague as not to be controversial or even of any interest at all.

Part IV of his book attends to Christology, and Ward argues for revelation in Christianity in terms of Jesus Christ. He maintains that Jesus was indeed sinless, following the testimony of the apostolic church, and in being sinless was unique in humankind. On this basis (rather than primarily the resurrection) he defends a high ontological Christology affirming Jesus to be a unique incarnation of the Word such that the Word is 'identical' with Jesus the human subject. This allows him to claim that 'Jesus alone, by the grace of God, is both uncorrupt and united to Divinity' (p.264); and regarding his two natures, 'Their perfect union is the foreshadowing of the future fulfilment of all humanity in the Divine Life' (p.267).

At this point two comments are worth making. First, it is not always apparent whether and how, if at all, Ward's doctrine of God is shaped by his Christology. When he speaks of other religions, Christological and trinitarian-shaped language tends to cease; it is replaced by terms such as 'Divine', 'Supreme Value', 'creativity' and 'dynamism'. This seems to undercut the implications of such a Christology. But he is ambivalent on this point, for at times he appears to recognise the implications of his high Christology, for example, when he writes: 'being set on the way to salvation does not depend on holding Christian beliefs; but being ultimately saved will depend on acceptance of the basic truths about Christ as Divine self-revelation – at least, if they are indeed truths' (p.317). Given that Ward says that he affirms such Christological truths, why does he not investigate or comment on the long Christian tradition regarding the *logos spermatikos* or the complex theologies of grace, especially prevenient grace? If Christology determines the meaning of 'revelation', rather than 'revelation' being determined by a trawl through the history of religions, then the discussion about 'revelation' in other religions must be linked to trinitarian reflection. Furthermore, Ward does not fully unpack the soteriology implicit in his Christological claims, so that the significance of Jesus Christ for all people is never made clear. At times the impression remains of an 'exemplary' Christology (p.239) which fails to illuminate the problem of how salvation is brought into the world by Christ (if at all).

An Asian Perspective

I will look at one more solution that is informed by liberation theology from an Asian perspective: the work of the Sri Lankan Jesuit, Aloysius Pieris. Pieris' entire project can be seen in terms of an Asian theology of liberation (the title of his major book).[30] Pieris contends that the Asian church is in a radically new situation, without comparison in the history of Christianity. It is a minority group within a sea of Asian faiths, committed to the liberation of the poor. It is this context that forces the church to be 'baptised' into Asia's grinding poverty and transforming religiousness (specifically Buddhism for Pieris) to find its own life and identity. Otherwise the church will remain a western multinational institution. Inculturation requires such risk. The liberative power of certain forms of Buddhism means that Christians and Buddhists must join together to create a new redeemed society. Mission will consist of educating 'the nations to fear the judgments of the victims they themselves create!'[31]

Pieris is deeply critical of his own church in terms of the Second Vatican Council's fulfilment theology. One reason is that it 'relegates other religions to a "pre-Christian" category of spirituality to be "fulfilled" through the church's missionary endeavour.'[32] This, he argues, is objectionable because such a claim is reversible and tends to lead to an impasse in dialogue. Furthermore, the fulfilment claim neutralises the uniqueness of other religions by seeing them as a lesser image of one's own.[33] The Second Vatican Council's fulfilment theology is also problematic because for Pieris the church's missionary endeavour has uncritically imported western conceptualities and practices, claiming gospel authority for its cultural imperialism. It is this unacceptable refusal to be fully immersed and 'baptised' within Asian poverty and religiousness which is at the heart of fulfilment theology, according to Pieris.[34]

Pieris' objections are also tied to his wider assumptions concerning Christology and the revelatory and salvific status of other religions. He argues that certain forms of Buddhism have revelatory and salvifically mediating structures. Pieris claims that Buddhist voluntary poverty, when employed as a resistance to Mammon, is evidence of its liberative and revelatory potential. This is especially seen in Buddhist monasticism and gnosis (understood as relativising, not denying the world) which allows it 'an engagement in a positive and practical programme of psychosocial restructuring of human existence here on earth in accordance with the path leading to nirvanic freedom.'[35] His thinking is informed by experience, as Pieris works alongside Buddhists in struggling for a just and fair society in Sri Lanka. Hence there is no uncritical endorsement of Asian religiosity for he fully recognises that there 'is also a *sinful* and *enslaving* dimension to Asian religion' insomuch as it hinders and obscures this liberative and revolutionary potential.[36]

All this obviously raises the Christological question and Pieris is unequivocal in denouncing the western 'obsession with the "uniqueness" of Christ.'[37] His argument is that the salvific reality denoted by 'Christ' and found in Jesus by Christians cannot be captured under any single revelatory categorisation. Pieris writes:

> What is absolute and unique is not the title [Christ], but what all major religions, some in theistic, others in nontheistic terms, have professed for centuries as the mystery of salvation manifesting itself at least in a trinal (if not trinitarian) form:
> (1) Salvation as the *salvific 'beyond'* becoming the human person's *salvific 'within'* (e.g., Yahweh, Allah, Tao, Nirvāna, Tathatā, Brahman–Ātman), (2) thanks to a *salvific mediation*, which is also revelatory in character (e.g., tao, *mārga*, *dharma*, *dabar*, image), (3) and a (given) human *capacity for salvation* or a saving power paradoxically inherent in the human person (*purusa*, *citta*, *ātman*, etc.) despite being sheer 'nothing', 'mere dust', 'soul-less' (*anātma*),

a part of created 'illusion' (*māyā*), immersed in this cosmic 'vale of tears' (*samsara*) from which one yearns for perfect redemption.

... I want to emphasize here that this 'triune' mystery constitutes the basic soteriological datum in many of our religious cultures.[38]

There are two points to note. Salvation is present and mediated in the world religions through their own structures. (Pieris here makes a rather sweeping claim, although most of his work is focused on Buddhism specifically.) And this salvation is known in Christianity through Father, Son and Spirit – but these are names, one set of human categorisations, which 'denote the mystery of salvation' that is found in all religions in different names and forms. Hence, any notion of a *Logos Spermatikos*, or *semina Verbi* is out of the question as this would be to fall back into old fulfilment categories.

Here again, we have a strong claim to many revelations. Is the challenge concerning the uniqueness of the revelation in Christ simply a western obsession, or is it central to the Christian faith? Pieris voices a deep concern of many Asians which must be taken with utter seriousness. Has this claim led to the lack of recognition of the revelatory and saving power of God within other religions and the pejorative encoding of the other in terms of *preparatio evangelica*? It is worth noting that a universal Council of the Church (the Second Vatican Council) found no resistance to proclaiming the uniqueness of Christ as central to Christian faith: that God has come in Christ to redeem the world through his Spirit and this good news is the message and life of the Catholic church. Bishops from Asia, Africa and South America were all present at the council and there is no evidence that this point was contested. Hence, uniqueness is not a western obsession!

So what is at stake in the claim of uniqueness? While Pieris acknowledges his siding with the poor is a consequence of his Christological commitment, he sees a similar processs in forms of Asian religions, so this aspect too could not be called unique. However, I would suggest that uniqueness is not to be predicated of Christ in the sense of making a comparison between him and other figures or other religious claims in this respect. In this respect, all religions are unique! Rather, uniqueness is a matter of saying that we live and breathe and have our being from Christ, in his Church through the grace of the triune God. It is to claim that the entire world is shaped by this drama of redemption that is always an inclusive and exclusive story of God's action towards us and for us.

What may be at stake in affirming the uniqueness of Christ is perhaps found by default in Pieris. – Pieris assumes a vantage point from which the religions, including Christianity, may be judged. He speaks of the life-giving power found in certain forms of Christianity and also in other forms of the world religions. This life-giving power may be characterised in terms of socio-political liberation from all forms of poverty and oppression, leading humanity into peace, justice and community. However, what is missing from this account is the specific rationale for such a characterisation of liberation and its fundamental relation to the Christian story.[39] In fact, Pieris' characterisation of liberation is in constant danger of being free-floating for it would be, for him, imperialist to causally locate it in the Christian story of redemption: hence Pieris' attempt to focus on the 'mystery of salvation' never known uniquely or definitively anywhere, but equally mysteriously everywhere. He fails to grapple seriously with 'the scandal of particularity' that caused the early church to be a folly to both Jew and Gentile alike. He seems to neutralise the dialectic of judgement and mercy borne in Jesus' cross, so that any Christological judgement on Asia's culture and religions is seen as imperialist – except insomuch as it is (rightly) a condemnation of Asia's structurally enforced poverty.

But in refusing to locate the story of God's redemption in Jesus Christ, there is the question: where then is the drama of redemption located? For Pieris, his fear of a starting-point that is Christian belies his desire to relate creation to soteriology in such a way that it seems to bypass Christ and conflate nature and grace entirely. In so doing, redemption sometimes seems to be a matter of women and men acting politically correctly. In refusing to acknowledge redemption in the name of Christ, but rather relativising all stories of redemption in favour of the overall 'mystery of salvation', there is a danger that revelation comes to mean a predetermined morality that the different religions embody. It is one thing to want rightly to avoid religious and cultural denigration in the name of Christ, but surely another to avoid the name of Christ, as a Christian, with the intention of granting soteriological equality to all religions. If the latter were in fact the case, then the Christian could only knew this in the light of Christ, for how else are we to discern the presence of the Spirit in the world?

Although Pieris does not explicitly adopt a Spirit theology, it is implicitly in present insomuch as he speaks of the life-giving liberating power to be found within all creation – as is seen in forms of Buddhism. However, Pope John Paul II interestingly warns theologians in this regard that affirming this life-giving force (of the Spirit) in all creation is not 'therefore an alternative to Christ, nor does he [the Spirit] fill a sort of void which is sometimes suggested as existing between Christ and the Logos.'[40] And besides this Christological relationship, he also underlines the ecclesiological relationship: 'Moreover, the universal activity of the Spirit is not to be separated from his particular activity within the Body of Christ, which is the Church.'[41]

Pieris is in danger of bypassing Christ and the Church in discerning the shape of revelation outside the Church, in affirming that other religions *per se* (even if only in certain forms) can be the means to salvation – for this is to say that God's story can be told in its redemptive fullness without the triune story of Son, Father and Spirit. The broader implication is that the particular drama of Christian redemption is disposable and not itself necessary for salvation. This is perhaps the deeper significance of the teaching regarding the unique self-revelation of God in Christ.

Many Revelations Within the One Revelation of Jesus Christ

Karl Rahner SJ has best formulated a position that both affirms the uniqueness of the trinitarian revelation and allows for 'revelation' within non-Christian religions, although in a necessarily limited manner. In this respect, he avoids the difficulties outlined above, but his own solution is not without problems.

Rahner's theological anthropology shapes his form of inclusivism. He argues that the precondition of finite (categorial) knowledge is an unconditional openness to being (*vorgriff*), which is an unthematic, pre-reflective awareness of God – who is infinite being. Our transcendental openness to being constitutes the hiddenness of grace. Men and women therefore search in history for a categorial disclosure of this hidden grace. In Jesus' total abandonment to God, his total 'Yes' through his life, death and resurrection, he is established as the culmination and prime mediator of grace: as true revelation, meaning God's self-communication to women and men. Therefore Christian revelation is the explicit expression of grace which men and women experience implicitly in the depths of their being when, for example, they reach out through the power of grace in trusting love and self-sacrifice, or in acts of hope and charity.

Rahner attempts to balance the *solus Christus* teaching with the universal salvific will of God, so as to maintain that Christ is the sole cause of salvation in the world, but that this salvific grace may be revealed within history without an explicit confrontation with Christ.[42] Such is the case in the history of Israel which Rahner calls a 'lawful religion' prior to the time of Christ. Rahner maintains it remains a lawful religion for those who have never been confronted historically (externally) and existentially (internally) with the gospel. If with Israel, may it not in principle be the case with other religions of the world? Rahner's answer is 'Yes', thereby extending the possibility of revelation outside the Church, but within carefully specified parameters.

Rahner argues that Christology and the doctrine of God should not be separated from the Church in which they are found, and therefore maintains that Christ is historically mediated through the Church. This means that Rahner must reconcile membership of the Church as a means of salvation and the possibility that revelation and salvific grace is mediated outside the historically tangible borders of the Church. He does this along the lines of the traditional Catholic teachings regarding the *votum ecclesiae* (a wish to belong to the Church), and the related notion of implicit desire.[43] He claims to be developing Aquinas' argument at this point.

Rahner argues that if revelation and salvific grace exist outside the visible Church, as he believes it does in the history of Israel, and in creation and through conscience, then this grace is both causally related to Christ (always and everywhere – as prime mediator) and his Church. Furthermore, given the socio-historical nature of men and women, grace must be mediated historically and socially. The incarnation is paradigmatic in suggesting this. Hence, if and when non-Christians respond to grace, then this grace must be revealed through the non-Christian's religion, however imperfectly. Rahner thus coins the term 'anonymous Christian' and 'anonymous Christianity'. The former refers to the source of saving grace that is responded to (Christ) and the latter refers to its dynamic orientation towards its definitive historical and social expression (the Church).

Because God has already been active within the non-Christian religions, Christians can be open to learning about God through engagement with non-Christians. Moreover, the Christian is also free to engage in active social and political co-operation, when appropriate. In this twofold respect, Rahner counters some criticism of Hick and Pieris. Rahner is able to affirm that the Church is given the one true revelation, while at the same time holding that other religions may have a provisional revelation which mediates salvation.

Rahner's achievement is considerable. However, there are two problems worth focusing on. (Clearly critics like Hick and Pieris have further and different problems which to some extent have been outlined above.)

The first is not dissimilar to the critique employed regarding Hick and Pieris, although its cutting edge is not so clear. Is Rahner in danger of severing grace from the specific and particular story of Jesus Christ? In one sense he is not, for he relates all grace causally and ontologically to Christ. But in another sense he is, for if salvation requires no explicit faith and response to the historically particular narrative of Jesus Christ, then this dangerously obscures the way in which the church claims to be formed and nourished by precisely its engagement with the self-revelation of God in Jesus Christ. Is the scandal of revelatory particularity evaporated in affirming salvific revelatory realities, however provisional, historically apart from the particularity of Jesus Christ?

I cannot attempt to answer this question here, but let me register another reservation. By relating revelation to experience via his transcendental anthropology, is Rahner in danger of conflating nature and grace so that finally, Christianity is just a better interpretation of the same experience of grace mediated differently in other religions? And what impact does such a view have other than to minimise the character of sin and tragedy which leads to an impoverished theology of the cross?[44] I leave these as open questions and turn to an extremely important attempt to steer beyond Rahner, yet avoiding a straightforward 'No' to the possibility of revelation within non-Christian religions.

The Uniqueness of Christian 'Revelation'

Besides positions that simply say, *a priori*, there is no revelation within the world religions, there have been some very sophisticated attempts to retain the uniqueness of Christian revelation and keep an open mind regarding the possibility of revelation within the world religions. This latter possibility is held in tension between a respect towards the 'Other', which is reticent to define what their religion is about beyond their own self-description, and to keep in mind the cultural–linguistic shaping of our realities. I shall examine a remarkable book by the dominican Roman Catholic scholar, Joseph DiNoia.[45] DiNoia closely follows George Lindbeck's cultural–linguistic model of religion, arguing that the specific way of life, determined by the actual doctrines held, uniquely shapes and moulds the religious practitioner.[46] This means that Christian revelation is precisely that – Christian. Hence the question of 'revelation' in other religions reduces itself to whether other religions are Christian, and at one straightforward level, they are manifestly not so. The goal and means of the religious way are intrinsically related and cannot be separated.

DiNoia maintains one cannot say anything about the meaning of another religion apart from specific and proper attention to the ways in which its doctrines regulate its practice and stipulate the goal to be achieved by that way of life. In Christianity, eternal fellowship with the blessed Trinity (revelation) can be said to be the goal (salvation) which is carefully orchestrated in minute detail through the liturgical life of the community. To claim that other religions attain the same salvific goal (or thereby have 'revelation') is obviously problematic. DiNoia's argument creates a space for other religions to really disclose what they are about in their doctrines and practice, without *a priori* categorisation, and this is to be welcomed. Hence the necessity of dialogue as the proper location for disclosure of the 'other'. Only in this process can we ask whether and how these ways of life relate to Christianity, if at all, and whether we wish to term them 'revelation'. (He criticises Hick and Rahner because they impose a soteriocentricism upon other religions where there may be none.)

DiNoia allows for the possibility that doctrinal truth and good actions can be found in other religions, without compromising the centrality of the incarnation as constitutive of salvation. But he is reticent as to whether this goodness and truth can be said to be in principle revelatory or the means of salvation for the non-Christian. He does not want to say 'yes', for this would tend to negate the view that doctrines constitute a way of life directed towards a particular goal which is not otherwise attainable. Nor does he want to say 'no', for this may limit the way in which God actually does work. What he prefers to say, when confronted by the question of non-Christian salvation and revelation, is that non-Christians will certainly have a chance to attain salvation after death in a purgatorial state. Since DiNoia accepts that purgatory does not provide an opportunity for the reversal of life-shaping decisions taken prior to death, he allows that other religions may therefore have a providential, 'rather than specifically salvific', role.[47] A religion may determine an individual's decision to 'acknowledge Christ'[48] in the purgatorial state. Hence other religions may, at their best, be a kind of *preparatio evangelica*. One might regard this as analogous to affirming the possibility of general revelation in other religions, but not special or saving revelation. DiNoia's solution allows for the universality of the offer of salvation and the specificity of its constitutive cause: Jesus Christ.

DiNoia's position is deeply attractive, although I should register some misgivings. Some of his criticisms of Rahner are problematic. DiNoia says that Rahner attributes to non-Christians the possibility of 'implicit acceptance of a revelation they explicitly reject or of which they are unaware.'[49] While Rahner argues that implicit acceptance of God is possible without explicit knowledge of God, he categorically denies that implicit faith could be attributed to one who knowingly and explicitly rejects Christianity.[50] Moreover, Rahner is clear that his reflections are *a priori*, covering only the possibility that revelation and salvation is available through the non-Christian's religion. He firmly states that the historian of religions and other specialists will have to investigate how far this may be true or false.[51] Thus DiNoia's characterisation of inclusivism as asserting the actuality rather than the possibility of soteriocentricism is false.

The real differences between DiNoia and Rahner lie in their different estimations of the possibility of implicit faith in a non-Christian, and thereby the possibility that such implicit faith may be mediated through revelation in the non-Christian's religion. For DiNoia, rightly I think, there is reserve about attributing 'revelation' outside of Christ. This is because the very term is Christologically determined, and if it were to be used it would have to be related explicitly to Christ. DiNoia's main argument against implicit faith being attributed to non-Christians is that there is no clearly specified 'potentially explicable and publicly identifiable body of teachings implicitly held' by a person 'on the authority of competent or official teachers.'[52] The teaching of implicit faith was historically developed in relation to catechumens or those who are actually in the Church but who have little intellectual grasp and understanding of its teachings. DiNoia argues that Aquinas is misused when this theory is extended to those outside the visible Church, or could only be plausible with more specification as to the beliefs that must be implicit that could engender such a *votum ecclesia*.

However, Rahner and Congar argue that implicit faith must be presupposed in true acts of love and charity, which are always filled with grace, that are often enjoined by revelatory/structural elements within another religion. Rahner argues that insomuch as true acts of love and charity are required by a non-Christian's religion, then the religion, in that instance, constitutes revelation and mediates salvation. DiNoia partially acknowledges this in his discussion of Aquinas and moral action, allowing that Aquinas admits the operation of grace in such acts.[53] But the problem revolves around the precise status of such grace and whether the correlative revelatory event engenders salvific grace or preparatory grace.

Finally, I have some reservations with DiNoia's purgatorial solution – not difficulties with the concept and possibility of purgatory, but with his use of it. The logic of his position would seem to require that non-culpable non-Christians end up in limbo rather than purgatory. They certainly do not merit eternal punishment and they certainly do not merit eternal salvation – or even seek it. This objection has a similar logic to the one DiNoia's employs against applying the category of implicit faith to non-Christians. Purgatory, properly conceived, is there for Christians who are not fully purified, not for those who are not justified. DiNoia appears to acknowledge this in a note: 'The doctrine of purgatory simply allows for some kind of interval in which the necessary purification can be undergone by persons who die in the "state of grace", with their sins forgiven, but with lingering effects of sin or any other spiritual deficiencies . . . rendering them unfit for the enjoyment of blissful, eternal fellowship with the Triune God.'[54] Furthermore, if purgatory does not allow for a change in fundamental decision there is an allied problem. If, in the best scenario, the providential revelatory role of another religion provides only a *preparatio evangelica*, then by definition the non-Christian will have actually made a fundamental decision for his or her own religion before death. To then require that a Buddhist, shaped by his or her specific form of Buddhism, become a Christian would require the altering of his or her previous fundamental decision, unless it could be shown that Buddhism was entirely in continuity with Christianity. But to assert this to any real extent would require acknowledging Buddhism as analogous to pre-Christ Judaism, a partial means to salvation with authentic revelation. To assert otherwise would acknowledge that if the practice of salvation is what constitutes salvation, then the Buddhist would have to learn a radically new language and pursue a radically new way of life – which surely constitutes a more fundamental shift, a more fundamental decision, than simply further purification which is all that purgatory can provide. DiNoia very briefly touches on these difficulties in the footnotes but not with enough detail.[55] However, these criticisms do not substantially affect his main thesis, except perhaps to clarify the difficulty of using or not using the term 'revelation' in regard to other religions.

Conclusion

Does revelation exist within other religions? I hope to have shown that the answer depends on how revelation is initially defined. If it is defined apart from Jesus Christ, then often a non-Christian ideology or philosophy will be promoted under the guise of revelation, as was the tendency in Kant, Hick and Pieris. If it is defined from Jesus Christ, then there are various alternative avenues that open up. These are exemplified in the work of Rahner and DiNoia, for example, although Rahner's transcendental anthropology does raise some problematic questions and shows how closely the relation of theology and philosophy might dictate various answers from within a Christological paradigm. It is also clear from the above that when revelation is granted as existing within non-Christian religions, it need not be equated with salvation within these traditions. The use and distinctions between general/special revelation and natural/supernatural theology indicate the complex and interrelated nature of revelation and saving grace.

In my opinion, if revelation is defined apart from Christ, then what follows cannot be called a Christian understanding of revelation. However, it is possible to see how revelation within other religions can be affirmed by the Christian theologian, but only if this is related to a trinitarian understanding of God's self-revelation, a suggestion I have tried to develop elsewhere.[56] If Christianity is not critically open to the voice of God within creation and culture, which therefore includes the religions, then Christians will fail to be faithful to God!

Notes

1. Avery Dulles, *Models of Revelation*, London, Gill & Macmillan, 1992, p.175. I do not think Dulles would hold this view today and was aware of many of the difficulties: see pp.174–6.
2. Ninian Smart, *The Phenomenon of Religion*, London, Macmillan, 1973.
3. Wilfred Cantwell Smith, *The Meaning and End of Religion*, London, Sheldon, 1978; Edward Said, *Orientalism: Western Conceptions of the Orient*, London, Routledge, 1978.
4. Dulles, *ibid.*, p. 175.
5. See, for example, the documents of Vatican II and the *Catechism of the Catholic Church* and for a good overview, Francis A. Sullivan, *Salvation Outside the Church? Tracing the History of the Catholic Response*, London, Geoffrey Chapman, 1992.
6. See my 'Whose Objectivty? Which Neutrality? The doomed Quest for a Neutral Vantage Point from Which to Judge Religions', *Religious Studies*, 29, 1993, pp.79–95; and 'The end of "Theology" and "Religious Studies" ', *Theology*, 1996, pp.338–51. The argument in both these is indebted more widely to Alasdair MacIntyre's recent work.
7. See Rosemary Ruether, *Faith and Fratricide: the Theological Roots of Anti-Semitism*, New York, Seabury Press, 1974, where she forcefully articulates

the challenge against Christian anti-Judaism. A good discussion of Ruether is found in Alan Davies, ed., *Anti-Semitism and the Foundations of Christianity*, New York, Paulist Press, 1979. I have questioned Ruether's thesis in 'One Covenant or Many Covenants? Towards a Theology of Christian-Jewish Relations', in Robin Gill, ed., *Readings in Modern Theology*, London, SPCK, 1995, pp.173–85.

8. See Paul van Buren, *A Christian Theology of the People of Israel*, Pts.1–3, New York, Seabury Press, 1983; Franz Mussner, *Tractate on the Jews*, London, SPCK, 1984.

9. See Paul Hacker, *Theological Foundations of Evangelization*, St Augustin, Franz Steiner Verlag, 1980, esp. ch.3; Sullivan, *ibid.*, chs.1–2.

10. See Sullivan, *ibid.*, ch.3 and for list of Augustine's primary texts.

11. See Montgomery Watt, *Muslim-Christian Encounters: Perceptions and Misperceptions*, London, Routledge, 1991.

12. See Said, *ibid.*, p.66; Norman Daniel, *Islam and the West: The Making of an Image*, Edinburgh, Edinburgh University Press, 1960.

13. See Sullivan, *ibid.*, ch.4 and for Aquinas' primary texts.

14. See Riccardo Lombardi, *The Salvation of the Unbeliever*, London, Burns & Oates, 1956, for an extremely detailed consideration of materials up to the 1950s; and Sullivan, *ibid.*; and the magisterial work of L. Capéran, *Le Problème du Salut des Infidèles*, 2 vols, Grand Séminaire, Toulouse, 1934.

15. See Dulles on revelation; and William J. Abraham, *Divine Revelation and the Limits of Historical Criticism*, Cambridge, Cambridge University Press, 1982; John Baillie, *The Idea of Revelation in Recent Thought*, London, SCM, 1964; Paul Knitter, *No Other Name?*, London, SCM, 1995, ch.4 re. Lutheran views on there being revelation, but not salvation.

16. See Philip Almond, *The British Discovery of Buddhism*, Cambridge, Cambridge University Press, 1988; Eric Sharpe, *Faith meets Faith. Some Christian Attitudes to Hinduism in the Nineteenth and Twentieth Centuries*, London, SCM, 1977.

17. See Sharpe, *ibid.*, especially his discussion of John Farquhar citing original texts.

18. See Almond, *ibid.*; R. Schwab, *Oriental Renaissance: Europe's Rediscovery of India and the East*, New York, Colombia University Press, 1984; H. Halbfass, *India and Europe*, New York, SUNY, 1988.

19. This phrase reflects Owen Chadwick's excellent charting of the process in *The Secularization of the European Mind in the Nineteenth Century*, Cambridge, Cambridge University Press, 1975. See also Michael Buckley, *At the Origins of Modern Atheism*, New Haven, Yale University Press, 1987.

20. See my *Theology and Religious Pluralism*, Oxford, Blackwell, 1986, for a definition of pluralism, inclusivism, and exclusivism.

21. See I. Kant, *Religion within the Limits of Reason Alone*, Indiana, Open Court, 1934.

22. John Hick, *God and the Universe of Faiths*, London, Collins, 1977, p.122.

23. *Ibid.*, pp.165–79.
24. John Hick, *An Interpretation of Religion*, London, Macmillan, 1988, pp.233–52.
25. *Ibid.*, pp.36–55.
26. *Ibid.*
27. See A. MacIntyre, *Whose Justice? Which Rationality?*, London, Duckworth, 1988; and *Three Rival Versions of Moral Enquiry*, London, Duckworth, 1990; and for MacIntyre's argument theologically transposed: Stanley Hauerwas, *A Community of Character: Towards a Constructive Christian Ethic*, Notre Dame, University of Notre Dame Press, 1981.
28. See my criticism of Hick on this count and his defence in Harold Hewitt, ed. *John Hick's Philosophy of Religion*, London, Macmillan, 1991.
29. A. MacIntyre, *After Virtue*, 2nd edn., London, Duckworth, 1985.
30. A. Pieris, *Towards an Asian Theology of Liberation*, New York, Orbis, 1989.
31. *Ibid.*, p.124.
32. *Ibid.*, p.47.
33. *Ibid.*, p.60.
34. *Ibid.*, pp.35–50.
35. Cited in *The Tablet*, 14 January, 1995, p.37.
36. Pieris, *ibid.*, p.60.
37. *Ibid.*, pp.59–65.
38. *Ibid.*, p.62.
39. See S. Hauerwas, 'Some Theological Reflections on Gutierrez's Use of Liberation as a Theological Concept', in Robin Gill, ed., *ibid.*m, pp.317–29; and my own critique of Knitter's liberation theology of religions in Paul Mozjes & L. Swidler, eds, *Christian Mission and Interreligious Dialogue*, New York, Edwin Mellin Press, 1991, pp.51–6.
40. *Redemptoris Mission*, 1991, para.29.
41. *Ibid.*
42. See Rahner's classic statement in 'Christianity and the non-Christian Religions', *Theological Investigations*, vol.5, London, DLT, 1966; and for a fuller bibliography, D'Costa, *Theology*, ch.3.
43. See the beginnings of Rahner's thought on this matter in relation to Pius XII's *Mystici Corporis Christi* in Rahner, *Theological Investigations*, vol.1, London, DLT, 1963, pp.1–89.
44. See the criticisms of G. Lindbeck, *The Nature of Doctrine: Religion and Theology in a Post Liberal Age*, London, SPCK, 1984, ch.3; H. von Blathasar, *The Moment of Christian Witness*, New York, Newman Press, 1969; and J.A. DiNoia, *The Diversity of Religions: A Christian Perspective*, Washington DC, Catholic University of American Press, 1992.
45. DiNoia, *Diversity.*
46. Lindbeck, *Doctrine.*
47. DiNoia, *ibid.*, p.90.
48. *Ibid.*, p.107.

49. *Ibid.*, p.101.
50. Rahner, *Investigations*, London, DLT, 1980, vol.5, p.120.
51. *Ibid.*, vol.17, pp.49–50.
52. DiNoia, *ibid.*, p.102 and pp.98–103.
53. *Ibid.*, p.97, and pp.95–8.
54. *Ibid.*, pp.191–2, my emphasis.
55. *Ibid.*, p.91.
56. See my essays 'Revelation and revelations: Beyond a static valuation of Other religions', *Modern Theology*, 10, 2, 1994, pp.164–84; and my chapter (2) in G. D'Costa, ed., *Christian Uniqueness Reconsidered*, New York, Orbis, 1990.

8

The Gospels as Revelation

Leslie Houlden

In 1964, F.G. Downing published a sustained attack on the appropriateness of 'revelation' as a term for the character of the Christian faith.[1] He maintained that it suggests a model for God's relationship with us which offers too much. Christianity just does not possess such clarity about God. If it did, how could it contain such diversity of beliefs and confusion of concepts? Also the 'revelation' model diverts attention from more profitable ways of picturing Christian faith. It is not a seeing of perfectly disclosed truth, but a sphere of existence, a way of living with others, bestowed by God through Jesus. As such, it is usefully seen as 'salvific', but it is always unfinished, *in via*. In new circumstances, it may take unforeseen turns.

In his article, 'Revelation', in the *Dictionary of Biblical Interpretation*,[2] he returned to the subject, focusing more specifically on the Bible. His main point is well taken. The language of revelation is less common in the Bible, in particular in the New Testament, than has often been supposed; and it is offset by the eschatological perspective of the New Testament. Whatever may have been given or communicated, more remains in store. However decisive the phenomenon of Jesus, it is a beginning as well as an end, and what it promises remains beyond us.

These cautionary proposals may be salutary, but nevertheless more remains to be said. In the first place, we may use the language of revelation in a stronger or a weaker sense; and an awareness of the inadequacy of the former need not preclude the usefulness of the latter. To speak of revelation is not to claim total revelation, though it may indeed lend itself to the exaggeration of what has been understood. It can even usefully be the idiom of an internal dialogue, a giving and a withdrawing, confidence without complacency. 'Revelation' expresses vividly an awareness of new perception which seems not self-generated; but its limitations must be speedily acknowledged, in case too much is

140

claimed. The gospel of John is adept at such toing and froing. In the second place, if we assume the legitimacy of this looser usage, we may assess different authors in relation to it. In the case of the evangelists, it is certainly worthwhile asking each of them how much they reckon to 'know' about God, and how far perception and disclosure have gone. We shall find that they differ considerably in the intensity and the character of their claims in this matter.

Recent study of the gospels has concentrated increasingly on treating them as whole and unified works, each with its own author – a person of distinctive theological outlook and particular underlying conceptions. This is a change from former methods which attended more to the gospels as composed of literary sources or as collections of stories and sayings of Jesus, circulating previously in oral form; in both cases, the evangelist was little more than the editor who made a coherent and presentable job of the available materials. That seems now to be inadequate as an appreciation of their work. Powerful theological threads are identified, and in each of the four cases the evangelist's mind is described as it is traced through the details of his ordering and wording of the material.

Within agreement on this 'holistic' interpretation, there is division as to whether to focus it on the author or the text. If the former, then one is led to read between the lines in the attempt to form a picture of the social and historical circumstances of the circles which produced a particular gospel. It is an enquiry which, though far from profitless, is starved of concrete information and invites hypothesis. To focus on the text is to ignore the historical element and simply to observe what is written, with as educated a literary eye as one can bring to the task, discerning patterns and sequences. In recent years, all the gospels have been the subject of illuminating studies along both these lines.

For the purposes of our limited subject it is, happily, not necessary to choose rigorously between them, but there will be a general tendency towards the latter method: an attempt to 'grasp' the text as text, in so far as it manifests an approach to our topic. How much, in effect, did each of these writers reckon to have seen and to know? And how did he see it as conveyed to him? Taking it as the first to be written and also as the principal source used by both Matthew and Luke, we turn first to the Gospel of Mark.

Mark and Mystery

If we are interested in what, if anything, is revealed, the passage about the sower (4:1–20) has a good claim to be the heart of Mark.[3] It is not only that in this passage many of Mark's recurring themes coincide ('the way', 4:3, 15; 'see', 4:12; seed/grain/bread; 'parable'/riddle/enigma, 4:2, 10); they all focus on a certain manner of perceiving. 'The way' suggests journeying, and this gospel is full of movement, above all Jesus' journey to Jerusalem (8:27; 10:32, 46, 52), which culminates in an end that seems not to be an end – though what it is instead is not wholly clear. 'Seeing' is problematic and precarious (8:18, 22–26; 10:46–52), though it may come as a gift (4:11). Seed is sown indiscriminately, just as bread is provided in abundance (6:34–44; 8:1–9); yet this giving is greeted with fear and incomprehension (6:52; 8:14–21), and even when this aspect of the riddle is given its solution in the bread of the supper (14:22–25) which is identified with Jesus-about-to-die, it cannot be grasped or acted on and those who eat with Jesus proceed to abandon him (14:50). The point of 'parables' is said to be to mystify outsiders (4:12), and the other uses of the word in Mark (except 12:1, 12) conform to this sense of it as 'riddle' or 'enigma'. Everything points to an understanding which is unclear, incomplete, and easily obscured. It coheres with this theory that the gift to insiders is not 'the kingdom of God' but (with Mark's only use of the word) 'the mystery/secret of the kingdom of God'. The kingdom, which Jesus came to preach and convey, is placed at a remove, held at arm's length. Similarly, the kingdom 'has drawn near' (1:15) – its arrival remains, not in doubt, but over the horizon.

We have identified in Mark a dominating sense of unfinishedness with regard to what the gospel has to communicate. That sense, which we centred on the parable of the sower, is both reinforced and mitigated if we look elsewhere or in other ways. It is reinforced by the long passage of formal apocalyptic character (13). It is crucial that Mark does not allow this theme the last word: our final attention is on Jesus' death and its puzzling, open-ended sequel. All the same, it is prominently displayed, and even if its prophetic element receives partial fulfilment in the story of the Passion[4] (e.g., the injunction to 'watch' of 13:35f. meets a specific opportunity in 14:32–42), it refers also to a future which still awaits us. Apparently informative, in that it contains a wealth of specific detail, and perhaps reflecting the writer's time, so that his gospel meets a crisis which he interprets as the moment of impending consummation (13:14), nevertheless the indications are not clear and there is no giving of days and times (despite 13:30, 'the end is not yet', 13:7). So the enigmatic tone is not disturbed; and even if the strong element of conventional apocalyptic 'furniture' in ch.13 puts us on the track of the idea that Mark is working in code to which we are not privy (though presumably his first readers were), the appeal to a possible historical scenario does not eliminate the centrality of mystery. Not only is it inescapable for us modern readers, it must have been present too for our first predecessors: for them too, 'way', inconclusive 'seeing', life-giving yet threatening bread, and 'parables' which conceal must have added up to anything but a neat package of religious knowledge.

Yet the sense of unfinishedness is also mitigated. First, though 'seeing' is difficult, it can be given in full: Bartimaeus sees in an instant and immediately follows Jesus 'in the way' (10:52). And if the women at the tomb (16:1–8) are confused and stunned into silence, there had been a woman who gave with total extravagance, an act as it were of total clarity (14:3–9; cf. 12:41–44). Second, the future promise, if obscure, is assured and unlimited in its scope: with apparently limitless expansive potential, the good ground brings forth its fruit (4:20, 26–29, 30–32). This future is actually referred to in terms of clarity (4:22–23).

Third, even if the account we read leads us through a tale of movement that remains obscure and incomplete and even, in a way, peters out, we are given from the start a fixed point which is, in itself, wholly complete: the figure and identity of Jesus, set forth plainly (1:1–11). While even close followers cannot or will not discern the truth about him (8:29–33) and about his character (10:35–45), we readers are left in no doubt. We are placed on an eminence from which we can comprehend the partly wicked, partly obtuse blundering that culminates in the betrayal, denial and abandonment of Jesus before his death. It is only possible for this to be true of us because it is true already of Mark, the narrator: he has already seen these things. Modern literary theory makes it easy to analyse these distinctions of standpoint within a narrative. We cannot suppose that Mark brought such conscious sophistication to his work. All the same, this combination of knowledge and uncertainty, of Jesus disclosed and the kingdom remaining somewhat 'beyond' – and of these contrasts reaching intolerable tension in Jesus' death, with its hopeless words (15:34–37) followed by an immediate, if tantalising, lightening of the scene (15:38–39; 16:6–7) – is pervasive in the gospel. It offers us a disclosure which is both defined and obscure. It is defined in that it concerns Jesus; but obscure in everything that concerns him – the kingdom of God to which he witnesses, the outcome of his death, the effectiveness of his call. It is a gospel of both the severest austerity and limitless horizons.

Matthew and Assurance

The dominant cultural context of the gospels of both Mark and Matthew is that of Jewish apocalyptic. That genre of writing was not homogeneous and the two gospels speak the one language with two distinct accents. If the disclosure of heavenly truth is to come from beyond, its interpreters may emphasise either its persistent obscurity or its clarity. The heavenly truth may appear either as a signal, leaving much to be discovered, or as a programme to be followed. In this regard, such writings might be placed on a spectrum. It is not surprising if, in the process of developing tradition, a work which highlights enigma seems to demand clarification – a reworking to provide more guidance and less austere assurance. This, it seems, was one aspect of the reaction of the author of Matthew to the gospel of Mark.

It has been recognised for some time[5] that if we are to give a professional classification to this author, then it must be that of 'scribe'. The references to such figures with approval as within the Christian sphere (13:52 and 23:34), are taken to be his cryptic (or not so cryptic) signature: scribal skills are, as it were, his modest boast. There is the question, however, of what such skills involved. That they included the interpretation of Scripture, using the sophisticated techniques current at the time, is common knowledge. Matthew's gospel gives ample testimony to their employment, especially in the so-called formula quotations which appear throughout the work and are concentrated especially in chapters 1–2.[6]

More specifically, scribal skills included the application of the law, especially to new cases and new circumstances. For Matthew, the coming of the Messiah certainly constituted a new circumstance, and it is consistent with his identification as a scribe that he devoted a major part of his attention to the repercussions of Jesus' life for the understanding of the law – to the nature of both the continuity and the novelty to which it gave rise. This is apparent both in his own writing and in his adaptation of Marcan passages.[7]

What has not been so clear is that a third aspect of the scribal 'package' was the gift of understanding and presenting heavenly mysteries, the esoteric truths associated with apocalyptic. Such an identification is to be seen in Ben Sira (e.g., Ecclus. 39:1–11), in apocalyptic literature itself (e.g., I Enoch 12:3f.), and in the Qumran writings.[8] It is evidently artificial and misleading to divide these functions. A scribe is one gifted with understanding, of several kinds. A training along these lines is bound to foster a concern with knowledge rather than adumbration, the explicit rather than the implicit, the given rather than the promised.

Much has been written about two major features of Matthew's adaptation of Mark. They are in line with two aspects of the scribal role as just described. First, in connection with the interpretation of Scripture. While he includes some direct quotations, Mark works more by way of allusions, some requiring a keen eye for their detection. Matthew prefers explicit quotation, in the major instances with formal introduction. Thus, Mark's use of Isa. 6:9–10 in 4:12 is formalised by Matthew (13:14–15) into a full quotation. The effect is to make the reference more authoritative and the point of the passage more compelling. In other cases, Matthew gives to Jesus' activity the backing of Scripture where Mark presented it as self-authenticated. So his speaking in parables is supported by Ps. 78:2 (13:35; cf. Mark 4:33–34) and his healings by Isa. 53:4 (8:17; cf. Mark 1:32–34). Other baffling matters are elucidated by Scripture, where Mark left them without comment. A notable case is the role of Judas, of whose fate Mark says nothing, while Matthew shows him receiving due recompense, in accordance with Scripture (27:3–10).

Second, Matthew seems deliberately to reverse Mark's depiction of Jesus as marginalising the law, or at least subordinating it to the figure of Jesus and the life of the kingdom. Thus, the abrogation of food laws is dropped (15:17; cf. Mark 7:19) and the case of *corban* is subtly transformed from an instance of a general ill to an isolated scandalous case of abuse (15:3–9; cf. Mark 7:9–13). The radical relativising of sabbath observance in Mark 2:27 is dropped, and the incident becomes a specific instance, an exercise of the Messiah's mercy (12:1–8, in the light of 11:28–30), from which general conclusions on the subject of sabbath law are not to be drawn. Passages like 5:17–20; 22:40; 23:2–3, 23 make the general Matthean doctrine on this matter abundantly clear.

A third feature of Matthew, this time more psychological or theological than professional, strengthens this impression. It is his reluctance to leave questions unanswered, loose ends untied. Sometimes it is linked with other concerns. For example, his wish to present Jesus' disciples as (at least in part) 'leadership models' combines with his dislike of enigmas to lead him to alter Mark's 'Do you not yet understand?' (8:20) to 'Then they understood' (Matt. 16:12). But often it is a matter of sheer information. What of the Galilee rendezvous promised in Mark

16:7 but never described? Was it literal or symbolic, and if the latter, what did it signify? Matt. 28:16 clears up the point. What is the status of the news of the resurrection if the women 'said nothing to anyone' and how did the news ever emerge (Mark 16:8)? In fact, 'they ran to tell his disciples' (Matt. 28:8). Why should anyone trust the testimony of a mere young man in a matter so momentous as the rising of Jesus from the tomb (Mark 16:5–7)? It was not a young man but an angel from heaven (Matt. 28:1–7). Why should the sinless Jesus receive John's baptism which was 'for the forgiveness of sins' (Mark 1:4)? That purpose applied to others (Matt. 3:6) and anyway the matter was discussed and resolved, presumably to Matthew's satisfaction (3:14–15). While cases can be found throughout the gospel, it is interesting that they concentrate at points of Christian sensitivity – where faith is challenged and seems to demand informative clarification. The story of the guards at the tomb shows that the circumstances of the resurrection were a prime instance of this difficulty, and the genealogy and birth stories, while they also have other purposes, probably indicate that Jesus' origins were another.

These three features of Matthew are subordinate to a fourth: the role of Jesus himself subsumes them all. Even deeper than his function as interpreter of the law and his being authenticated by Scripture is his unique insight as Messiah. This is nowhere so sharply focused as in 11:25–27. Whether the passage derives from the tradition of Jesus' teaching (formally, for Luke shares it, 10:21–22) or is the evangelist's composition, Matthew certainly believes it wholeheartedly. It occupies a key position in the narrative. Like Ben Sira, Daniel, Enoch and the teachers of Qumran – and more so, for so many and such lofty roles concentrate on him – Jesus is the recipient of special understanding. His unique position, implicit in his being Messiah and 'God with us' (1:23), is confirmed by the affirming of his total and universal authority (28:18). This was always latent (26:53), though partly held back in the time of his lowliness (12:18–21; cf. 11:29; 21:5). The divine purpose is to pass on this understanding to Jesus' followers ('babes', 11:25; cf. 'little ones', 18:6, 14; 'least ones', 25:40, 45), and Jesus chooses to whom it is to be 'revealed' (11:25, 27).

The subject of this insight seems to be many-sided and in part refers back to our earlier topics. Matthew speaks of it, with an appearance of generality or vagueness, as 'these things' (11:24) or 'all these things' (13:52; cf. 'all authority' in 28:18), but the appearance is misleading.[9] It includes the message of the parables (13:34–35), which in Matthew is marked less by enigma and more by plain truth than in Mark, as we can tell especially from his own additions to the collection in ch.13

('tares', 'dragnet', 'precious pearl', and 'hidden treasure'). If we may take 'these words' as equivalent to 'these things', Jesus' teaching is included (7:28). So, clearly and more specifically, is the apocalyptic teaching in ch.24 (8, 34; cf. 23:36). It amounts to a comprehensive deliverance of heavenly guidance, stamped by divine authority and mediated by Jesus.

Given the multiple character of this guidance it is not surprising that Matthew changed Mark's use of the singular, 'mystery'/'secret' (4:11), to the plural, 'mysteries' (13:11): for Matthew, the 'kingdom of heaven' is an entity which may be expressed and apprehended in a set of items of knowledge, not simply a single gift of insight. And given this detailed treatment, in terms that are indeed open to human reception and action, it is not surprising that Matthew adds the verb 'to know': 'to you is given to know the mysteries of the kingdom of heaven'; and that Peter's affirmation of faith is greeted with the conferring of decision-making powers (16:13–19; cf. 18:18). As for those who receive this ample revelation and live in the light of it ('pure in heart'), they will receive the supreme reward that is reserved for the virtuosi of the religious world of apocalyptic: 'they shall see God' (5:8).

Luke and Visitation

Like Matthew, Luke shows evidence of discontent with the intangibility of Mark when it comes to religious knowledge, to arriving rather than travelling. Indeed, to follow up that aspect, while Mark does not quite say where 'the way' finally ends, Luke presents identifiable destinations at two levels – Jerusalem (19:41ff.) then Rome (Acts 28) on earth, and heaven to which Jesus departs and from which he reigns, with palpable and triumphant effects (Acts 1:1–11). It is true that Mark depicts Jesus as the 'proclaimer' and his message as 'proclaimed' (1:14, 38, 39), and attributes this character also to the Christian faith (13:10; 14:9); but in the impression left by the Gospel as a whole, it is overshadowed by 'parable' and 'mystery' – the element of uncertainty and incompleteness. In Luke it is otherwise: notably, he brings forward to the head of Jesus' public ministry the keynote event of his visit to Nazareth (4:16–30; cf. Mark 6:1–6), and fills it with content. For Mark, Jesus simply 'teaches': Luke defines what he teaches, and we can see precisely why his words were the cause of deep offence. The incident has something of the character of a theophany – a genre with which Luke is not at all unfamiliar (Acts 14:8–18). It is temporary (4:30), yet decisive, informative and paradigmatic. Already Luke has spoken of the total 'Jesus event' in terms of 'visit' (1:68, 78; cf. 7:16); and in the use of this language, it is on a par with the coming judgement (19:44).

Like Matthew, Luke sees Jesus (and by implication the truth he communicates as well as the acts he performs) as authenticated by prophecy (1:70; 24:26–27, 44–47), though he is less inclined to specify passages and to demonstrate their bearing on Jesus. Again like Matthew, Luke knows the role of angels in effecting communication from heaven to earth, above all in the stories of Jesus' origins which set forth his identity (1:11, 26; 2:9, 13), a role also performed by 'the holy spirit' (2:26). Comparable angelic visits occur at less momentous stages of the spread of the Christian preaching, still guaranteeing its protection from harm and its power to save (Acts 5:19; 8:26; 10:3; 12:7–11; 27:23). At certain key moments, supremely in the call of Paul, Jesus himself speaks from heaven (Acts 9:4ff.). In other words, angels, spirit, the heavenly Jesus and visionary experiences all combine to form and maintain secure lines of communication between heaven and earth throughout the crucial events which Luke describes.

While the function of the course of events described in Acts in relation to Luke's present situation is uncertain (is it a peak from which there has been decline and to which Luke hopes to inspire a return? or a paradigm which he sees as somehow true for the church always?), the career of Jesus is, as we have seen, the 'visit' par excellence. During it, Jesus' own lines are constantly open: the spirit is 'upon him' (1:35; 4:18), and he is constantly at prayer (3:21; 9:28; 10:21–22; 11:1), addressing God as 'father' (22:42; 23:34, 46). For us then, the visit is dependable, a veritable presence of the kingdom of God (11:20; 17:21; 22:29) and of sure 'salvation' (7:50; 18:42; 19:9–10).

This prolonged visit from heaven and, in Acts, the subsequent briefer visits by angels and voices and the imitative visits to city after city by apostles and others are clamped together by the continuous, pervasive presence of the spirit, which guides, guarantees and empowers all that is done.

Though the visit and the presence are the chief realities given by God, there is also definable information outlining a way of life and even social priorities, as the Nazareth sermon already indicates. In the passage about parables, Luke too can use the same adaptation as Matthew ('to you is given to know the mysteries of the kingdom of God', 8:10), signifying a perception of a collection of items of truth which can be grasped and acted upon. While this is spread out for us in the teaching material of the gospel, Luke focuses more on a few strong directions in the moral life (generosity of heart and with money, width of human sympathy and sensitivity to need) than on the regulatory and disciplinary needs of Christian communities (cf. Matt. 18, especially 12–14, alongside Luke 15:4–7). All the same, in both story and instruction, this gospel (and Acts in its thoroughly edifying narrative) provides firm outlines of knowledge of God and of his purposes. It is information that would otherwise have been denied, and it is to serve largely for the present, though, as in Mark and Matthew (but perhaps more as filling in a corner of the picture which should not be left blank), the consummation is also envisaged (21:25ff.).

John and Completeness

As far back as we can go, the gospel of John has been seen to make more far-reaching claims both for Jesus and for the present status of those who believe in him than any of the other gospels. This is true, whatever the idiom of thought used to interpret the gospel. It is plainly the case with the classical orthodoxy of patristic times, when John was read as if written in the Platonist terms then current.[10] It is also the case when the gospel is read in the historically more realistic terms suggested in modern criticism – whether the Jewish context of thought, in terms of which Jesus is seen by John, is identified as that of the law of agency ('an agent is like the one who sent him')[11] or of heavenly visitant, perhaps after the manner of speculation concerning Moses.[12]

This impression can be put more precisely by saying that John's gospel has a more thoroughgoing and self-contained quality than the others. No doubt the impression is not wholly just and further examination makes us modify it. All the same, it has its measure of validity, at two levels. The first is in the book itself, where the constant reiteration of a limited range of concepts and words, endlessly associated and re-associated, has the effect of satiating the reader, so that we feel we are initiates of a world sufficient to itself. But, second, this reflects the doctrine of the book, which describes the sufficiency of Jesus to mediate God, from every possible angle, and the comprehensive adequacy of the 'life' conveyed. So dominant is this pure adequacy that it seems to eliminate the merely informative character of anything conveyed (such as we found in Matthew and Luke). Bultmann gave the celebrated judgement: 'it turns out in the end that Jesus as the Revealer of God reveals nothing but that he is the Revealer'.[13]

Yet there is a measure of reticence. We referred in the opening section to the way in which this gospel makes claims only to withdraw or limit them. Revelation and veiling go hand in hand. This is notable in the case of the most lofty claims of all. In each of the three passages where the term 'God' is applied to Christ, there is both identity and distinction between the two. The Word is not only 'God' but also 'with God' (1:1); not simply the 'God' who has made the Father known but (taking the probable text) 'God only-(begotten)',[14] the adjective qualifying the noun (1:18); Jesus is not only 'my God' (20:28) to Thomas but also the one who can himself, alongside his disciples, speak of God as 'my God and your God' (20:17). Similarly, while 'he that has seen me has seen the Father' (14:9), it is also the case that 'no-one has seen God at any time', even though Christ has now 'made him known' (1:18).

Nowhere does the author reconcile these dialectical statements, and we are left to make our own attempts to rationalise them. So we may say, for example, that Jesus is identical with God, as far as the medium of 'flesh' (human conditions?) allows. But there is no theory given of what that limitation amounts to. For the purposes of our relationship with God, it is evident that, in John's view, it is an irrelevant limitation – it does us no harm. Whatever that relationship consists of and achieves for us (e.g., 'eternal life'), it is wholly sufficient, and abstract speculation is not encouraged: enough for us to be sure that it is perfectly grounded in God and in his activity 'from the beginning' (15:27). So implicitly, as far as the gospel goes (though there is nothing to indicate that the author considered the matter), any reconciliation, perhaps into blandness, of affirmation and qualification is left aside in favour of strong statements which invite us into a new world of perception – a world open also for us to inhabit and act in (e.g., by 'loving one another', 13:34, and performing 'greater works' even than Jesus, 14:12).

This dialectic which we have observed in John arose within an overall impression of self-containedness. In so far as that impression is a valid view of the gospel, it stands in contrast to the unfinished vision of Mark, ever urging the reader to look and move beyond what has been given. There are, however, statements in John which stand apart from the dialectic itself and testify either to completeness or, as it seems, to unfinishedness. There has long been discussion whether the latter element, found often in isolated statements, and easily understood as intruded into the text for some corrective purpose and as alien to its main conception, should be left aside in forming a view of the gospel's picture of things. It is not hard to interpret items of futurist eschatology, such as 6:39, 40, 44, in this light; less easy with a statement like 'the hour is coming and now is' (4:23; 5:25), where future and present, the unfinished and the finished, are side by side. And there are strong signs that, in many of his statements concerning the future, the author has exercised interpretative skill to draw their reference back into, if not the present of 'gospel time', then into the present and even the past of 'readers' time'. Thus the departure of Jesus to 'where he was before' (6:62) appears not to involve his removal from the enclosed circle of disciples (14:15–18); and the discussion of the 'little while' (16:16–18), almost feverish to our eyes and so probably a matter of intense exegetical importance to the evangelist and his readers, seems to signify a similar drawing back of reference from the future to the readers' present. Indeed, it is likely that the supper discourses as a whole (chs.14–17) should be read in this way. They present knowledge, insight and a scene of existence (alongside Jesus) which embrace the whole of the believer's being.

The affirmation of completeness is clear too in the often recognised 'realised eschatology' – the application of the images of the End to the career of Jesus and the believers' association with him; in relation to judgement (3:17–19), to life (5:24), and to resurrection (11:25), most notably. The application of the language of heavenly splendour ('glory') to the presence and, audaciously, the death of Jesus is as vivid an expression of this perspective as any (1:14; 12:28; 13:31). 'Knowing' God is also brought within the sphere of the given and received (17:3, 8).

The gospel of John, then, depicts, by means of the story of Jesus, a disclosure of God, which, while not without limits, is as complete as it needs to be to fulfil human needs and aspirations.

Conclusion

Though human needs and aspirations, viewed in a religious light, are doubtless capable of being described in general terms, it is both more instructive and more interesting to recognise their diversity. Written within approximately half a century of the events they reflect on, the gospels illustrate that diversity in innumerable ways, not least in their understanding of what has come to them through Jesus by way of illumination, as from God.

Assuming that human desire, religiously, is for as much illumination as possible, the desire is bound to be conditioned both by specific mental and cultural formation and by the particular needs of an individual or social group. Thus the scribal formation of Matthew seems, rather clearly, to determine the character of the guidance that he sought from

Jesus. And it has been plausibly suggested that Luke's concern with the poor is dictated by a need felt by him to unify the better-off and the worse-off in the Christian group to which he belonged.[15] Of course, the operation of neither of these conditioning factors implies that they were simply foisted on the tradition about Jesus and that he was made to dance, quite unfairly, to a Matthean or a Lucan tune. While some aspects of Matthew's scribalism seem to be very much his own, there is every likelihood that, perhaps in other forms, at least some of those skills were shared by Jesus, so that he himself gave an impulse welcomed and developed by Matthew. Again, it is unlikely that a historical Jesus unyielding in his devotion to the conventions of rigid social hierarchy was transmogrified by Luke into the friend of the poor and the enemy of the rich; more likely that an impulse was developed and applied, even if with exaggeration. Though history is littered with illustrations of the principle that Jesus is created anew in all kinds of interests, however bizarre,[16] the account just given of these aspects of the gospel tradition remains the most commonsensical, and some scholars would say it was all but demonstrable.

Nevertheless, the fact remains that the gospels show remarkable divergence in the styles of 'demand' for illumination which they reflect. While these different styles are best seen in the gospels as entities (their shape and pattern of narrative, dominant concerns and tendencies), they are naturally expressed also in details of wording, perhaps most vividly in changes carefully made by Matthew or Luke to the Mark which both inherited. They are evident not just in four total 'pictures' of Jesus but also in the evangelists' readiness to produce their own material, whether in response to 'impulses' from Jesus or not. Though each of the gospels belongs to the specific circumstances in which it arose, on which we can now only speculate, it is neither unfair nor unhelpful to see each as pointing ahead to certain broad styles of approach in Christianity through the years.

Mark's combination of fervent commitment with relative indifference to detailed information, of knowledge of God as essentially 'mystery' with its statement as marked by enigma ('parable'), of a journeying always in progress with a future sure but not identified, is echoed, albeit in quite different intellectual contexts, in the *via negativa* and the apophatic element in much theology and spirituality, both Western and, especially, Eastern. Matthew's perception of divine provision in terms of many-sided information, making possible detailed moral and spiritual obedience, together with his sense of orderly structure both in the conduct of life and in the map of history and of the human race, have found possibly more successors than any of the others, in teachers and governors of the Church, in the draftsmen of rules for religious orders and syllabuses for neophytes and trainees. Luke's sense of an order, historical and ethical, that can be known is not dissimilar – again it answers to a human need for secure paths – but there is here also a sense of the illumination as occasional and special, yielding memory to be cherished and inspiration to be acted upon. Luke too, with his warm yet demanding picture of Jesus, has not lacked disciples, notably among those whose faith is nourished by experience apparently received unbidden or experience interpreted with hindsight as salvific – a kind of visitation, in the midst of the ordinary and setting it in a new light. John's rather enclosed world, yet universal in its extent, has always appealed to those seeking a total 'solution' here and now, a picture of all reality in the light of God, though it discourages them from seeking detailed mapping either of conduct or of the future, and leads them rather to the fundamentals of intellectual and spiritual perception.

In describing the positive features of the styles bequeathed by the evangelists, we should not disguise that each has its weaknesses as well as its strengths. Partly, as we reflect on the illumination the gospels mediate, we must be aware also of our reciprocal initiative; in it, 'seek and you will find' turns all too easily, and in a measure inevitably, into 'seek and you will find what you need and want to find'. Awareness of the risk, and candour in realising that the evangelists have, long ago, run it before us, can be salutary.

All the same, 'revelation', whether from the gospels or anywhere else, is always a matter not only of sheer transforming novelty but of what those receiving it are capable of grasping. Yet there is novelty too; and Mark, the first evangelist, is surely the one most deeply aware of it. He writes in a mood of surprise. For quite other reasons than this (for the gospels have not been read in quite this way for long), Mark's gospel has been in practice largely ignored through most of Christian history: it was so brief, so lacking, compared with Matthew, in useful teaching from Jesus, and, compared with John, in beneficial statements of doctrine. Scholarship has done much to atone for this neglect in the past century and a half. Christian theological and spiritual perception, not to speak of Church awareness, have not yet caught up. It is a debt worth paying.

Notes

1. F.G. Downing, *Has Christianity a Revelation?*, SCM Press, 1964.
2. R.J. Coggins and J.L. Houlden, eds, SCM Press, 1990.
3. J.G. Williams, *Gospel against Parable*, Almond, 1985.
4. R.H. Lightfoot, *The Gospel Message of St Mark*, Oxford University Press, 1950, ch.IV.
5. M.D. Goulder, *Midrash and Lection in Matthew*, SPCK, 1974, ch.1; D.E. Orton, *The Understanding Scribe*, JSNT Supplement Series 25, Sheffield Academic Press, 1989.
6. Goulder, *op. cit.*, ch.6.
7. G. Barth in G. Bornkamm, G. Barth and H.J. Held, *Tradition and Interpretation in Matthew*, SCM Press, ET 1963.
8. Orton, *op. cit.*
9. Orton, *op. cit.*, p.146f.
10. M.F. Wiles, *The Spiritual Gospel*, Cambridge University Press, 1960; T.E. Pollard, *Johannine Christology and the Early Church*, 1970; J.L. Houlden, 'The Gospel of John', in eds R.J. Coggins and J.L. Houlden, *op. cit.*, n.2 above.
11. P. Borgen, 'God's Agent in the Fourth Gospel', in ed. J. Ashton, *The Interpretation of John*, SPCK, 1986; A.E. Harvey, 'Christ as Agent', in L.D. Hurst and N.T. Wright, eds, *The Glory of Christ in the New Testament*, Oxford University Press, 1987.
12. M. de Jonge, *Jesus: Stranger from Heaven and Son of God*, Scholars Press, 1977; W.A. Meeks, 'The Man from Heaven in Johannine Sectarianism', in J. Ashton, ed., *op. cit.*, n.1 above.
13. *Theology of the New Testament*, vol.2, SCM Press, ET 1955, p.66.
14. It has become common to translate *monogenès* by 'only'/'unique', but for the traditional rendering, which comports well with the image of sonship here and in other passages where the word occurs, cf. D.A. Fennema, 'John 1:18: "God the Only Son",' in *New Testament Studies*, 31, 1985, pp.124–135.
15. P. Esler, *Community and Gospel in Luke–Acts*, Cambridge University Press, 1987.
16. J. Pelikan, *Jesus Through the Centuries*, Yale University Press, 1985.

Bibliography

Barton, S.C., *The Spirituality of the Gospels*, London, SPCK, 1992.
Best, E., *Mark, the Gospel as Story*, Edinburgh, T. & T. Clark, 1983.
Burridge, R.A., *Four Gospels, One Jesus?*, London, SPCK, 1994.
Hooker, M.D., *The Message of Mark*, London, Epworth, 1983.

Kingsbury, J.D., *Matthew as Story*, Philadelphia, Fortress, 1986.

Kysar, R., *John's Story of Jesus*, Philadelphia, Fortress, 1984.

Maddox, R., *The Purpose of Luke–Acts*, Edinburgh, T. & T. Clark, 1982.

Painter, J., *John: Witness and Theologian*, London, SPCK, 1975.

9

Revelation in Feminist Theology and Philosophy

Esther Reed

Why all the fuss recently about God and bodies? Is it the familiar story of those early Christian fathers who supposedly found the body a burden, a prison, a source of temptation, and who longed for the freedom of death and heaven? Are women, brought up within a predominately male tradition, still having to break the taboos of childhood by talking about body parts and bodily functions, especially the messy ones? Are Christian feminists who write about the body capitalising on a secular trend? Or, is the subject of urgent importance if Christian feminists are to insist upon the indispensability of embodiment to an understanding of revelation?

In this essay, I argue that this matter is of too great consequence to be ignored. This is for two reasons. The first is the perception in feminist circles that Christian talk about revelation is problematic. The second is the elliptical use of the word 'revelation' in non-Christian talk about spirituality of the body. This leads to confusion and other potential difficulties when reference is made to the human body in relation to 'god'/the divine/spirituality/transcendence. With these issues in mind, I am interested in the following questions. Far from being a 'problem' for Christian feminists, why is talk about revelation essential if an adequately Christian understanding of gendered bodiliness is to be sought? How can exploration of the themes of embodiment and gender in Christian theology be of help in coming to new perceptions of revelation? What challenges might a Christian feminist pose to contemporary forms of materialist spirituality in which the body is construed as a direct source of revelation?

Feminist Problems with Talk about Revelation

The concept of revelation has been, and continues to be, problematic amongst many feminist writers. Daphne Hampson rejects Christianity as untrue because its understanding of revelation entails fundamental ethical and philosophical problems. If God is known through revelation as other and outside the self, and if God is in relation to humanity by subjecting it to laws that derive from beyond human experience, then an unacceptable heteronomy is built into Christianity which precludes full human autonomy. Neither, she says, can Christian claims for the particularity of God's revelation in Christ Jesus be allowed to stand because they clash with modern knowledge, violate the laws of physics, and interrupt the causal nexus of history and nature in unbelievable ways (Hampson, 1996a, esp. ch.1; 1996b, esp. ch.1). In place of traditional Christian notions of revelation as the unveiling of something hidden, the making manifest of that which is concealed – namely, the absolutely mysterious and inaccessible God – Hampson sets the attaining of self-knowledge.

Hampson is not the only woman to have baulked at traditional Christian notions of revelation. Rosemary Radford Ruether has defined revelation, or that which is 'revelatory', as meaning 'breakthrough experiences beyond ordinary fragmented consciousness that provide interpretive symbols illuminating the means of the whole of life.' (Ruether, 1983/1992, p.13) For Ruether, revelation starts in an individual's consciousness and has more to do with the quest for full humanity than with the self-communication of the living God whom the Bible names Lord. In opposition to the scandal of particularity in which God communicates utter otherness in the person of Christ Jesus, Ruether asserts that that which is revelatory endows all human beings.

Sallie McFague has recognised the importance for theology of the historical claims about Jesus in Christian tradition but confined revelation to a past event in history. (McFague, 1987, pp.45–57) For McFague, the figure of Jesus of Nazareth remains a constant that constrains the Christian theologian, but the construction of new metaphors with which to speak of God overtakes the history of revelation to which the Bible bears witness. She conceives of revelation as a point in linear time and not as the way in which God travels with believers. This does not detract from her perception of Christianity as 'the religion of incarnation *par excellence*. Its earliest and most persistent doctrines focus on embodiment . . .' (McFague, 1993, p.14) She refuses, however, to perceive the history of revelation as the history of salvation; McFague contests that what God has done for humanity in the past is less important than what humanity, with God, does now.

Feminist Revisioning of Talk about Revelation and Embodiment

Some feminists have responded to these challenges by suggesting that there are other ways to conceive of revelation within Christian theology. Mary Grey invites inquiry into a model of revelation as connectedness. In *The Wisdom of Fools*, she recognises that revelation in Christian tradition has never been a monochrome truth but has stood for a variety of conceptions. She argues that Christian talk of revelation has been dominated by *Logos*/reason/rationality, at the expense of *Sophia*/subjectivity/connectedness. A new understanding of revelation is needed which has relationship at its heart and makes 'connected knowing' (i.e., the state of being aware of the organic links between all living things and advocating an ethic of care rather than control) a way of making divine communication intelligible. Gender is a primary factor in her analysis of the concept of revelation as she stresses women's experience as an important *locus* for talk about God. She investigates how embodiment is intrinsic to divine/human communication and articulates a Christian feminist understanding of revelation 'within a theology of mutual relation, as divine communication for our times, the "filter" through which we understand our culture, our identity' (Grey, 1993, p.1) Her broad concern for issues of social justice serves as a reminder that Christian doctrine of revelation will not be confined to the individual's experience of bodiliness, but will seek connections with every aspect of human existence, especially the needy.

Elisabeth Moltmann-Wendel's *I am My Body: New ways of embodiment* is a more explicit engagement with the individual's physicality of human existence. In it she argues that the body is the medium through which the self experiences manifold relations; the experience of embodiment is an irreducible given wherein all human beings are interconnected (Moltmann-Wendel, 1994). The assertion 'I am my body' is a polemically phrased reminder that: there are no Christian reasons to be ashamed of 'being in the body'; western post-Cartesian philosophy has tended towards obsession with rational consciousness at the expense of bodiliness; Christian pastoral ministries might benefit from fresh appreciation of Jesus' sensitivity to his own embodiment and that of others; and Christian churches need to rethink creedal confession of the resurrection of the body. She denies that women need notions of goddess for body thought and, instead, invokes the Christian doctrine of incarnation as an untapped resource for feminist theology. She gently ruffles the feathers of conventional Christian theology; she is a pioneer who urges suspicion of abstractions in theology which dissociate God-talk from embodiment.

More recent is Elizabeth Stuart's *Just Good Friends*, which is noteworthy in this context because of her distinction between primary and secondary modes of revelation. The former, I assume, comprises the testimonies of believers whose experiences of life throughout generations bear witness to God's love. She writes: 'the Spirit has been blowing through history for thousands of years, inspiring the spinning and weaving of theology' (Stuart, 1995, p.14). Primary modes of revelation are traditional patterns of God-talk that function to inspire, test, and make sense of, contemporary (secondary) modes that are woven by people of faith today. The former is incomplete without the latter, and *vice versa*, because Christian experience in the present involves relationship with the past, and hopes for the future: 'Revelation occurs between persons, but it can also occur when those persons, having taken their experience and analysed it using tools available to them, then take it to the past, take it to their ancestors for their comment and wisdom' (Stuart, 1995, p.14). Stuart does not minimise the fact that Christian tradition has, at best, been clumsy in talking about the body. She makes the important point, however, that a model of revelation as connectedness will include connectedness with others who have walked the path of faith in generations past.

More examples of feminist revisioning of Christian talk about revelation and embodiment could be given, for example, Janet Martin-Soskice's paper 'Blood and Defilement', delivered to The Society of the Study of Theology in 1994, in which she interpreted the nature of Jesus' wounds on the cross with reference to female experiences of bleeding and giving birth. Similarly, we could recall the connections between revelation, embodiment and liberation made by María Clara Bingemer, professor of theology at the Pontifical Catholic University of Rio de Janeiro. She approaches trinitarian theology through meditation upon the life-praxis of Jesus, especially in relation to women, and argues that Jesus' egalitarian behaviour reveals new conceptions of God (Bingemer, in King, 1994, p.314). Of note also is Herlinde Pissarek-Hudelist's hint in *Wörterbuch der Feministischen Theologie* that women need to remain watchful and self-critical in their continuing articulation of perceptions of God's revelation. The subject remains, she suggests, an 'open question' (Pissarek-Hudelist in Gössman, *hrsg.* 1991, pp.309–310). Rather, than list more instances of Christian feminist writing in which women have perceived connections between revelation and embodiment, I shall proceed by articulating some criteria of coherence and clarity that might be of assistance in these reflections.

Notes on a Dogmatics of Revelation and Embodiment

By way of a preliminary, let me comment briefly on terminology, especially the terms 'dogmatics' and 'systematics'. Despite negative associations of the former word with arrogant declarations of tenets of faith by ecclesial authorities, I choose to use it rather than the latter for the following reasons. First, 'dogmatics' conveys a sense of interaction between personal experiences of God, and the witness to God's revelation in Christ within Christian tradition, as handed down from generation to generation in the churches. The Greek word *dogma* (δόγμα) means opinion or public decree, and can be understood as interpretation(s) of the life of the Holy Spirit in the church; it involves reciprocity between present experiences of God and a heritage from previous ages. With this in mind, I use the word 'dogmatics' to describe the practice of observing common patterns of opinion in multiple experiences of faith, including both past and present. Second, it avoids negative associations connected with the word 'systematics'. In particular, I think of objections that a theology that is at the same time feminist and systematic is a contradiction in terms, i.e., that to articulate Christian truth as a self-consistent whole is to squeeze God into preconceived forms of thought, and that this contradicts feminist concerns to recognise different experiences of revelation. I wholeheartedly agree that no Christian theology can be adequate if it is not sensitive to different experiences of God, and concerned to articulate the complexity and vibrancy of God's reality for each person; an appreciation of difference can illuminate and challenge individual perspectives of faith. Hence, the following is a personal exercise in dogmatics, i.e., in sensitivity to, and the noticing of, difference and commonality in Christian feminist witness to the reality of God's revelation.

• It is not enough for 'male-stream' theology to assert Christian truths about revelation as statements or formulae without engaging with experiential aspects of faith; the Christian's primary relationship to God is one of faith and trust, rather than information and knowledge.

• The *doctrine* of revelation is secondary to the experience and knowledge of salvation. This statement must be qualified to the extent that, in existential terms, there is a dialectical interaction between the epistemic dimensions of faith and the soteriological and experiential. Any theory concerning knowledge of salvation presupposes the reality of salvation. On the other hand, some conceptual grasp of doctrine is needed if personal experiences of salvation are to be named, and acknowledged, as such. Within this interaction, however, it is important to remember that a properly Christian doctrine of revelation serves, first and foremost, to convey the message of God's love. Doctrine is best conceived of as in service to the movement of God's Spirit.

- God and revelation are less than adequately construed by radical feminists as 'objects' or 'things' to be received in unqualified passivity. Feminist critics of Christianity often reduce a Christian understanding of revelation to the status of an 'object', 'thing', or 'phenomenon', that is experienced always as coming 'from above' and is to be received in unqualified passivity. This fails to appreciate that revelation in Christian tradition is about connectedness and communication between God and humankind.

- It is important to remember that a Christian doctrine of revelation has at its heart the message of God, the bringer of love and grace into each and every situation. It can be helpful for believers to remind themselves of this through individual and corporate meditation upon the historical presence of God in Christ Jesus, and the continuing presence of Christ Jesus in the Holy Spirit.

- The Spirit of God makes the revelation of God knowable in all its diversity and difference. This is independent of whether or not human beings perceive, recognise, or acknowledge it.

- In order to take seriously Christian experiences of diversity and difference, it is beneficial, amongst other things, to listen to the history of testimony about relationship between God and God's people throughout many generations. There is much wisdom concerning revelation within Christian tradition (as well as much bigotry and sexism) that can serve to attune us to the diversity that characterises the movement of God's Spirit.

- Revelation in Christian tradition was, and continues to be, about a

161

form of personal relationship with God. The quality of this relationship is characterised by the vulnerability of embodiment that God chose in the incarnation. Love required a body; God took a human body, assumed human flesh in the person of Christ Jesus, bore in that body the sins of the world, to open the way of salvation to all.

• From Jesus' ministry we learn that revelation in Christian tradition is not primarily about propositional truths or epistemic theories, but about the embodying or 'making real' of healing, cleansing, and the restoration of relationships. In practical and pastoral terms today, this requires a willingness to take seriously the manifold dimensions that make up the human experience of bodiliness. It requires sensitivity to experiences of violence and pain, as well as delight in pleasures of the body; concerns about frailness, sickness and disability, as well as intimacy and ecstacy; ubiquitous and iniquitous pressures to conform to our materialist and consumer culture, as well as the simple joys of delight in another person, sights and sounds of beauty, good food or laughter.

• Revelation in Christian tradition continues to be about embodiment because God's Spirit enables ever new perceptions and expressions of life-giving relationship. The Holy Spirit continues to be at work in bringing to birth justice, mercy and knowledge of God, across the face of the whole earth (Isa. 11:4b, 42, 49–52; Rev. 21:1). In practical and pastoral terms this involves discernment and anticipation of the presence and work of the Spirit of God. This difficult task belongs to the whole church and has no easy answers. However, it can be expected that persons and institutions who are Christ-like will bear the wounds of love.

• The human body is no hindrance to wisdom or truth (cf. Plato, *Phaedo*, 54A) but is neutral – it can be either a temple of the Holy Spirit (1 Cor. 6:20) and life-loving, or dominated by 'fleshly' lusts (Rom. 8:7) and oriented towards death,.

• Christian talk about embodiment does not begin with sexuality but centres on personal identity, self-esteem, and loving relationship, because God first communicated this kind of love to us.

162

Putting a Christian Feminist Dogmatics to Work

So much for an attempt to articulate aspects of an understanding of divine revelation in Christian theology in relation to feminist principles. However, the matter does not end with seemingly abstract formulations. How might a Christian feminist understanding of intrinsic connections between revelation and embodiment show itself in dialogue with contemporary non-Christian feminist discourse? In particular, what challenges might a Christian feminist pose to contemporary forms of materialist spirituality in which the body is construed as a direct source of revelation? Recently, a number of feminists have started writing about the body, especially the female body, as a site of revelation. New forms of spiritual materialism are emerging in which women claim to be rediscovering the body, and recoding it with significance, for what they deem to be their experience of the 'divine'. Instead of the supposed negativity of Christian confession, according to which the body is in some way associated with imprisonment, darkness, and bondage, some feminist writers are asserting that the body mediates the divine. What is a Christian feminist to make of this? Why, and to what effect, has sexuality become an object of spiritual discourse? What happens to understandings of the female body when sexuality constitutes a spiritual domain? Are new forms of spiritual materialism potentially more harmful for female well-being than traditional Christian doctrine(s)?

The Body as Source of Revelation?

On this topic, the readers of feminist theological/thealogical/spiritual literature will have noticed the emergence of two schools of thought. One is the new French feminism of Luce Irigaray, Hélène Cixous, Annie Leclerc, Julia Kristeva, Monique Wittig, *et al.*, which introduces fresh perspectives in women's writing from the body. Each, in her own way, not only opposes women's bodily experience to phallic symbol patterns in western thought, but articulates the body as an enigmatic source of self-knowledge. Having lost the 'God' that died with Nietzsche, these writers replace 'God' with the body and make it an object of faith. The other is the goddess spirituality of, e.g., Carol Christ and Judith Plaskow, C. Spretnak and Starhawk, for whom the body is a site of revelation because it is alive with sacral powers which manifest divine fecundity and creativity. Melissa Raphael's book, *Theology and Embodiment: The Post-Patriarchal Reconstruction of Female Sacrality*, expounds examples of goddess spirituality which reconfigure the divine as female as specifying generative energies. Women in both camps seek 'god'/the divine/spirituality/transcendence through the body.

It is not possible here to discuss each of these thinkers, and I shall concentrate upon some ideas of Luce Irigaray. The intention is to identify points of shared concern, but also of difference and disagreement, between a Christian feminist understanding of revelation, embodiment and gender, and Irigaray's endeavour to recode the body with spiritual significance. Irigaray's exploration of the relationship between 'god'/the divine/spirituality/transcendence and the body is of interest to Christian feminists for several reasons. One is her resistance to Christianity's rendering of the body as spiritually inarticulate. Her accusation is that differences between male and female are not taken into account positively in Christianity, and silence is imposed on women because the measure of women is lack: 'a/one logos that connotes her as castrated, especially as castrated of words' (Irigaray, 1985, p.142). She registers resistance to both Freud's account of female sexuality and Christianity's depriving women of anything to say about God. Because 'God – absolute (self)principle *is*, in the very purity of conception, then he will be able to serve as a paradigm . . . for the representation of all being' (Irigaray, 1985, p.142). The God of men binds spiritual discourse to ideas in a fleshless intellectualism which starves the body of its vibrancy. Chantal Chawaf expresses Irigaray's sense in the lament: 'Too often GOD was written instead of LIFE' (Chawaf, in Marks and Courtivron, 1981, p.177).

Christian feminists will probably agree that there has been a lamentable absence of women in traditional paradigms of revelation which has impoverished Christian resources for God-talk. There is a category leap, however, between Irigaray's diagnosis and her tendency to speak of 'god'/the divine/spirituality/transcendence as experienced in, through, and at the limits of the body. As we have seen, many Christian feminists attest truths about revelation in ways that are embedded in various life experiences of bodiliness and gender. This is not the same, however, as making the body a sacral place where self-knowledge and revelation of the divine are to be sought. For Irigaray, the givenness of the body speaks of that which lies beyond the individual human and tends towards infinity. Nothing is ever finite. Nothing is limited or bounded such that it has no reference to that beyond it. According to her perception, the God preached within Western philosophical and theological traditions is extrapolated to infinity and reduced to that which cannot be reached or influenced by humanity. By contrast, her 'god' is envisioned in/at/

as the abyss concealed within woman's body: 'The bottom, the center, the most hidden, inner place, the heart of the crypt to which 'God' alone descends when he has renounced modes and attributes' (Irigaray, 1985, p.196). 'God', for Irigaray, is/is in/is in-between the flame of desire and flow of excess pleasure.

This means that she conceives of the female body as a direct source of revelation; women are 'the richest in revelations' (Irigaray, 1985, p.192). If women are to experience 'God', they must begin with their bodies, and their bodies begin with sexuality. They have contact with the divine force or searing light that is divine because their pleasure and sense of selfhood exceeds all representation. Christian teaching is hijacked as language about the incarnation and revelation is taken over to express the *jouissance*, or pleasure that derives from but exceeds the physical: 'But if the Word was made flesh in this way, and to this extent, it can only have been to make me (become) God in my jouissance . . . she is transformed into Him in her love' (Irigaray, 1985, pp.200–201). The limits of the female body are permeable as female flesh mingles with the divine and 'she' is 'God'. Autoeroticism assumes a quasi-liturgical status, as the unapproachable and ungraspable within the body becomes an object of faith, and is celebrated as such.

Irigaray owes no allegiance to any particular religious tradition and there is no reason to accept unquestioningly the validity of the questions and challenges that she raises. She cocks a snook at Christian tradition, and mystically names the body 'god', in such a way as to exceed the poetic and breach the idolatrous. For this reason, some might dismiss her work without further comment because the 'god' discovered through the body is different from God experienced through that which Christian faith calls revelation; the 'god' who is the mystical or poetic excess of materiality is not God the Giver of all things good, and Life that gives life to the body. I, for one, maintain that she turns the body into an object of faith and makes an idol of the female self. In losing the distinction between 'subject' and 'Other', (Irigaray, 1985, p.191) self and God, she renders her work incompatible with Christianity's confession of God as the one who reveals and communicates God-self in the person of Christ Jesus. Yet there are reasons to read her books.

Feminist theologians were originally slow to respond to her work. Possibly this was because her work is difficult to read in the original French. Possibly it was because a whiff of essentialism suggests that women's experience is bound to biological make-up and processes. Possibly it was because a lurking idealisation of the body as inherently divine threatens to denigrate women's real experiences of bodiliness.

Possibly it was because the tendency to make female and male libidinal differences spiritually significant hinders rather than helps talk of revelation that can contribute to the healing of relationships between women and men. Nevertheless, her work has recently aroused considerable interest amongst theologians, linguists, philosophers, psychoanalysts and feminist theorists. It has a creative energy that conveys a certain *joie de vivre*, especially in relation to bodiliness, that, speaking personally, makes me curious about what she is trying to achieve, and its likely implications for female well-being. For this reason, I set out to explore, in the remainder of this essay, some experiential effects upon female selfhood of her material spirituality. To do this, more methodological considerations need to be brought in; more specifically, concerning how she perceives spirituality in relation to its object the body.

Lack, Sameness and Utility in Irigaray's Material Spirituality

So far we have been discussing the idea of 'spirituality' in general terms without dealing with the word's ambiguity. With reference to Irigaray, I have used the word 'spirituality' to refer to that which exceeds human sign systems and tends to the inscrutable. This is close to the definition given by Kathryn Bond Stockton (Bond Stockton, 1994, pp.7–9). It includes the mystical sense in which the body appears as something enigmatic, opaque, and which both conceals and reveals the presence of the divine; it is malleable enough to encompass categories of the mysterious in Christianity, Marxism, post-structuralism, psychoanalysis, and other spheres of discourse. The obscurity of the term has to do with the subjective character of the self's contact with 'divine' force, but the universality of its application derives from biological reference to the body. Reference to the body becomes spiritual when, in Kathryn Bond Stockton's phrase, she places 'god' 'between the lips' (Bond Stockton, 1994). For Irigaray, spirituality is not really about God at all. It is about woman's physical 'lack' and 'absence' redefined as possibility. Woman's lack of visible genitalia is interpreted not as emptiness and want, but as a fathomless abyss that is a source of wonderment and exhilaration.

My dogmatic contention here is that Irigaray collapses 'god' into the body and the body into 'god'. Given, however, (as explained above) that is not enough to assert Christian truths about revelation as statements of formulae without engaging with experiential aspects of faith, my further question is whether women can prosper spiritually through her theory of female selfhood. It would be easy to assert at this stage that, in Christian confession, revelation is not reducible to bodiliness and that this rules out further investigation, period. If, however, there are detrimental consequences that follow from her advocacy of a 'spiritual' way for women to accept and live with their bodies, these should be considered. What experiential and pastoral implications are consequent upon the kind of dialectical relationship she frames between use and enjoyment of the body? I argue that she cuts female spirituality off from transformative relationship with the divine by reducing woman and the divine to a self-enclosed sameness. She wants to leave God behind but, in so doing, devolves the female self's relationship between body and spirituality to one of utility and self-exploitation.

These questionable consequences for women's spiritual well-being occur because her materialism is strongly tied to notions of 'sameness' and 'lack'. I venture to suggest that her work tends both to reification that encloses female spirituality within a circle of self-affirming sameness in which difference and relationality cannot thrive, and also to abstraction that reduces woman's spirituality to an unattainable 'beyond bodiliness' or impersonal divinity that is a form of nothingness. The consequence of both is that revelation is devoid of life-giving relationality. She asserts that to confess a God, who is both transcendent beyond and immanent within the world, is to exist in thought rather than matter, i.e., to abstract oneself from reality and to flee from the world. Christianity is seen as a form of depressive thought or behaviour in which neurotic individuals are abnormally hostile to the body and physical pleasure. I suggest the contrary, namely, that she both diminishes the body to a usable object in the pursuit of spiritual pleasure, and tends towards nihilism in making absence, within and beyond the body, the horizon of spiritual meaningfulness.

This is not to say that Christian women are unaccustomed to speaking of absence, emptiness or silence, as places where God is sought. On the contrary, many Christian women have found spiritual blessing in the paradoxical experience of the presence of God in absence. Christina Georgina Rossetti (1830–1894) wrote (Rossetti in Gardner, 1972, p.728):

> Sometimes I said: 'It is an empty name
> I long for; to a name why should I give
> The peace of all that days I have to live?'

Simone Weil, in the twentieth century, accepted the experience of emptiness as part of her spiritual journey: 'We must take the feeling of being at home into exile. We must be rooted in the absence of a place' (Weil in Runcorn, 1989, pp.6–7). Catherine de Hueck Doherty develops an appreciation of absence as a place of spiritual growth when she writes: 'We all need to create a *poustinia* in the heart – a desert place of silence and prayer.' (Hueck Doherty in Runcorn, 1989, pp.6–7) For these women, God's presence, or at least non-absence, in absence, suggests a discovery of self, in and through communion with God, in moments of silence wherein quietude is found. The exchange between emptiness and presence is the possibility of heaven within.

Nor is it to devalue the quest for self-transcendence that Irigaray observes in human being and expresses in the language of revelation. There is a general consensus amongst Christian and non-Christian spiritual writers that humans aspire towards that which is other than the self; reaching out to that which is beyond is constitutive of human being. For the Christian feminist, this is due to a central principle in anthropology, namely that human beings are created 'in the image and likeness of God.' Human beings are constituted to be in relation to God which bestows upon them a capacity to seek and enjoy God who/which is other than human existence. For non-Christian feminists, or those who describe themselves without reference to Christianity, this intuition takes different forms. For Irigaray, it means positing that which guarantees the infinite in particular, the infinity of the female gender. The finite, or that which sets (male) limits to human expression, must be avoided because it constricts development of the female self: 'In order to become, it is essential to have a gender or an essence (consequently a sexuate essence) as *horizon*. Otherwise, becoming remains partial and subject to the subject' (Irigaray, 1993, p.61). For Irigaray, care of the self involves both respect for the ineffable depths within the self, *homo absconditus*, and the desire to transcend, or soar beyond, the limitations of present existence. These two quests for self-transcendence need not be torn apart into the goody-goody Christian mode and the stroppy, erotogenic feminist mode. The real discussion is about which discourse liberates, promotes, and enables life.

Nor is this questioning of Irigaray to deny that spiritual and/or psychic, and bodily, aspects of human being exist within one another. Pre-modern theological thinkers spoke readily of reason and intuition as faculties of the soul, and of the soul's union with the body. Even the supposed arch-enemies of feminism, Augustine and Aquinas, affirmed that no human faculty is isolated and sealed up, but is open to every other. In Augustine's words that were cited by Aquinas: 'In any body whatever the soul is whole in the whole and whole in every part'.

(Augustine, *De. Trin.* VI, 6, in Aquinas, *S.T.*, 1a. 76, 8). They both suggest that there is a coherence and continuity between each aspect or faculty of human being that renders the body transparent to the spirit, and makes corporeal existence spiritual. By extrapolation, the Christian may affirm that bodily pleasure can be a spiration of the Holy Spirit, i.e., a grace or charism that defines a human being in her or his relation with another. A holy spiritual life can include bodily pleasure that is grounded in love (Gen. 2:18; S. of S. 1:2–4; 1 Cor. 7:4–5, 11:11; Eph. 5:25–33).

Rather, this questioning of Irigaray is to suggest that there are reasons to be suspicious of her positing of revelations of 'god'/the divine/ spirituality/transcendence, experienced as the void. These become clearer if we look at her ideas of 'sameness' and 'lack'. By 'sameness', I refer to her enclosing of the female self within a circle of self–identity in which finite and infinite are merged. By 'lack', I refer to her recasting the age–old designation of woman as lack, i.e., that 'woman is a woman as a result of a certain lack of characteristics', in terms of potential (Irigaray, 1985, p.112). With reference to 'sameness', consider how for Irigaray the body as revelation is conceived within self-relation, and within relation with others through the body. The 'body' is the totality of all that is and can be experienced, including the 'divine': 'Onward into a *touch* that opens the "soul" again to contact with divine force' (Irigaray, 1985, p.193).

My question is whether this construal of female bodiliness can do justice to the spiritual essence of human being. I suggest that it cannot because, in trying to think 'god' out of absence, she equivocates within a dilemma. Either she reduces 'god' to the sameness that is woman; spirituality acquires an egocentric stamp as 'god' becomes either a bodily kind of aspiration. Or she purports that 'god' is a movement in the gap between the body, human ideals of pleasure, and the reality of disappointment. In trying to find a new life-metaphor she aspires to see the divine within women, but does so in a highly speculative fashion; 'god' is the rebounding of light as self reflects self and produces an image of that which lies beyond but includes the physical. 'God' is not a power that delivers, helps, and liberates, but which stays hidden in a dark 'beyond' that is identical to human aspirations.

With reference to the idea of 'lack', consider how, for all her apparent rebellion, she is closer to the Western philosophical definitions of women which she repudiates than might be supposed. Woman, she writes, has been regarded as genitally deficient, and this absence or want of visible reproductive organs has resulted in depraved perceptions, held by women and men, of her value within the sexual economy. This is not disputed. On the contrary, I welcome her diagnosis of pathological attitudes to women. As she suggests, Western thought forms have, for centuries and without good reason, ascribed the darkness of 'un-knowledge' and ignorance to women. Freud's supposed demonstration of a castration complex in women is simply a twentieth-century manifestation of much older Western notions. In response, however, she claims that the negativity in Western and phallocentric perceptions of the dialectic of the sexes is subsumed and superseded by female sexuality. She wants to move beyond traditional Western philosophical and Christian representations of women as 'lack' with the language of *jouissance* and fruitful possibility. Women, she writes, are the privileged guardians of what has not yet been revealed; Plato's cave imagery is recast as the womb and breaking forth from the womb is akin to male imagery of entry into knowledge and light.

In this context, I do not wish to decry Irigaray's intention to transvalue familiar definitions of women. Rather, I am concerned with the manner in which she proceeds and where she ends up. Her spirituality, I suggest, climaxes on a false, hollow note, with a sad feeling of unpromising emptiness. By refusing all transcendence other than the *pour-soi* ('for myself') of women, she associates revelation with indeterminacy within finitude. Revelation is an idea used to express a spiritual disposition that is also physical. Her materialist spirituality is an exchange process that depends upon utility, rather than a reciprocal giving and receiving, and yields an unattainable ideal. Consider how Irigaray repeats the ancient definition of woman as lack but reinterprets lack as the plenitude void of woman's womb. This lack, or absence, becomes a place or idea that is used for experiencing the divine: 'Mystery, me-hysteria, without determinable end or beginning . . . quietude and rest in herself-God' (Irigaray, 1985, p.201). An exchange is set up between female bodiliness and ideas of 'god'. Exchange (between self and a self-projected idea of 'god') is effected in order to derive spiritual pleasure; the body is used by the woman to take pleasure in the idea of her own divinity. Irigaray wants us to believe that the functional relationship she sets up between 'god' and enjoyment of the body is a good rather than bad exchange. In her essay, *La Mystérique* this is because 'nothing has a price in this divine consummation and consumption' (Irigaray, 1985, p.195. See also Stockton, 1994, ch.1). The currency of bodily spirituality pertains to a mystical medium of expenditure in which woman invests in herself.

For Irigaray, the value of spiritual currency is not determined by an alien economy, external to the self, but is set according to the woman's own utility. Woman sets her own rates of exchange and is subject to no external forces; she finds real value in expenditure on her own hidden desire for divinity. It is still the case, however, that she uses the body to take pleasure in the divine, and uses the idea of 'God' to enjoy the body. The self uses the self in order to derive pleasure in selfhood. This, is not necessarily destructive but is a recursive, and less fully relational, exchange than that which is Christian. Irigaray's exchange is between the female self and the idea of 'god', and is mediated through a void. What a Christian feminist might dub the reality of revelation, i.e., the self-communication of God in a real exchange between human and divine, has been reduced to speculative conjecture.

What follows from all this is that she commits herself to a relationship between the female self and the divine which is one of non-reciprocal exchange and utility. I am not suggesting that the notion of exchange *per se* is problematic in feminist spirituality. On the contrary, relationships characterised by reciprocity and mutuality involve various types of exchange: exchange of self-communication, exchange of gifts of kindness and caring, exchange of risk-taking and trust. This cannot be fully demonstrated here but has been argued convincingly by John Milbank (Milbank, 1995). Suffice it to say that a relationship of love will include the giving of a gift or gifts. The giving of a gift is inseparable from exchange because, in order for a gift to be given, it must be received and, in some way, returned. Of itself, the notion of exchange in relationship is not problematic. For Irigaray, however, the relationship between woman and the divine (i.e., a relationship of sameness) becomes one of sameness and utility-exchange rather than gift-exchange. Utility is the determining motivation. 'God' is no real partner but a projection that arises because of lack within the self: 'She is transformed into Him in her love: this is the secret of their exchange' (Irigaray, 1985, p.201). She offers a materialistically modified identity philosophy in which the finite–infinite relationship relies on the female subject being both subject and object, finite and infinite, for itself.

Summary

In the first part of this essay, I reviewed why talk of revelation is a 'problem' for Christian and post-Christian feminists, and explored how themes of embodiment and gender in Christian theology can be of help in coming to new perceptions of revelation. In the second part, I put some of these revisionary ideas to work by discussing what challenges a

Christian feminist might pose to a contemporary form of materialist spirituality, in which the body is construed as a direct source of revelation. By problematising Irigaray's notions of a spiritual relationship between the female self and 'god'. I illustrated how her search for 'god' in the physical might be less beneficial for women's spiritual well-being than Christian teaching about the relationship between creator and created, in which the body is accepted as God's gift and re-given in the holy living. The reinvocation of revelation, as envisaged by Irigaray, is a spiritual option for women, but might always leave an aching need for reciprocity and relationality. Without an original relationality, there can be no revelation of anything other than 'sameness' or 'lack'. Such an original relationality is already attested within Christian tradition, where revelation involves precise knowledge about the God one loves, and the experience of being loved already by God.

Bibliography

Bingemer, María Clara, 'Women in the Future of the Theology of Liberation' in Ursula King, ed., *Feminist Theology from the Third World*, London, SPCK, 1994, ch.32.

Bond Stockton, Kathryn, *God Between Their Lips: Desire Between Women in Irigaray, Brontë and Eliot*, California, Stanford University Press, 1994.

Chawaf, Chantal, 'Linguistic Flesh' in Elaine Marks and Isabelle de Courtivron, eds, *New French Feminisms: An Anthology*, New York, Harvester Wheatsheaf, 1981.

Grey, Mary, *The Wisdom of Fools: Seeking Revelation for Today*, London, SPCK, 1993.

Gössman, Elisabeth, hrsg., *Wörterbuch der Feministischen Theologie*, Gütersloh, Gütersloher Verl.-Haus Mohn.

Hampson, Daphne, 'On Autonomy and Heteronomy' in Daphne Hampson, ed., *Swallowing a Fishbone? Feminist Theologians Debate Christianity*, London, SPCK, 1996a.

Hampson, Daphne, *After Christianity*, London, SCM, 1996b.

Hueck Doherty, Catherine de, 'Poustinia', in D. Runcorn, *Silence*, Nottingham, Grove Books Limited, 1989.

Irigaray, Luce, *Speculum of the Other Woman*, transl. Gillian C. Gill, New York, Cornell University Press, 1985.

——, *Sexes and Genealogies*, transl. Gillian C. Gill, New York, Columbia University Press, 1993.

Kim, Maggie, C.W., St Ville, Susan M., Simonaitis, Susan M., (eds), *Transfigurations: Theology and the French Feminists*, Minneapolis, Fortress Press, 1993.

McFague, Sallie, *Models of God*, London, SCM, 1987.

——, *The Body of God: An Ecological Theology*, London, SCM, 1993.

Milbank, John, 'Can a Gift be Given? Prolegomena to a Future Trinitarian Metaphysic' in *Modern Theology*, vol.11, no.1, January 1995, pp.119–161.

Moltmann-Wendel, Elisabeth, *I am my body*, London, SCM, 1994.

Rossetti, Christina Georgina, 'A Pause of Thought' in Helen Gardener, ed., *The New Oxford Book of English Verse*, Oxford, Oxford University Press, 1972.

Ruether, Rosemary Radford, *Sexism and God-Talk*, London, SCM, 1983/1992.

Stuart, Elisabeth, *Just Good Friends: Towards a Lesbian and Gay Theology of Relationship*, London, Mowbray, 1995.

Weil, Simone, 'Gravity and Grace', in D. Runcorn, *Silence*, Nottingham, Grove Books Limited, 1989.

10

Jesus the Revelation of God

Richard Bauckham

'Whoever has seen me has seen the Father,' claims Jesus in the Fourth Gospel (14:9), encapsulating the dominant theme of that gospel: that it is in God's incarnation as Jesus that God truly makes Godself known. The idiom is a little different but the claim is the same when Paul speaks of 'the knowledge of the glory of God in the face of Jesus Christ' (2 Cor. 4:7). For both John and Paul – as for the Christian tradition after them – it is in the particular human personal identity of Jesus that God can be known. An understanding of divine revelation which claims to be Christian must not only include an account of Jesus as the revelation of God. The search for an appropriate understanding of what it means to call Jesus the revelation of God must be its central task, decisive for its whole enterprise. In the modern period it has proved a difficult task. Again and again the theological enterprise has abstracted what is revelatory about Jesus from his particular identity. Again and again it has lost sight of 'the face of Jesus Christ' – the particular identity in which Jesus is who he is and no one else. But it is in this face of Jesus that the face of God is to be seen. It is in the particular identity of Jesus – who Jesus himself is – that the identity of God – who God is – is revealed. The search for an appropriate understanding of Jesus as the revelation of God must avoid all paths which lead away from the unique particularity of Jesus. Its task is to understand precisely this unique particularity of Jesus as the revelation of God.

This chapter has three sections. The first outlines and discusses the three principal ways in which the idea of Jesus as the revelation of God has been understood in Christian theology in the modern period. The third of these three options, which corresponds most adequately to the place of Jesus Christ in Scripture and Christian tradition, is then further explored in the second and third sections of the chapter. The second section engages with previous theological discussion of one key issue within our topic: in what sense God is revealed in the humanity of Jesus. The third section presupposes the insights gained in the first two sections from the critical engagement with recent theological discussion of the topic, and moves beyond these insights to offer a creative restatement of the Christian understanding of Jesus as the revelation of God.

1. Three Views of Jesus as Revelation of God

The idea of Jesus as the revelation of God has a long history in Christian theology since the New Testament, but it has become especially popular in the modern period. In this period it has taken widely divergent forms, which relate to widely divergent understandings of God, God's relation to the world, and the place of Jesus in God's relation to the world. In what follows we shall exclude from consideration views which focus largely or exclusively on Jesus' teaching as revelatory of God, rather than on Jesus himself, in his person and history, as revelation of God. Such views portray Jesus as the *revealer* of God, but can scarcely be considered views of Jesus as the *revelation* of God. The various ways of understanding Jesus as the revelation of God we shall classify in three broad categories. In sketching these categories, we shall indicate also how each relates to three other important christological themes: the uniqueness of Jesus Christ, the incarnation of God in Jesus Christ, and the role of Jesus Christ in salvation. The relationship to these other themes will enable us to understand and to assess each of the three views more adequately.

(1) Jesus Illustrates the Moral Character of God

According to the first of the three views, Jesus is revelation of God in the sense that he illustrates for us what God is like. As it has sometimes been put, Jesus is a parable of God. Since the moral attributes of God are those which can also be attributed to a human being, it is these that Jesus reflects in his human life. (For some, though not all, versions of this view, the moral attributes are the defining attributes of God.) So as well as teaching, in his parables and other sayings, that God is compassionate and forgiving, Jesus practised compassion and forgiveness in his own life and death. From Jesus' human love we can see what God's love is like.

Such an understanding of revelation in Jesus entails the view that

175

God is similarly revealed in other human lives to the extent that they, too, display such moral characteristics. As revelation of God, Jesus can therefore be unique only in degree. He may reveal God to a greater extent than all other human beings. He may be the fullest revelation of God. But, as revelation of God in this sense, he cannot be unique in kind. Some theologians who understand revelation in this way may hold Jesus to be unique in kind for other reasons (usually because they understand him to be the incarnation of God in a unique sense), but this view of revelation does not itself require Jesus to be unique in kind. Nor is it easy to see why it should require Jesus to be unique in degree, unless the traditional doctrine of his sinlessness is maintained as a constituent of this view. As has often been pointed out, we not only do not but, in the nature of the case, could not have the historical evidence to show that Jesus was in fact morally superior to any other human being. More importantly, the gospel stories, whose portrayal of Jesus must in practice be the medium through which God is revealed in this way, hardly seem concerned with showing Jesus as more loving, more compassionate, more forgiving, than any other human being.[1] The fact that nineteenth-century versions of this view (for example, in German Liberal Protestantism) generally held Jesus to be unique must be attributed to the strong nineteenth-century European sense of Christianity's inherent superiority to other religions and cultures. In a quite different context, where claims to the uniqueness of Christ are perceived as an impediment to open dialogue between the religions or as implausible in the light of other religions, this view of Jesus as revelation of God now commonly takes the form of seeing him as one outstanding illustration of God among others. Furthermore, on this basis, whether Jesus is the fullest revelation or only one of the fullest revelations of God so far available to us, one could reasonably hope for a yet fuller revelation of God in the future. The logic of this view of revelation is inevitably away from the uniqueness of Jesus.

This understanding of Jesus as illustrating what God is like is readily combined with a view of salvation as revelation. The emphasis may either be on Jesus as showing us God's love so that we may respond to it, or on Jesus as an inspiring example of God's love reflected in a human life which we can follow in reflecting God's love in our own lives. In either case, the human plight is ignorance of God, which Jesus remedies (as other people may also do in various degrees) by revealing God to us. Not all who take this view of what it means to call Jesus the revelation of God reduce Jesus' soteriological role to revelation. They may combine this view of revelation with other soteriological themes.

But in that case these themes have no intrinsic relationship to the understanding of Jesus as revelation of God. In other words, this view of revelation has no relationship to soteriology unless salvation is defined as revelation.

This first of our three views of Jesus as revelation of God does not require a doctrine of incarnation. However, an influential form of it connects revelation with divine immanence in human life, and takes the incarnation of God in Christ to be the (or a) supreme instance of the immanence of God in all humanity. God is incarnate in all human life to varying degrees, and correspondingly reveals Godself in all human life in varying degrees. As revelation is a matter of degree, so incarnation also is redefined as a matter of degree (in contradistinction from the traditional definition of incarnation as uniquely true of Jesus). Early in this century such a view cohered easily with a kind of evolutionary immanentism, which identified God with the process of evolution and progress in nature and human culture. One of the (Anglican) English Modernists, Hastings Rashdall, who also famously espoused the purely revelatory (or 'moral influence') view of the atonement which he attributed to Peter Abelard, well expresses this complex of ideas:

> We cannot say intelligibly that God dwells in Christ, unless we have already recognized that in a sense God dwells in and reveals Himself in Humanity at large, and in each particular human soul . . . [But] men do not reveal God equally. The more developed intellect reveals God more completely than that of the child or the savage: and the higher and more developed moral consciousness reveals Him more than the lower, and above all the actually better man reveals God more than the worse man. Now, if in the life, teaching and character of Christ . . . we can discover the highest revelation of the divine nature, we can surely attach a real meaning to the language of the Creeds which singles him out from all other men that ever lived as the one in whom the ideal relation of man to God is most completely realized. If God can only be known as revealed in Humanity, and Christ is the highest representative of Humanity, we can very significantly say 'Christ is the Son of God, very God of very God, of one substance with the Father,' though the phrase undoubtedly belongs to a philosophical dialect which we do not habitually use.[2]

This line of thought, with a background in idealist philosophy, easily leads to the kind of thorough-going immanentism which treats divinity itself as a matter of degree: God progressively actualises Godself in the process such that the perfection of humanity is at the same time the fullest realisation of human potential and the fullest actualisation of deity.[3] As another of the English Modernists, H.D.A. Major, put it, 'the difference between Deity and Humanity is one of degree.'[4]

The first view of revelation in Christ readily serves such a conclusion (though by no means all who take it reach such a conclusion). If the most perfect human life reveals God most fully just because it is the most perfect human life, then deity is human perfection and human perfection is deity. In that case, however, the understanding of Jesus as revelation of God with which we began can now be revised. It is not merely that Jesus illustrates what God is like, but that, as the (or a) supreme instance of the universal phenomenon of divine incarnation in humanity, he reveals the coincidence of human perfection with the fullness of divine self-actualisation. At this point we have in fact reached what I wish to distinguish as the second view of Jesus as the revelation of God.

(2) Jesus Reveals the Universal Possibility of Divine-Human Union

The second view is that Jesus reveals God-in-humanity as a universal possibility of human life. As we have seen, there is an easy progression from the first view, when presented in terms of the immanence of God in human life, to this second view. Nevertheless the two views are distinct. It is possible to hold the first view – that Jesus illustrates what God is like – without any trace of the second view. For the second view, it is not primarily the character or attributes of God that Jesus reveals, but rather the possibility of divine–human union, a possibility which is actualised in Jesus himself as a revelation of its possibility for all people.

Though not necessarily taking the idealist or evolutionary forms it took in English Modernism, all forms of this view share with the English Modernists an understanding of the incarnation of God in Jesus as a special instance of that divine–human relationship which is the fulfilment of human nature in all people. It is by actualising this universal possibility that Jesus reveals God. He reveals precisely this universal possibility of divine humanisation and human divinisation. Thus John Macquarrie, in one of the most recent statements of this view, writes:

> Only if there is *in all human beings* a possibility for transcendence and a capacity for God, can there be such a possibility and a

capacity in the man Jesus; and only if God makes himself present and known in and through the creation generally can there be a particular point at which he is present and known in a signal way. Jesus Christ would not be a revelation if he was only an anomaly in the creation. He is revelation because he sums up and makes clear a presence that is obscurely communicated throughout the cosmos.[5]

The claim in the second sentence of this quotation must mean that only if incarnation in Jesus is the (or a) signal instance of incarnation as a universal possibility can incarnation in Jesus be revelatory of incarnation as a universal possibility. It is tautologous, taking for granted a particular view of the meaning of the claim that Jesus is a revelation. As we shall see, there is a quite different possible way of seeing incarnation in Jesus as revelatory of God.

Some versions of this view, such as Macquarrie's, maintain the uniqueness of Jesus as revelation of God and as Saviour, but do so in the weak form of a degree Christology, structurally similar to the first view. The complementary movements of human self-transcendence into God and divine self-transcendence into humanity take place, to some degree, throughout human life, independently of Jesus. As the most perfect instance of their occurrence and coincidence, Jesus makes clearer to others this possibility of human fulfilment and so facilitates the salvation which is nevertheless already available. The archetype of fulfilled humanity, of which we are all implicitly aware, gains new power when it appears as realised in Jesus as the representative human being.

Karl Rahner, whose Christology is the most fully elaborated version of this structure of thought, aims to maintain the uniqueness of Jesus as revelation of God and as Saviour in a stronger form, designating him the 'absolute Saviour' towards whom the universal human orientation to the divine self-communication is implicitly orientated. There needs to be an historical individual in whom the divine self-communication and the free human acceptance of it are fully realised. Therefore Jesus is unique as the 'final cause' of salvation: the goal at which all human aspiration to fulfilment in God implicitly aims. As the one in whom the divine self-communication and the free human acceptance of it were fully realised, Jesus also constitutes God's definitive and irrevocable self-offer of the same absolute self-communication of God to all other people. The incarnation is unique only as the first instance, but as the first instance it is God's definitive offer of salvation to others. This formulation aims to preserve the uniqueness of Jesus as revelation, but other elements in Rahner's thought throw doubt on the extent to which it is successful in doing so. A prime example is his well-known theory of 'anonymous Christians' – people (adherents of other religions or of none) who respond to the divine self-communication without explicit Christian faith. The 'anonymous Christian', it seems, is capable of as full an acceptance of the divine self-communication as the explicit Christian, without knowledge of Jesus as God's definitive self-offer.

(3) Jesus Reveals the Unique Presence and Action of God which is Jesus' Own History

We turn to the third of the three broad categories we are distinguishing. According to this third view, Jesus is revelation of God in the sense that he reveals that unique gracious presence of God with us and that unique saving activity of God for us which are Jesus' own history. Jesus reveals the *unique* presence of God in human life, which he himself *is*. Jesus does not merely illustrate what God is like, nor is he merely the representatively fullest instantiation of humanity united with God. His unique human life, death and resurrection are at the same time uniquely God's human history, in which God's unique act of self-giving love for all humanity took place. God's self-giving love is revealed by Jesus, not simply in a representative instance, but in a unique act of self-giving love, in which God gave Godself in becoming this human being, living this human life, dying this human death and rising from death. The love which God is and which God shows in all relationships with creation here takes the specific form of God's loving self-identification *as* actually a human being with all other human beings. Only because the incarnation *is* this unique act of God's love does Jesus reveal God as the love which takes this step of radical self-identification with humanity.

With regard to the uniqueness of Jesus, this view differs from the others in that it understands – indeed, entails understanding – the incarnation of God in Jesus in the traditional way, i.e., as indicating a difference in kind between Jesus and other humans, not a difference of degree. God's immanent presence in all creation and all human life is not incarnation. Incarnation is God's unique presence as the human being Jesus of Nazareth. Correspondingly this view understands the revelation of God in Jesus as unique not simply in degree. It is not merely a fuller revelation of what can be known of God apart from Jesus Christ (though this view does not need to deny that revelation of God occurs apart from Jesus Christ). If it is precisely God's humanity that is revealed in Jesus – God's radical being with us and for us through living and dying as this human being – then it is *possible* for this to be revealed *only* by its occurrence in Jesus. On the basis of the other two views, maintaining the uniqueness of the revelation in Jesus seems in the end an arbitrary limitation: why should not what is revealed in Jesus be just as well revealed elsewhere? But for the third view, what is uniquely revealed in Jesus is precisely what uniquely occurs in Jesus. The limitation is not arbitrary but logically necessary.

Consequently, this view also connects revelation very closely with salvation, though not by reducing salvation to revelation. In Jesus God enters the human situation, in all its godlessness and godforsakenness, identifying with it in order to redeem and to transform. This salvific act is more than revelatory, but in it God is revealed as the God who in this way is with us and for us. By acting for our salvation in the history of Jesus, God reveals Godself as our Saviour. By giving Godself in radical self-identification with us in the life and death of Jesus, God reveals Godself as this self-giving love. In other words, the kind of revelation that is involved is inextricably connected with salvation.

Two other differences, not unrelated to each other, strikingly distinguish this third view from the other two. First, according to the other two views, what Jesus reveals is separable from Jesus. Even if we require Jesus in order to come to know God in this way, having done so we can know God in this way without thinking of Jesus. Jesus is not intrinsic to the knowledge of God he reveals. For the third view, he is. Secondly, according to the other two views, what is revelatory about Jesus are features he shares with other people, differing only in degree. According to the first view his moral qualities reveal the character of God; according to the second, his union with God reveals union with God as a universal possibility. These views can value what is particular about Jesus only as representative of what is universal or universalisable. This is why so many exponents of this view who wish to maintain some kind of uniqueness for Jesus fail to do so convincingly. According to the third view, on the other hand, it is the particularity of Jesus that is revelatory of God. Admittedly, a version of the third view is possible which reduces this particularity to the mere claim that one particular human being was, uniquely, God. According to Kierkegaard's well-known statement, if we knew only that God appeared in history as a human being,[6] it would be sufficient. But for most exponents of the third view, it is not sufficient. God is revealed in that this particular human history, which the story of Jesus narrates, is the human history of God. The story of Jesus' activities and encounters and relationships, of his crucifixion and resurrection on the third day, is the story of God's self-giving love in historical occurrence. It does not reveal some generality abstracted from it. It reveals God as human in this way, as this human being, in this human story. That God is also more than this and in every respect consistent with this, the story reveals only inseparably from this.

2. God Revealed in the Humanity of Jesus

The third view of Jesus as revelation of God, as we have outlined it above, is the one which the rest of this chapter will explore. A useful point of entry into some of its theological implications is what Karl Barth called 'one of the hardest problems of Christology': 'Is the *humanitas Christi* as such the revelation?'[7] Does the humanity of Jesus Christ as such reveal God? Barth denied that it does. He has often been misunderstood as denying that the humanity of Jesus reveals God,[8] whereas what he denied is that 'the *humanitas Christi* as such,' simply as humanity, 'as it were in itself,' reveals God. He had in mind nineteenth-century versions of our first two views, according to which it is Jesus' humanity as such which reveals God. Such views exemplified what Barth so entirely and consistently rejected: the nineteenth-century route to knowledge of God by way of the affinity and continuity of humanity and deity. If, for example, it is the moral perfection of Jesus that reveals God, and this moral perfection of Jesus is the finest example of human goodness, then God is conceived as a projection of human goodness, and no revelation occurs of the God who is wholly other than humanity.

As the finest recent exponent of our second view, Karl Rahner illustrates clearly what happens when Jesus' humanity, understood as the common humanity he exemplifies, is understood to reveal God. Rahner speaks of the humanity of Christ as the self-expression of God, as what the divine *Logos* becomes when expressed in what is not God. But because he thinks not of the particularity of Jesus' history, but of his humanity as human nature in general, this understanding of revelation makes humanity as such the self-expression of God:

> Human nature in general is a possible object of the creative knowledge and power of God, because and insofar as the Logos is by nature the one who is 'utterable' (even into that which is not God); because he is the Father's Word, in which the Father can express himself, and, freely, empty himself into the non-divine; because,

when this happens, that precisely is born which we call human nature . . . So that we may and should say, when we think our ontology through to the end: man is possible because the exteriorization of the Logos is possible.[9]

Although Rahner also states that human nature, which is the same in us and in Jesus, is only in Jesus' case, not in ours, uttered as God's self-expression,[10] it is very difficult to see either on what basis this distinction is possible for him or that he in fact maintains it. The logic of this view is that it is as ideal humanity that God is revealed.

The matter is quite different if God is revealed, not by general characteristics of humanity which Jesus shares with others and exemplifies supremely, but by the particularity of Jesus' human history which in its *particular* humanity is uniquely God's human history. Then *as God's humanity* it expresses and reveals its divine subject, or, rather, God reveals Godself through God's own particular human history. When – and only when – the story of Jesus is understood as God's human story, then God is revealed as the God who is other than humanity but in grace has chosen to identify with us, to be with us and for us, to give Godself in love for us and to us.

Since Karl Barth is a major exponent of the view we have expounded as the third view of Jesus as revelation of God, we turn now to the contribution his own work may make to our understanding of the issue he called one of the hardest in Christology. Two aspects of what Barth has to say about the humanity of Christ are relevant here, and correspond respectively to his early stress on the 'wholly otherness' of God and his later stress on 'the humanity of God.' Just as this later emphasis qualifies, without invalidating, the earlier, so we need to consider not only the way the humanity of Christ features in his earlier theology of revelation but also the way in which his later thought about the humanity of Christ may qualify that theology of revelation without revoking it.

God as wholly other

The structure of Barth's understanding of revelation was not designed with the Christological issue of the humanity of Christ specifically in view, but came, in the increasingly Christological concentration of Barth's theology, to be applied to it. It is characterised by a dialectic of veiling and unveiling, hiddenness of God and self-disclosure of God.[11] (Revelation, it is important to remember, Barth consistently conceives as event.) Revelation occurs in a creaturely medium which, because it is not God, conceals God, until and unless God draws back the veil and makes Godself known. There are two main concerns in this understanding of revelation. One is for the absolute distinction between God and all creaturely reality. In revelation God reveals Godself, and so the creaturely means of revelation, which is not God, cannot as such be the content of revelation. Simply as creaturely reality it conceals the God who is wholly other than it. God is revealed truly as God only when God is known as wholly other than the creaturely medium of God's revelation. This is true even of the humanity of Christ, which as such is creaturely, not God. Deification of the creaturely medium of revelation would only lead in the direction we have seen our first two views of revelation in Christ take: to the knowledge of a God who is no more than perfect or ideal humanity.

The second concern in Barth's revelatory dialectic of concealment and disclosure is for the freedom of God to be the subject of revelation. It is God who reveals Godself in the event of revelation. Barth's epistemological concern is that revelation does not make God an object of human knowing, grasped and controlled by the human knowing subject. Therefore, even when God in some sense becomes an object in the world by taking form in a creaturely medium of revelation, God retains the freedom either to remain hidden or to disclose Godself. 'God's self-unveiling remains an act of sovereign divine freedom.'[12] (One could argue that freedom is intrinsic to self-disclosure as a personal act. Human persons do not have absolute freedom in becoming known to others, but do exercise freedom in the most personal aspects of self-disclosure. The divine self-disclosure must be free in the fullest sense.) Again, what Barth says of the creaturely media of revelation in general is true even in the case of the humanity of Christ. Even in assuming this creaturely form God 'remains free to become manifest or not to become manifest in this form.' Barth rightly points to the fact that 'even Jesus did not become manifest to all who met Him but only to a few.'[13]

From all this it would be easy to derive the impression that the creaturely form of revelation functions only as the veil behind which God hides in order to preserve God's freedom, and has no positive function in revelation. But this is not Barth's intention. Revelation is possible only because God takes a form in which God becomes something in the world, in which 'He Himself, as God, exists for men exactly as other things or persons exist for them.'[14] Barth speaks of 'the real objectification of God in His revelation.'[15] As creaturely the form is unlike God, but in assuming this form God exercises precisely 'the freedom to be unlike Himself.'[16] God's Lordship in revelation includes this freedom to 'become unlike Himself in such a way that He is not tied to His secret eternity and eternal secrecy but can and will and does in fact take temporal form as well.'[17] Unfortunately, the largely formal nature of this account of revelation leaves it quite unclear how the form positively functions in the event of revelation. For example, is the fact that Jesus was crucified – as distinct from, say, dying in his bed – intrinsic to the revelation when it occurs, or merely the occasion for it? It is only when Barth moves on from his formal account of divine revelation to his later concern with 'the humanity of God' that a clear answer to this question becomes possible.

God as human

God's divine freedom to be unlike God in revelation is in Christ God's divine freedom to be human. It is this thought that enables Barth's development from a theology of revelation in which the concern is for the otherness of God as truly God, not creature, to a theology of incarnation in which the concern is for God's free choice to be also human. Now the role of the humanity of Christ is no longer merely formal: 'It is when we look at Jesus Christ that we know decisively that God's deity does not exclude, but includes His *humanity*.'[18] This is not because the human nature of Christ as such reveals God, but because God as its subject is revealed in it as the God who condescends in self-humiliation to unity and solidarity with creaturely, sinful and perishing humanity. His becoming 'unlike Himself' is not merely the means of revelation, but the content of revelation. In God's becoming human in solidarity with sinful and condemned humanity, God's very deity is revealed as the freedom of divine love to be humble, to choose to be with and for humanity, to be God in such a way as to include humanity in God's deity. Barth's insistence that the humanity of Christ is not God and, in the sense of being creaturely, is unlike God,[19] is not in the least superseded in this doctrine of the humanity of God. God is not revealed as like humanity, but as the sovereign Creator who chooses in the freedom of God's grace to be not only the 'wholly Other' but also the God who is with and for humanity to the point of accepting the human situation as God's own.[20] There is thus no independent epistemological route from humanity to God, not even from Jesus' humanity as such to God, but only the God-given revelation that in this particular human being Jesus, God has made humanity God's own.

Epistemology and soteriology

It is noteworthy that this development occurs as Barth's theology moves from a primary concern with the epistemology of revelation to a primary concern with soteriology (reconciliation). When the primary concern was with the epistemology of revelation, what God reveals is Godself as Lord. But when the primary concern becomes reconciliation in Christ, then God's Lordship is revealed as also Servanthood. The creaturely form of revelation – 'the form of a servant'[21] – is thus intrinsic to the revelation. For this way of thinking, the particularity of Jesus' human history – at least in broad outline – must be seen as intrinsic to what is known of God in Christ. It is no mere occasion for the revelation of the God who is other than human, but intrinsic to the revelation of the God who includes humanity in his deity. That God in Jesus Christ is human in this way reveals God's true deity. God is most truly God's self in being also this human being Jesus, and therefore is most truly revealed as God's self in this human being Jesus.

What perhaps escapes notice in Barth's development is that from this perspective it is possible to see the *incognito* of the incarnation – the fact that Jesus is not revelation to all and sundry who encounter him in his earthly life – as primarily soteriological rather than epistemological. It is not so much that God's hiddenness in the humanity of Christ preserves God's freedom to be Lord in revelation, but rather that God's free grace in Christ takes the form of solidarity with humanity. In the freedom of God's love God becomes human, becomes not God, unlike God, and therefore *incognito*. Only in the God–given recognition that *this* man is *God*'s humanity – which entails the recognition *both* that God is wholly Other *and* that God truly identifies with the human other that is not God – is God's radical grace in Christ perceived and received.

A further step can be taken, in a direction taken already by Martin Luther's early theology of the cross and by Jürgen Moltmann's understanding of the crucified God.[22] This step brings into even closer correlation the epistemology of God's revelation in hiddenness in incarnation and the soteriology of God's identification with humanity in incarnation and cross. In incarnation and cross God becomes unlike God and so not humanly recognisable as God, not merely through becoming a creature, but also through identifying with sinful and suffering humanity, humanity in its opposition to God and its abandonment by God. God identifies with God's opposite.[23] To recognise God in the degradation and abandoned suffering of the crucified Christ is therefore to see God revealed in what contradicts God: in godlessness and godforsakenness.

To recognise God in this is to recognise God's love as the love which identifies with its opposite, which undertakes humiliation and suffering and abandoned death in solidarity with the wretched and the condemned. At precisely the point at which God is most hidden – on the cross – God's deity is most fully revealed in the lengths to which in this event God's love actually goes. And recognising God thus in the cross is saving recognition of the God whose radically identifying love is salvific. In this recognition the proud aspiration to godlike self-transcendence in imitation of the ideal humanity modelled by Jesus must be abandoned. Those to whom the crucified God is revealed are the wretched of the earth, whose abandonment he shares, and the godless of the world, whose condemnation he bears. To recognise God in the crucified Jesus is to find oneself among the lowly and the godless with whom he is identified. Thereby one finds the love which lifts the abandonment from suffering and the grace which liberates from sin. Thus the route to true humanity runs through the revelation of God's incarnate and crucified identification with us in our alienated humanity.

3. God as Identifiable in Jesus

In this section we presuppose the insights gained from engagement with previous theological discussion in our first two sections. We offer here a fresh restatement of the Christian understanding of Jesus as the revelation of God, placing this Christological climax of the biblical history of revelation in relation to the broader biblical understanding of God's self-revelation.

Revelation in the biblical tradition

Essential to any account of Jesus as the revelation of God must be the continuity between the New Testament's understanding of Jesus and the Old Testament revelation of God. The Jesus of the gospels does not, like Marcion's Christ, reveal a previously unknown God. The God he calls Father is the God of Israel whom his Jewish hearers already knew. It is also true that, according to the New Testament, the events of Jesus' history make the God of Israel known as God throughout the world, beyond the boundaries of Israel, as the prophets had expected. But it is the God of Israel who thus becomes in Jesus Christ the God of Gentiles also. Both for Jews and for Gentiles the God revealed in the

187

history of Jesus is the God who had made Godself known in the Old Testament story. So if the gospel story of Jesus is to be read as revelatory of God it must be read as the climax of the Old Testament story of Israel. The sense in which Jesus is revelation of God must be in continuity with the way in which God was revealed to God's people in the Old Testament period. In what follows, therefore, we shall first characterise the biblical understanding of revelation with primary reference to the Old Testament before, secondly, relating this understanding of revelation to Jesus. Three points will serve to characterise the main outline of this biblical under- standing of revelation.

(1) God is identifiable through God's identity in the world

First, revelation in the biblical tradition can usefully be understood as God's making Godself *identifiable*. God becomes known when God gives Godself an *identity*[24] within the world and thereby becomes *identifiable*. Without such an identity God remains the incomprensible mystery, knowable only negatively as what lies beyond the limit of all things finite. What happens in revelation is that God comes out of God's mystery by becoming identifiable. God becomes identifiable as the God of . . . or the God who has done this . . . or the God who promises that . . . or the God who is such-and-such . . . or the God who dwells in this place. In this way God is known as the universal God related to all worldly things, identifiable as the God who created all things and is sovereign over all things. But God is also much more specifically identifiable through relationship to particular worldly realities – events which are particular acts of God, places in which God appears or dwells, people to whom God relates in specific ways. God in an important sense *particularises* Godself and gives Godself a *particular* identity by which God may be known. By appearing to the patriarchs, giving them commands and promises, entering into covenant with them, God becomes the God of Abraham, Isaac and Jacob. By bringing Israel out of Egypt, by giving Israel the law at Sinai, by giving Israel the land, by being accessible to Israel in the temple, God identities Godself as the God of God's people Israel. In the covenant formulary, 'I will be your God and you will be my people', God not only gives Israel her identity as God's people but also gives Godself God's own identity as Israel's God. It is this particular identity of God which enables God to be known, not in abstraction, but in encounter and relationship.

Of course, this does not mean that God is reduced to this identity.

Just as God's presence in the temple does not confine the God whom heaven and earth cannot contain, so God's identity as the God of the patriarchs or the God of Israel in no way reduces God's transcendence of all created things. For God's particular identity to be properly understood, God must be recognised as the one who is truly God in *both* having *and* transcending this identity. God is the God of Israel only as the Holy One of Israel. God is not reduced to God's particular identity, but God does truly own it. God remains the incomprehensible mystery, but becomes identifiable as the one who, remaining the incomprehensible mystery, is *also* the God whose identity can be specified.

(2) God is identifiable as Saviour

The second aspect of this biblical understanding of God's identifiability is that *revelation and salvation* are closely interconnected. When God becomes identifiable, it is as the God who is with and for God's people; the God who acts graciously towards them; the God who judges but whose grace exceeds judgement; the God who goes with them and dwells in their midst. It is therefore God's acts of salvation for Israel and God's saving presence with Israel which reveal God's identity. YHWH who brought Israel out of Egypt is who God is, and this identity will be demonstrated again and again as God proves consistent with it in new acts of salvation and judgement. God demonstrates Godself to be the God of justice and abundant grace, the God who fulfils God's pledges to act with justice and abundant grace, the God who remains faithful to the covenant with God's people, in concrete acts whereby people will 'know that I am YHWH' (e.g., Exod. 14:18; Ezek. 16:62; 20:26, 44) or 'that I, YHWH, am your Saviour and your Redeemer, the Mighty One of Jacob' (Isa. 60:16).

We should not imagine here a contrast between who God is in Godself and who God is in relation to God's people, as Saviour. In acting in righteousness and grace towards God's people, God is truly Godself. It is important not to construe the divine identity in the 'postmodern' sense of an arbitrarily constructed identity, malleable and changeable at will. Rather, in becoming identifiable in the world God is true to God's eternal self.[25] God's identity as the Saviour of Israel, as the God who is with and for God's people, is truly revelatory of who God eternally is. To put it another way, God truly puts Godself into this identity.[26] But for this reason, Israel does not, in order to know who God is, have conceptually to abstract God from the relationship to Israel in which

God is revealed to Israel. YHWH who brought Israel out of Egypt is who God is.

For understanding New Testament theology, it is very significant that, in Deutero-Isaiah's great vision of the future revelation of God to Israel and to the ends of the earth, this same integral relationship of salvation and revelation obtains. By an unprecedentedly new act of salvation (cf. Isa. 43:18–19) YHWH is going to demonstrate YHWH's unique deity to Israel and to the nations. Thus, in parallel passages, the universal revelation of God can be described either as seeing God's saving action or as seeing God's glory (Isa. 52:10; 40:5). For the first Christians, this was what came about in Jesus, when God acted for the salvation both of Israel and of all the nations, and thereby became identifiable as God to all the nations.

(3) God's narrative identity

The third aspect of the biblical understanding of revelation is that God's revealed identity is rendered in the Old Testament primarily by *narrative*. God is identifiable from the stories of God's acts and relationships. This point can be overdone since, especially in the Wisdom literature, God's relation to the created order plays an important part in rendering God's identity. But God's specific identity as Israel's God is conveyed primarily by narratives in which God speaks and acts in concrete relationships with Israel, other nations, and a very large number of specific individuals. Law and prophecy, which in different ways convey God's word to God's people, relate intimately to the narratives. The prominence of narrative in rendering God's identity is certainly not an accidental matter of literary form. Since it is as personal agent and personal presence within the world that God becomes identifiable within the world, God's identity can only be adequately conveyed by narratives of God's agency and presence with God's people. Such narratives portray God as a character in the narrative, using in many respects the same kinds of literary means of rendering character as narratives deploy for all of their characters, while in this case giving sufficient indication that this character uniquely also transcends the narrative. Just as human personal identity can only be adequately depicted by narratives in which intentions are enacted and character established in relationships with others, so too the divine identity: who God is as God with us and for us. What it means – that God is merciful and gracious – is only adequately conveyed by narratives in which God acts mercifully and graciously in a profuse variety of ways which establish a consistency of divine character and activity. Whereas human identity may show radical inconsistency in the course of the narrative that renders it, God's narrative identity demonstrates, even in surprising ways, God's faithfulness to Godself and to God's promises.

In summary, it is in saving activity and saving presence, conveyed by narrative, that God makes Godself identifiable within the world. With this biblical understanding of revelation we must resist the persistent theological tendency to drive a wedge between the concrete forms of God's acts and presence in the world and what they reveal about God apart from them. God puts Godself into these concrete forms of God's acts and presence in the world. God puts Godself into an identity which is defined by relationship to worldly realities just as truly as it is by transcendence of worldly realities. Similarly we must resist the persistent theological tendency to abstract universals of God's relationship to the world from the particular forms of God's acts and presence in the world which reveal them, as though the universals which are revealed can then be known separately from the particulars which reveal them. Then the Exodus, for example, would be merely the occasion for recognising that God is righteous and gracious, a truth then knowable without reference to the Exodus. The biblical perspective is rather that through the Exodus God has identified Godself as the God who brought Israel out of Egypt and has enacted righteousness and grace for Israel in this way. God makes Godself identifiable precisely in a particular identity which must be narrated to be properly known. It is true that the consistency of divine character and activity which emerges in the biblical narratives can be summed up without explicit reference to the narratives. It is also true that, because God is the God of all reality, God can be expected to act outside these narratives consistently with God's identity in them. But such generalisations from the narratives cannot replace them. They can be understood only by constant reference back to the narratives from which they derive. It is into God's particular identity that God has put Godself so that God may be identifiable thereby.

Jesus the revelation of God

With the benefit of this biblical understanding of revelation, which we have formulated from the Old Testament, we may now attempt an appropriate understanding of Jesus as the revelation of God. The gospel narratives of Jesus are the continuation and the climax of the Old

Testament narratives of God's self-identification as the God of Israel. In the history of Jesus, God becomes identifiable in a way which is both continuous with God's narrative identity in the Old Testament and also radically novel. The same God who brought Israel out of Egypt and thereby identified Godself as Israel's God now identifies Godself as the God of the one Israelite Jesus, and further defines this identity as God's identity for all people. God's identity in Jesus is, by Israelite standards, both radically particular – in its focus on the one Israelite Jesus – and radically universal – in being an identity for all people. The narrative of one human being now renders God's identity definitively for all human beings. We shall explicate this with reference to the three aspects of the biblical understanding of revelation which we have established from the Old Testament.

(1) God's particular human identity

First, the radical particularity of Jesus as the revelation of God is both continuous with the Old Testament in being a particularisation of God and novel in the radical form which this particularisation takes. It is the most radical form of that particularisation of God which God's identity in the Old Testament revelation involves. There God identifies Godself in relation to particular realities in the world. There God has an identity within the world as the God of Israel, who brought Israel out of Egypt; gave Israel the law; settled Israel in the land; dwelt in the temple; and so on. Similarly, in the New Testament God is identifiable through close identification with a particular worldly reality – as the Father of Jesus Christ, who sent Jesus Christ and raised Jesus Christ from the dead. The God of Israel is now also the God of Jesus Christ. But, more than this, more radically than this, God's self-identification as a reality within the world now also includes God's self-identification *as* a particular worldly reality, as Jesus of Nazareth himself. God in Jesus is identifiable not only through identification with a particular worldly reality, but also through identification as that same particular worldly reality, the human being Jesus. As the human being who is himself included in the identity of God, Jesus is God's *human* identity, rendered for us by the gospel story.

God is not, of course, reduced to this human identity. God is identifiable in the history of Jesus as Father, Son and Holy Spirit – as the Father of Jesus Christ, as Jesus Christ, and as the Spirit of Jesus Christ. The gospel story, by rendering the human identity of Jesus, renders also this triune identity of God. It depicts God as truly Godself in all three ways – identified as Jesus and identified in relation to Jesus as his Father and his Spirit.[27] The notion of incarnation which is involved here is not at all inconsistent with the Old Testament understanding of God. Incarnation – meaning God's identity as the specific human being Jesus – is the most radical form of that particularisation of God which the Old Testament itself depicts in its narratives of divine identifiability. But for a notion of incarnation to retain this fundamental continuity with Old Testament theology, it is essential that the particularity of Jesus be kept sharply in view, as it is in the New Testament. Incarnation is not a deification of the creature which compromises the otherness of God. Incarnation is God's self-identification as this particular worldly reality, Jesus in his particular personal history. God of course transcends this particular human identity, yet also truly owns it as God's own identity in the world for us. In this identity as Jesus, God is truly Godself.

(2) God's identity in salvific identification with all people

However, both the radical particularity of Jesus as the revelation of God and the way in which in this radical particularity Jesus is the *universal* revelation of God can be fully understood only *soteriologically*. (This is the second of our three aspects.) It is in order to be savingly present in human life that God gives Godself a particular human identity in Jesus. It is in order to be savingly present for all human beings that God identifies Godself for all people in Jesus.

At this point we can again make use of the concept of identity, along with the related notion of *identification*. Identification can occur either when one identifies oneself *as* So-and-so, or when one identifies oneself *with* others. In the first case, it is a matter of one's own identity as oneself and no one else. In the second case, it is a matter of close association with others such that one's own identity is inseparably linked with theirs. In the case of the divine identity these two forms of self-identification come together. God identifies Godself *as* the God who identifies *with* others. In this concept, as we shall now see, we have the key to the relation of particularity and universality in Jesus and to the relation of revelation and salvation in Jesus.

As we have seen, in the biblical tradition revelation occurs when God gives Godself a particular identity within the world and thus becomes identifiable. Since this identity is a worldly identity, it involves a kind of identification with worldly reality. For example, God becomes the

God of Israel and is identifiable as Israel's God. God's identity includes the close relationship with the people of Israel which God has established by delivering them from Egypt, giving them the law and the land, dwelling among them, and so on. We could say that God becomes identifiable *as* the God of Israel by identifying *with* Israel as her God. Moreover, this self-identification of God is both revelatory and salvific. It is in acting savingly for Israel and in being graciously present with Israel that God identifies with Israel. Salvation and revelation are inseparably related in that it is by identifying with Israel (salvation) that God identifies Godself as the God of Israel (revelation). Both in self-identification with Israel and in self-identification as Israel's God, God is the God who is with and for Israel. God's identity is as Saviour. God's identity is in gracious self-identification with others.

In incarnation in Jesus, God's self-identification becomes even more radically a self-identification with worldly reality. What we have previously described as the radical particularisation of the divine identity – God identified as this particular worldly reality, the person and history of Jesus – we can now redescribe as the radical identification of God with worldly reality. In covenant with Israel God is identified – in the sense of closely associated – with a worldly reality, Israel. In incarnation God is so identified with a worldly reality, Jesus, as to be identical with that same worldly reality. In incarnation *self-identification with* and *self-identification as* coincide. God not only identifies Godself with Jesus; God identifies Godself as Jesus.

This self-identification of God *with and as* the one human being Jesus is precisely the way in which God's universal self-revelation and salvation occur. In identifying Godself with and as Jesus, God identifies Godself for all people (revelation) and with all people (salvation). This one human being is God's saving presence with and for all human beings. This radical grace which consists not only in God's close association with human beings, but in God's presence actually as a human being with and for other human beings, required the radical particularity of God's self-identification as the one man Jesus which is at the same time the fullest universality of God's self-identification with all human beings.

(3) The story of Jesus renders his identity as God's identity

Finally, we turn to the third aspect of the biblical understanding of God's identifiability which we have established from the Old Testament in order to relate this also to Jesus as revelation. This is that God's revealed identity is rendered primarily by narrative. Just as God's identity as Israel's God is rendered by the Old Testament story of God's relationship with Israel, so God's new identity as the God of Jesus Christ is rendered by the story which the gospels tell in detail and which is summarised in various ways elsewhere in the New Testament and in the later Creeds of the church. In this story God is identified not only in relation to Jesus – as the Father of Jesus and the Spirit of Jesus – but also as Jesus. Jesus' own human identity is *God's* human identity. Thus it is precisely in the narrative rendering of his particular human identity that Jesus is revelation of God. Into this particular human identity which, like any particular human identity, can only be adequately depicted in a narrative, God has truly put Godself in order to be identifiable thereby.

It is of the greatest importance that the gospel narratives render the identity of Jesus precisely as the unsubstitutable personal identity of this particular human being.[28] They do not tell a story of Everyperson. They do not even downplay the particular in order to highlight the respects in which Jesus represents common human characteristics or typifies human possibilities or instantiates a way of being human. (This is what the first two of the three views of revelation which we sketched in the first section of this chapter would require.) Rather they constitute a unique identity description. They relate Jesus' particular mission from God, his particular life and relationships and fate. Read as narratives of divine revelation, they make the human particularity of Jesus intrinsic to the divine identity. God is revealed as the one who is human in this way. What is revealed is not what God is like apart from Jesus nor what human beings may be in parallel with Jesus, but God's identity as this one human being. Therefore the narratives which render this unique human identity of God are not replaceable.

The story has a highly distinctive shape. It tells initially of Jesus' earthly life lived in such a way as to end in death by crucifixion, and subsequently of God's raising and exaltation of Jesus. On the one hand, the narrative up to and including his death tells of Jesus' loving identification with other humans,[29] culminating in giving his life for them through dying in humiliation and abandonment. On the other hand, the claim that, through resurrection, Jesus was exalted to the divine throne in heaven identifies Jesus with God.[30] For the first Christians, the exalted Jesus' participation in the uniquely divine sovereignty over the world, to which his sitting on the heavenly throne of God refers, could only mean that Jesus was included in the identity of the one God.[31] But if Jesus in his exaltation is identified with God, then Jesus' identification with people in his life and death is God's identification with them. God's identity as Jesus, revealed in Jesus' resurrection and exaltation, is therefore an identity in identification with others, which took place in Jesus' life and death of loving identification with others. In this way the gospel narratives should be read as the story of God's radically identifying love, in which God as this human being Jesus identified with all human beings. This loving self-identification of God with us took place in this unique history. In Jesus, therefore, in his story and in his person, God is identifiable as, in this uniquely radical sense, the God who is for us and with us.

Definitiveness and openness in God's identity in Jesus

When understood in this way, it is clear that the revelation of God in Jesus is unique. This does not mean that God cannot be identifiable in other ways apart from Jesus. It does mean that the revelation of God in Jesus is *definitive* for human knowledge of God. In Jesus God has defined God's identity for all people. But the concept of definitiveness is here much more helpful than the more traditional notion of finality.[32] Unlike the latter, it can be combined with a certain kind of openness to the world and to the future. The key to this is to recognise that it is in *relation* to all people and to all reality that Jesus is revelation of God. The gospel narratives themselves, like all narratives of human identity, render Jesus' identity in relationships[33] – to God, to other human persons, and to non-human creatures. This identity-in-relationship is the identity God has given Godself in incarnation. In principle, the relationships of Jesus are to all reality, and in his death for all people and his exaltation to rule over all things the gospel story claims this universality of relationship for Jesus already in principle. However, in human experience Jesus' relationship to all people and to all reality is not yet completed. It is constantly taking place in new ways as the gospel story is told in new contexts. As the story that renders Jesus' identity is told in an endless variety of new contexts, Jesus' identity itself, as an identity in relationship to those who hear the story, as an identity for them, in a certain sense develops. And so God's identity as the God who is for us and with us in Jesus is constantly becoming known afresh – not just in the same way again and again, but in ever new dimensions. Similarly, the definitiveness of this identity of God in Jesus takes place as believers continually recognise and explore Jesus' relationship to all truth and value, all needs and opportunities, all that may be known of

God in whatever way, all aspects of reality as they are constantly experienced in new ways.

This openness of God's identity in Jesus to relationship with all reality[34] corresponds to the way in which the gospel story itself is not concluded. Jesus' own narrative identity, as the gospels tell the story, is open to the continuing story of his presence, in the Spirit, with his followers, and to his coming in glory. It is notable that, in the New Testament itself, Christological use of the words 'to reveal' and 'revelation' is mostly with reference to the *parousia*, when Jesus will be revealed to the world. Then God's identity in Jesus will not only be identifiable to faith, as it is within history, but openly revealed for all people to see. Furthermore, only then, when the goal of God's salvific purpose in Jesus is realised in the renewal of all creation, will Jesus' relationship to all things be finally achieved and revealed. Until then Jesus' identity retains its openness to relationship to all things, and his definitiveness as revelation of God entails this openness.[35]

Notes

1. Therefore G.W.H. Lampe, *God as Spirit*, Oxford, Clarendon, 1977, who speaks freely of the 'sinless perfection' of Jesus, does not escape the problem which all degree Christologies that wish to assert this have, by applying his degree Christology to the Christ of faith rather than to the Jesus of history.

2. H. Rashdall, quoted in A.M. Ramsey, *From Gore to Temple*, London, Longmans, 1960, p.69.

3. Among the English Modernists, this view is expressed by J.F. Bethune-Baker, quoted in Ramsey, *From Gore*, p.72, and in A.M.G. Stephenson, *The Rise and Decline of English Modernism*, London, SPCK, 1984, p.119.

4. H.D.A. Major, quoted in Ramsey, *From Gore*, p.73.

5. J. Macquarrie, *Jesus Christ in Modern Thought*, London, SCM Press, 1990, p.381. For a fuller critique of Macquarrie's Christology, see my review in *JTS* 42 (1991), pp.793–7.

6. In fact, Kierkegaard (or rather his pseudonym) says a little more: 'If the contemporary generation had left behind them but these words: "We have believed that in such and such a year the God appeared among us in the humble figure of a servant, that he lived and taught in our community, and finally died," it would be more than enough': S. Kierkegaard, *Philosophical Fragments*, transl. D.F. Swenson and H.V. Hong, Princeton, New Jersey, Princeton University Press, 1967, p.130. In context, the point is that no amount of additional historical detail can produce faith.

7. *Church Dogmatics*, I/1, p.323.

8. J. MacIntyre, *The Shape of Christology*, Philadelphia, Westminster Press, 1960, pp.157–61, seems to make this mistake.

9. K. Rahner, *The Trinity*, transl. J. Donceel, London, Burns & Oates, 1970, pp. 32–3.

10. K. Rahner, *Theological Investigations IV*, transl. K. Smyth, New York, Crossroad, 1982, p.116.

11. For this dialectic in the development of Barth's theology up to the *Church Dogmatics*, see B.L. McCormack, *Karl Barth's Realistic Dialectical Theology: Its Genesis and Development 1909–1936*, Oxford, Clarendon, 1995, pp.248–50, 269, 315–52, 362–3, 371, 459–60.

12. *Church Dogmatics*, I/1, p.321.

13. *Ibid.*, I/1, p.323.

14. *Ibid.*, I/1, p.316.

15. *Ibid.*, I/1, p.318; cf. *Church Dogmatics* II/1, p.207.

16. *Ibid.*, I/1, p.320.

17. *Ibid.*, I/1, pp.319–20.

18. K. Barth, *The Humanity of God*, London, Collins, 1961, p.49.

19. Cf. *Church Dogmatics* IV/1, p.178: 'Its [the revelation's] form does not correspond to it but contradicts it.' In context this means specifically that the humanity of Jesus contradicts the claim to 'unlimited omnipotence' which he makes in Matt. 11:27. At *Church Dogmatics* IV/1, p.187, Barth says that the freedom of God's love to be human, even in solidarity with the sinful humanity that contradicts him, 'corresponds to and is grounded in His divine nature.' Becoming human *corresponds* to God's nature because his nature is the gracious love that chooses solidarity with the creatures that *contradict* him.

20. Cf. especially *ibid.* IV/1, pp.186–8.

21. Philippians 2:7. Barth has Philippians 2:6–8 in mind throughout *Church Dogmatics* IV/1, § 59.1.

22. See R. Bauckham, *Moltmann: Messianic Theology in the Making*, Basingstoke, Marshall Pickering, 1987, pp.65–72; *idem*, 'Cross, Theology of the', in S.B. Ferguson and D.F. Wright, eds, *New Dictionary of Theology*, Leicester, Inter-Varsity Press, 1988, pp.181–3. While Luther, like Barth, speaks of revelation of God in God's hiddenness 'under opposite form', Moltmann speaks only of God's 'revelation in contradiction'. In both cases the dialectic is close to Barth's, but in focusing the epistemological issue especially on the cross both sharpens it and makes it more explicitly soteriological.

23. For this thought also in Barth, see, e.g., *Church Dogmatics* IV/1, p.185.

24. For the notion of identity as I use it here, cf. H.W. Frei, *The Identity of Jesus Christ*, Philadelphia, Fortress Press, 1975; *idem*, 'Theological Reflections on the Accounts of Jesus' Death and Resurrection', in H.W. Frei, *Theology and Narrative: Selected Essays*, ed., G. Hunsinger and W.C. Placher, New

York/Oxford, Oxford University Press, 1993, pp.45–93; D. Patrick, *The Rendering of God in the Old Testament*, Philadelphia, Fortress Press, 1981; R.W. Jenson, *The Triune Identity*, Philadelphia, Fortress Press, 1982; R.F. Thiemann, *Revelation and Theology: The Gospel as Narrated Promise*, Notre Dame, Indiana, University of Notre Dame Press, 1985, chs.6–7; R.A. Krieg, *Story-Shaped Christology: Identifying Jesus Christ*, New York, Paulist Press, 1988, ch.1; K.J. Vanhoozer, 'Does the Trinity Belong in a Theology of Religions? On Angling in the Rubicon and the "Identity" of God', in K.J. Vanhoozer ed., *The Trinity in a Pluralistic Age*, Grand Rapids, Eerdmans, 1997, pp.41–71. As Vanhoozer notes, ' "Identity" is, of course, susceptible of several meanings: numeric oneness, ontological sameness or permanence in time, and the personal identity of self-continuity' (p.47). The last is the meaning employed here. Reference to God's identity is by analogy with human personal identity, understood not as a mere ontological subject without characteristics, but as including both character and personal story (the latter entailing relationships). These are the ways in which we commonly specify 'who someone is'. In view of God's transcendence, for us to be able to specify 'who God is', God must give Godself an identity in our world for us. This is revelation. The meaning I give to notion of divine identity will unfold as the argument proceeds.

25. In traditional theological terms, God in God's 'economic' relationship with the world corresponds to God in God's immanence in Godself. In trinitarian terms, the economic Trinity corresponds to the immanent Trinity. To construe God's identity in the 'postmodern' sense rejected here would be Sabellianism.

26. This concept of revelation as God's identifiability in a worldly identity in which God is true to Godself meets some of the difficulties which F.G. Downing, *Has Christianity a Revelation?* London, SCM Press, 1964, finds in the idea of divine self-revelation. He does not find the latter in the Bible (prior to the *eschaton*) because he understands it as manifestation of a transcendental divine self and requires of it a clarity which biblical identification of God does not have. Consequently, he advocates the notion of salvation to the exclusion of revelation. Thus he drives a wide conceptual wedge between God's self-revelation and God's saving activity. Our proposal enables us to see that in God's saving action and presence in the world, God becomes identifiable, within all the unclarities of worldly history, as the God who is with us and for us, and that this identity is truly who God is.

27. A fuller treatment of our subject, impossible here, would, of course, have to consider in far more detail the relation of Jesus as God's human identity to God's triune identity.

28. This point has been made and developed magisterially by H.W. Frei, *The Identity of Jesus Christ*; cf. *idem*, 'Theological Reflections'; *idem*, 'The Encounter of Jesus with the German Academy,' in H.W. Frei, *Types of*

Christian Theology, ed. G. Hunsinger and W.C. Placher, New Haven/ London, Yale University Press, 1992, pp.133–46.

29. For development of this notion, in relation to particularity and universality in Christology, see R. Bauckham, 'Christology Today', *Scriptura* 27, 1988, pp.20–8.

30. Frei treats the resurrection as 'the climactic eatablishment of Jesus' identity' ('Theological Reflections', 47), but in the New Testament it is Jesus' exaltation to the right hand of God which really merits this description. In resurrection as such, Jesus pioneers the destiny of all who will rise to life in him, but in exaltation to the divine throne he is uniquely identified with God.

31. See further my 1996 Didsbury Lectures, to be published as *God Crucified: Monotheism and Christology in the New Testament*, Carlisle, Paternoster/ Grand Rapids, Eerdmans.

32. Both notions have been used in somewhat varying ways in this connexion, and some uses of the term 'finality' are not far from my use of 'definitiveness'. The latter includes the requirements both that all other knowledge of God must be consistent with God's identity in Jesus, and that all other knowledge of God (and all other knowledge of reality) will be fully understood only in relationship to Jesus as God's definitive identity for all. But my argument also implies that since God's identity in Jesus is an identity-in-relationship, it is fully understood only in relationship to all reality. Jesus in his *parousia*, revealed in his final relationship to all reality, will be the final revelation of God.

33. For Jesus' identity in relationships, see J. Moltmann, *The Way of Jesus Christ*, transl. M. Kohl, London, SCM Press, 1990, ch.3, esp. pp.74, 142–9; D. J. Georgen, *Jesus, Son of God, Son of Mary, Immanuel*, A Theology of Jesus 4; Collegeville, Minnesota, Liturgical Press, 1995, p.212.

34. P. Avis, *The Methods of Modern Theology*, Basingstoke, Marshall Pickering, 1986, pp.210–11, criticises Barth and T.F. Torrance for 'isolating' Jesus Christ as containing all the data of theology. If Jesus is understood as definitive revelation of God precisely in his relationships to all reality, this problem is avoided.

35. I am indebted to my colleague Trevor Hart for stimulating discussion and helpful comments on an earlier draft of this chapter, and to members of the Thursday theological discussion group in St Andrews, who devoted three meetings to discussing the chapter with me.

11

Revelation Reaffirmed

William J. Abraham

Our Unease with Divine Revelation

Attempts to articulate a substantial doctrine of divine revelation are inherently implausible in contemporary theology. The matter is forthrightly expressed by Stanley Hauerwas in a revealing aside: 'The very idea that the Bible is revealed (or inspired) is a claim that creates more trouble than it is worth.'[1]

The reasons for this aversion to the idea of divine revelation are manifold. First, the neo–orthodox attempt to rehabilitate divine revelation has not carried the day. Despite its extraordinary impact, neo–orthodoxy did not have the intellectual resources to argue a case for divine revelation, not least because it rejected in principle that arguments could be given for divine revelation. Where a case has been attempted, as is true of the work of Thomas Torrance, the argument rests essentially on the validity of theology as a science; even then, the whole operation is a dubious one.[2] Second, the centre of gravity in theology has shifted from concern with the content of the recovery of the *kerygma* to concern with the social and political context in which the church must act and witness. In liberation theologies there is little interest of the first degree in a vision of divine revelation. Where it is mentioned, it tends to perpetuate the popular vision of revelation as the mighty acts of God in history for the liberation of Israel. In addition, the quest to interact positively with the great non–Christian religions has made it difficult to deploy ideas of revelation which belonged to earlier generations. Finally, the deep animosities which divided philosophy from theology until very recently have meant that revelation has been something of a conceptual orphan. Theologians have, of course, deployed the idea, for it is difficult to avoid all talk of divine revelation – if only for old time's sake – but it has not generally carried the cognitive freight which philosophers are wont to put on it.

For the philosopher of religion, revelation is not generally a marginal notion. Both atheistic and theistic philosophers of religion are drawn to it for the same, very good reason: revelation is an inherently epistemic idea. Talk of divine revelation is invariably construed as talk about how God is made known. Hence the philosopher will be driven to spell out the content and implications of a doctrine of divine revelation with precision and thoroughness. In this way the claim to knowledge embodied in discourse about divine revelation can be articulated, scrutinised, and evaluated. In itself this interest does not settle the issue for or against the view that all knowledge must be fitted into a foundationalist perspective. It is perfectly possible to be an anti-foundationalist and yet to insist that the whole point of a doctrine of revelation is to lay bare the grammar of Christian discourse about how God is made known on earth.[3]

Understandably, the theologian is nervous and critical of the philosopher's ways of deciphering and exploring divine revelation. This is expressed in a variety of modes. At one level, it will be feared that the ineffable mystery of God will be ignored or eroded in the quest to set forth in propositional form what is supposedly known about God. At another level, the concern is that conceptions of divine revelation developed in philosophical laboratories will be used as distorting lens through which the sacred traditions of the faith are misread or even mutilated. At a third level, theologians are rightly worried that a preoccupation with epistemological questions will displace the primary content of the faith with apologetic proposals which undermine precious dimensions of Christianity. At a fourth level, they are naturally suspicious that focusing on the objectivity of revelation and its cognitive import will leave no room for the place of either divine grace or historical community in the reception and transmission of sacred tradition. At a fifth level, those contemporary theologians who are interested in the quest for human transformation and liberation are wont to dismiss the philosopher's quest for some kind of special knowledge enshrined in divine revelation as a cover for a deeper commitment to oppression or to the political status quo. Finally, if we pay attention to the work of deconstructionists like Derrida or pragmatists like Rorty, the very idea of knowledge will be set aside as unavailable. The idea of revelation will be construed as inextricably tied to the fortunes of classical foundationalism, a tradition under heavy fire in contemporary discussions of epistemology. So developing and sustaining a doctrine of divine revelation is an arduous affair.

Yet revelation remains a crucial part of our discourse about God. This claim does not turn on word studies about the use of the word 'revelation' in Scripture, but on the whole fabric of Christian discourse manifest in the Christian tradition over the centuries. Moreover, it is extremely difficult to dislodge the idea of revelation from Christian theology, not least because the concept is often deployed in an indirect fashion. It arises very naturally because of a great variety of things Christians say about God – about how God is made known to human beings, about what God has done in various and sundry ways, and the like. In doing so I am interested in both first order discourse about God and in attempts at the level of academic theology to make sense of the idea of revelation.

The Importance of Historical Considerations

In debates about the nature of revelation it is entirely legitimate that at least two sets of issues be kept in mind, namely, the historical and the conceptual. Doctrines of revelation need to be compatible with what we know about the matrix of tradition and experience within which revelation is transmitted. It is far from easy to satisfy this requirement. Strictly purist interpretations of sacred tradition and religious experience which do not trade on contested conceptual and metaphysical assumptions are extremely difficult to secure. Yet it is obvious that doctrines of divine revelation can quite easily be overturned by historical findings concerning canonical texts. It was common in much post-Reformation theology, for example, to insist that divine revelation took the form of the divine dictation of the Bible. Even Calvin can be cited in this respect.[4] The abandonment of this and its replacement by the sophisticated account of divine inspiration commonly found in conservative theologies of the last century took place, sometimes very quietly, under pressure from detailed observations about the style and character of Scripture. We cannot therefore pretend that our views of revelation can be affirmed in the teeth of well-grounded discoveries about the nature of sacred tradition.

Yet great caution is needed as we seek to develop an account of divine revelation which will fit naturally with Scripture and experience. This is especially the case where critical readings of Scripture are linked to metaphysical convictions about what can and cannot happen in history.

One influential trajectory of critical scholarship, which stretches from Hume through Treoltsch and Bultmann to many contemporary biblical scholars, rules out certain possibilities with respect to divine action as 'mythological' and impossible. The resolution to treat talk of divine intervention as inadmissible is pervasive in this tradition. Clearly in this case certain limits are set as to what the genuine historian can allow in the present and this will serve as a test of adequacy in evaluating one's appropriation of historical investigation. The contemporary theologian or philosopher should not be constrained by the strictures of this trajectory. So long as he or she is prepared to deploy comprehensively and appropriately an alternative trajectory of critical assumptions, together with the historical conclusions they yield when put to work in investigation of the tradition, he or she cannot be faulted on historical grounds. At this point we all have to face the fact that we live in a situation where there are competing accounts of what is formally and materially available to us as a result of historical inquiry. Nothing is gained by dogmatically insisting on one such account as the only one available. In this context it is especially important to eschew the use of pejorative terms to carry the argument. Each side must carry the argument as charitably, fully, and succinctly as it can.

The Importance of Conceptual Considerations

History, however, is not the only factor that matters in any account of divine revelation. Indeed, an accurate depiction of the complex character of historical investigation should not only make us sensitive to the competing sets of results available to us; it should also alert us to the crucial role of conceptual considerations in any inquiry into the nature and status of revelation. Any vision of divine revelation which is theologically interesting will eventually, for example, have to identify what it posits as divine revelation. Philosophers can be content with the discussion of formal possibilities; theologians cannot. To be true to their vocation they must say where revelation is to be found. In the past they have not hesitated to do so. They have claimed that divine revelation has taken place in creation generally; in the activity of the human conscience; in the mighty acts of God in history; in the word spoken by the prophets of Israel; in the life of Jesus of Nazareth; in the text of Scripture; in the hearts of those who listen to the gospel; in the historic councils of the church; in the teachings of the bishop of Rome; in mystical traditions; and so on. The vital point to note now is this: all of these presuppose some conception or preunderstanding of what revelation is. To say, for example, that certain historical events or a certain book is a divine revelation already presupposes some regulative idea of divine revelation without which the claim is hopelessly vacuous. Or, to express it in different terms, in searching in history for divine revelation we would not be able to identify certain events or religious experiences as divine revelation if we did not bring to our inquiry some prior conception of divine revelation.

It is at this point that the philosopher very naturally gets a toehold in the discussion, for conceptual analysis has been a vital element in the toolbox of philosophy from Plato to Wittgenstein. What is of interest to the philosopher at this level is what is going to count as divine revelation in the first place. To resolve this issue, it is totally inadequate to point to a body of tradition, say, in Scripture, name it as the *locus* revelation, and then seek to resolve the question of the nature of revelation by assembling information from history about the origins and character of the biblical traditions. Such a move assumes that we already know what revelation is and that we already know that the Bible is revelation. Until we give some content to the concept of revelation, such claims are empty.[5]

What is needed is a careful elucidation of how the verb 'reveal' is to be applied to God. With this in hand – and only then – can we begin to identify responsibly how and to what degree Scripture or events in history or creation, or the like, can be construed as divine revelation. Moreover, as a result of our work we may need to refocus the way in which we locate divine revelation in order to do justice to its sheer complexity. It is truly astonishing in this regard how many books can be written on divine revelation without a single reference to the incarnation of God in Christ.[6] It is also amazing how quickly debates about divine revelation slide without notice into debates about divine inspiration.[7] This inevitably happens when sensitive conceptual analysis of particular divine actions is totally ignored as irrelevant, or is displaced by an inductive study of sacred texts and past events. Even very sophisticated analyses of revelation can be grossly misleading when they fail to attend to certain basic features of our discourse about divine revelation. It requires an uncommon commitment to bring together the results of both comprehensive conceptual analysis and rigorous historical investigation so that they can bear fruit in the development of an adequate doctrine of divine revelation. Let us now pause and explore some basic conceptual considerations.

The Polymorphous Character of Revelation

An especially salient feature of the concept of revelation is that it is a polymorphous concept. Agents reveal themselves through what they do. They reveal themselves in word and deed. Imagine for a moment asking someone to take five minutes and reveal herself. This is a very odd request compared, for example, to asking someone to take five minutes and read a book, or pop round to the shop. We can only make sense of it by imagining someone taking five minutes and telling us who she is, where she is from, and what she has done over the years. Some kind of narrative of action will be crucial in any attempt to secure something significant or revelatory of the person in question. Hence one reveals oneself in, with, and through the various acts one performs. In this sense 'reveal' is akin to other polymorphous concepts like 'teach', or 'farm'. One teaches by giving lectures, holding tutorials, setting papers, and requiring set texts to be read; one farms by ploughing fields, planning what crops to plant, driving tractors, and cleaning out byres. Teaching and farming are not activities done after these activities have been performed; they are done in performing these other activities.

This elementary point about the concept of revelation sheds immediate light on the whole sweep of Christian accounts of divine revelation. For one thing it helps to explain the amazing diversity of claims made about the *locus* of divine revelation. Doctrines of divine revelation invariably pick out and focus on a slice of divine action or activity construed to reveal God. In short, they concentrate on those acts in, which, and through God reveals himself. These acts reveal what has previously been hidden.

Hence a hallmark of classical claims about divine revelation is its stress on divine revelation in creation. The starry sky above and the moral law within have both been seen as avenues into the divine mind. The natural order displays the wisdom and power of God and the voice of conscience makes manifest the moral character and will of God. Within creation revelation is said to occur in a variety of situations. It is found in God's word to prophets and apostles. It is enacted in the mighty acts of God in the history of Israel and in the life, death, and resurrection of Jesus of Nazareth. Revelation also takes place in the human heart as the veil of ignorance and sin is removed through the activity of the Holy Spirit and people are enabled to behold the light of the glory of God in the face of Jesus Christ. Finally, revelation will take place at the end of time when the ultimate purposes of God for creation are consummated and fulfilled.

Christian accounts of revelation are in part extended footnotes on these various *loci* of revelation. So we have a theory of general revelation to account for revelation in conscience and the natural order; a propositional theory to do justice to the revelation to prophets and apostles; a *Heilsgeschichte* theory to deal with revelation in the 'mighty acts of God in history'; a theory of illumination to make sense of the hidden work of the Holy Spirit in restoring spiritual sight to the blind; and a proleptic theory to accommodate the revelation of God at the *eschaton*. Given the possible combinations and permutations of these various elements, it is not surprising that the history of the doctrine of revelation appears somewhat chaotic. The obvious temptation to simplify and limit revelation to one set of acts of God – say, in creation or in history – is exceedingly and understandably strong. The pressure from, say, historical studies can have exactly the same effect; deists, ancient and modern, bear ample witness to this fact.

In my judgement such single-focus accounts are generally arbitrary. As we correlate conceptual sensitivity with the extraordinary richness of talk about revelation available in the tradition, the natural way to proceed is to see all of these positions as viable so long as they are not developed in an exclusive fashion. There might, of course, be good reason for dismissing some putative *loci* of revelation as empty of content and significance. In the absence of such reasons, however, it is natural to see these competing accounts as held together by the formal assumption that divine revelation is mediated through divine action, and by the material claim that each of the *loci* of revelation are instances of quite specific action or activity of God. Reference to the various locations of divine revelation is therefore a way of signalling those particular acts in and through which God reveals himself.

The Significance of the Word of God

Once we begin to spell out the content of the particular revelatory acts attributed to God, we are in a position to make sense of a second feature of accounts of divine revelation which is very striking, namely, the tendency to gravitate towards the word of God and the incarnation of God in Christ as especially significant. In fact, these two merge in an interesting way when the revelatory significance of the incarnation is captured by stressing that Jesus is the Word of God *par excellence*.

We can make a start in manifesting this by noting that some of the actions we perform cast extraordinary light on what we do and hence on what we truly are like as people. Consider the miser who hoards all his money and steadfastly refuses to give away a penny to help the poor. He refuses all kinds of pleading made on their behalf. Then he dies and leaves all his money to the local vicar, who is required by the terms of the miser's will to distribute it to the needy of the parish. This is accompanied by an explanation; unbeknown to others, our miser had made a rash promise to his father on inheriting the family fortune that he would never give away a penny to the poor so long as he lived. Moreover, he was honour bound to keep this promise a secret during his lifetime. The final will and testament of the supposed miser totally alters our reading of his life and character. Precisely because of this, we naturally want to say. 'Well I never thought old Jones had it in him. Fooled me, he did! What a revelation of the old fellow!' It is in situations like these that the concept of revelation takes root. By examining them it is immediately plain that some acts are revelatory while others are not. Some stand out as windows into the character of a person and are identified precisely by their capacity to illuminate otherwise dark or ambiguous tracks of action. It is surely because of this that we say in common parlance that actions speak louder than words.

It was this insight that lay behind the *Heilsgeschichte* conception of revelation developed by such scholars as G.E. Wright, Reginald Fuller, Bernard Anderson, Alan Richardson, John Baillie, and others. Revelation was a matter of God's action in history, rather than of mystical experience, or static propositions in an ancient book, or rickety philosophical argument, or precarious noetic insight. The Bible was the book of the acts of God; God's action in Jesus was the centre of God's action in time; faith was the God-given ability to discern divine action in history; and the task of the Church was to celebrate, declare and even join in God's action in the world. These theologians were clearly on to something of enormous significance, for actions even in the case of God do often speak louder than words. Trouble arose, however, when this feature of our very rich discourse about revelation was pressed too hard and too far. Theologians tried to extract too much out of a useful slogan which captured only one dimension of the issue.

The *Heilsgeschichte* position in so far as it constituted a distinctive, coherent tradition fell apart for extremely interesting reasons. We need not tell the whole debatable story here but suffice just to say this. On the one side it suffered a penetrating attack and analysis from Langdon Gilkey, whose primary concern was the emptiness of its talk about the mighty acts of God.[8] Somehow, after the critical, historical work was done on the tradition, it was far from clear what God had actually done in history. At one level there was a lot of supernaturalistic talk about God's action; but this was not really integrated with the naturalistic, humdrum discourse which showed up at a historical level. Gilkey's initial solution to this was to reach for a general theory of divine action which could be put to work in figuring out God's particular actions in history.

Perhaps the most devastating criticism, however, came from the pen of James Barr.[9] Barr argued more directly from the biblical traditions, insisting that the *Heilsgeschcichte* position could not cope either with the Wisdom traditions nor with the recurrent emphasis on the divine word which one finds in the Bible as a complement to the mighty acts of God in history. In turn, Barr set out to develop an account of Scripture which saw it as the classic literary expression of the people of God's experience in their contact with God. This sounds like a typical liberal understanding of Scripture, but to treat it in such a way is not only anachronistic, it fails to capture the subtlety and richness of Barr's understanding of Scripture. Unfortunately, it is not always easy to decipher Barr's positive proposals, given the stridently polemical character of some of his writings; it is obvious that for a generation he has championed a thoroughly inductive understanding of Scripture which would prevent it from being imprisoned in the procrustean beds of various doctrinal or conceptual frameworks. In and through this he has assembled a variety of brilliant suggestions which hang somewhat loosely together.

Conceptual work, however, is inevitable and inescapable in theology. So it is surely not surprising that Gilkey and a whole host of theologians have embarked on a quest for a theory of divine action in the wake of their queries about divine action in history. In my view this has its merits, but general theories of divine action have inherent limitations in their content. It is much more promising to pause and pick up on the conceptual import of Barr's reference to divine speaking, even though he may have great misgivings about the direction we may travel. The crucial issue at stake is that the emphasis on the speaking God is not accidental, once we place it in the conceptual field of revelation. The action of speaking takes us into a class of actions which are characteristically revelatory. We often clear up queries about what a person is doing and the rationale for their actions by asking them to tell us what is going on. Personal avowals and confessions are virtually essential data we need to know if we are to have any idea of what agents have done on various occasions. Indeed, in the case of God, this is extremely important because, generally speaking, we do not have the functional equivalent of bodily actions or bodily movements in our endeavours to discern God's action in history. The main point can be worked out here very simply by imagining what it would be like to live in a universe where all agents, including the embodied agents we know, are dumb. Speaking, whether human or divine, is characteristically revelatory; which is one reason why we use 'speaking' as a vivid metaphor when we say that actions speak louder than words.

This important insight went badly astray in conservative theories of revelation and inspiration. The deep issue at stake here is the natural place which God's word to prophet and apostle has in the unveiling of God's action in history. Given God's decisive action in Israel and in Jesus for the liberation of the cosmos, it is entirely fitting that this was accompanied by a form of verbal revelation which identified and articulated what God has done and is doing. Unfortunately, this observation went awry. Protestant scholastics of the Reformation and their fundamentalist offspring translated this into a theory of divine dictation and divine inspiration which created enormous problems for the critical investigation of the Bible. Few have seen the ramifications of this conceptual confusion.[10]

What everyone now wants to know is how to cash out empirically the claim that God spoke to the prophets and apostles. Did the airwaves change? Did they hear voices? Did they see visions? Was there a telepathic communication and an inward hearing of the message from God? Did God just bring it about that the prophet thought certain thoughts, and thought of those thoughts as coming directly from God? The short answer to this is that we rarely know. This does not mean, however, that we cannot imagine all sorts of conceptual possibilities. After all, divine speaking is not something that simply stopped with the prophets and the apostles. There are legions of case studies in the history and phenomenology of religious experience which we can draw on. Think of Paul's experience on the road to Damascus or Augustine's experience in the garden or many instances of a divine call to the Christian ministry. To be sure, we face here exactly the same blinders and blinkers which eschew all reference to divine intervention as mythological. The suppression from the record of the Church of whole tracts of religious experience as enthusiasm, fanaticism, Pentecostalism, and the like, is all the offshoot of the same prejudice, and we cannot pause here to set that story straight. What we must accept is the historical limitations which confront us. What we have are precious traditions within and without Scripture in which the word of the Lord has come down to us in such a way as to save our souls and initiate us into the reign of God. Those who heard the word of God had more on their minds than the issue of the recording of the phenomenological features of their experience. What mattered was the content of what God had promised and demanded. It was more important to heed the summons of the Lord of hosts than to preserve the record of the material forms of God's word for posterity, even though we can at times catch a glimpse or two of these in the traditions of God's people.

The Significance of Incarnation

Moreover, the word has a kind of ancillary purpose. The really crucial word from God has come not in the word to a prophet, or in the verbal content of some ancient book. The true Word has come in the flesh of a Jewish labourer, who was anointed of God, who died on Golgotha, and who was raised by God on the third day. The epistle to the Hebrews captures the matter brilliantly:

> In many and varied ways God spoke of old to our fathers by the prophets; but in these last days he has spoken to us by a Son, whom he appointed the heir of all things, through whom he also created the world. He reflects the glory of God and bears the very stamp of his nature, upholding the universe by the word of power. When he had made purification for sins, he sat down at the right hand of the Majesty on high, having become as superior to angels as the name he has obtained is more excellent than theirs.[11]

It was this revelation of God in Jesus which caught everybody off guard and which, when properly appreciated, became the centre of the church's revelation. This is where the intellectual storm was let loose theologically, rather than on debates about the exact nature of the word to prophet and apostle. In insisting on this unique act of revelation, the very being of God was at issue, rather than the contingency of this or that way of God speaking to the fathers. It is most fully reflected in the Nicene creed, where considerable attention is given to the nature of Christ while the nature of God's speaking to the prophets is barely mentioned. Over time, the church came to believe that it was here where the intellectual homework had to be done thoroughly. Ontological and metaphysical questions were and are inescapable. To this day the debate continues as hot and ferocious as ever.

It is at this point that the philosopher and the theologian concerned about revelation can very easily go astray. As I mentioned earlier, whole books can be written about revelation without any reference to the incarnation. We can see why. The thirst for knowledge, especially for a propositional revelation which will fill our minds with correct information about the divine, becomes a kind of obsession. We disclose ourselves therein as children of the Enlightenment, looking for one more book to bring us light and salvation. Many become uneasy if the revelation is not cast in a form which is neat and tidy. It is difficult to tolerate a revelation which is transmitted in the life of a Jewish carpenter; it is hard to accept a revelation transmitted through human witnesses who enshrine it in a varied set of traditions which are so mundane and unspectacular. Moreover, the accompanying requirement about prayer and fasting, about repentance and faith, are dismissed as pious afterthoughts.

Our problem, we assume, is an intellectual problem, and it must, therefore, have a conventional intellectual solution written down in an appropriate text which all can read and understand. Our quest for revelation, that is, tends to entail a set of assumptions about the human predicament which casts our ideas about the nature of revelation in a certain mould. Hence even if we think that Jesus is the Word of God, we take it as read that his work is that of a teacher – if not of ethics, then of some prosaic scheme of salvation that will bring us happiness in the life to come, as we find in Locke and Paley. Being of a rationalistic turn of mind, we then look for proofs of Christ's divinity, or we discuss at length whether such an evidentialist approach to divine revelation is appropriate; having settled these, we then move on to another subject. In the process we set aside the sheer intellectual audacity of the Christian claim about incarnation and we run the risk of misreading the nature of God's action in Christ.

Our dilemma in this is very subtle. We are right to press the cognitive dimension of the issue. Christians claim that God has revealed himself uniquely in Christ. There is no going back on this cognitive claim; the determination with which Christians have explored the background and ramifications of this claim is staggering and even appropriate in its proportions. Yet we must move circumspectly as we attempt to articulate how divine revelation in this instance is achieved. This is where our conceptual work becomes, once more, quite crucial.

Our actions including our acts of revelation, are not performed in a vacuum. Even our speaking is done with certain people in view, and it is related intimately to the problems, dispositions, issues, and forms of life of those addressed. The Christian claim about revelation in Christ has to be understood, then, as part of a comprehensive vision of ourselves and our predicament which shapes the very form and character of that revelation. God did not send a library of books for our enlightenment, even though we find the books of Scripture indispensable in one way or another for maturity in the faith. Nor did God send his Son so that we might hold extended seminars on ontology and metaphysics, even though these may throw valuable light on what is at stake. He sent the Son to liberate the cosmos from sin and to grant us eternal life. Hence the crucial first-order verbs which are deployed to describe God's action in Christ focus not so much on revelation as on salvation and redemption. It is in and through these actions that God is truly revealed and made known. To develop a doctrine of revelation independently of them is profoundly misleading and distorting. Reminding ourselves of the conceptual connections between our actions, our intentions, and our contexts brings this readily to mind.

We can pursue this further by noting that revelation is characteristically an achievement verb. In the case of speaking, for example, someone has to grasp and pick up on what is said in order for there to be a revelation. At the very least, something could have been picked up or grasped. Otherwise all we have are certain locutionary acts. In the case of speaking, the agent needs to perform the illocutionary act of revealing himself or herself. For this to happen something has to be picked up and received, or it must be such that it could have been picked up and grasped. Hence revelation, to be revelation, has to be in principle, subjectively effective. It has to be such that it can find its away into the life of the individuals and communities to which it is directed.

The implications of this in the case of divine revelation are clear. Hearing God speak, or being confronted by the incarnation, is not a casual affair like reading the local newspaper or switching on the television. In the long run we are inevitably confronted by our darkness and rebellion. Our initial natural reaction to divine revelation is not one of welcome but one of awe and even terror. As Kierkegaard laid out so brilliantly a century ago, we invariably put into action a host of devices to keep the offence of the Word of God in Christ at bay. Hence it is not surprising that classical Christian accounts of coming to faith and belief are concerned to stress the inner working of Holy Spirit as part of the total process of revelation. We cannot come to see in a deep way what Christ has done, and thereby what God has revealed through him, without a profound immersion in the Holy Spirit. Such an immersion makes possible the kind of repentance and conversion which enables us to bear the full truth about ourselves without hopelessness and despair. It is surely no surprise, therefore, that accounts of divine revelation can easily collapse into a theory of inner illumination. We undoubtedly do need the veil of darkness about ourselves and the world to be removed by the Holy Spirit if we are to see what God has done for the healing of the world.

We return again to the polymorphous nature of both the concept and nature of God's action in history. God is indeed revealed in, with, and through what God does; manifold and wondrous is the form and diversity thereof; and one ingredient in that diversity is the hidden work of the Holy Spirit in our hearts and minds. A Christian account of divine revelation will gather up all that God has done to reveal himself to the world and relate it in rich and surprising ways both to the means of grace which transmit divine revelation, and to the tasks and projects of ecclesial and everyday existence.

Notes

1. Stanley Hauerwas, *A Community of Character*, Notre Dame, University of Notre Dame Press, 1982, p.57.
2. For a sensitive review of Torrance see Ronald F. Thiemann, *Revelation and Theology*, Notre Dame, University of Notre Dame Press, 1985, pp.32–46.
3. Foundationalism is the view that there are some beliefs which are properly basic beliefs, that is, they are not in need of support from other beliefs. The obvious alternative to foundationalism is coherentism, the view that all of our beliefs are supported by other beliefs, i.e., there are no properly basic beliefs. Classical foundationalism is the view that only those beliefs which are self-evident, evident to the senses, or incorrigible can be properly basic beliefs. The unwary should note that overturning classical foundationalism by no means destroys foundationalism as a serious option in epistemology.
4. John Calvin, *Institutes of the Christian Religion*, Philadelphia, Westminster Press, 1960, IV, VIII, 6, p.1154.
5. This is the most obvious weakness in David Brown's approach to revelation in *The Divine Trinity*, La Salle, Illinois, Open Court, 1985, p.54. Brown follows Barr at this point in misunderstanding my earlier efforts to develop a viable concept of inspiration and revelation. What is especially interesting about Brown's analysis is that after rejecting the idea of divine speaking as a mode of revelation, he promptly turns around and introduces the concept of dialogue as a better model. But this entails return to divine speaking, for dialogue belongs to the same family of concepts as speaking and communicating.

6. See, for example, George Mavrodes, *Revelation in Religious Belief*, Philadelphia, Temple University Press, 1988.
7. Note, for example, how Hauerwas conflates the two in the quotation above.
8. Langdon Gilkey, 'Ontology, Cosmology and the Travail of Biblical Language', *Journal of Religion* 41 (1961), pp.194–205.
9. James Barr, 'Revelation through History in the Old Testament and in Modern Theology', *Interpretation* 17 (1963), pp.193–205.
10. Brown is wide of the mark when he tries to see my own work as allowing fundamentalism back in again in the form of a new inner canon of *ipsimma verba* of God. See his *The Divine Trinity*, p.57. In my work on inspiration and revelation I have very deliberately steered clear of a comprehensive account of canon in Christian theology, so his inference at this point is invalid. Brown is also worried that I do not engage more fully with the biblical material. But this is also wide of the mark. I am well aware of the debates about the meaning of the biblical traditions, but one can often best get access to the conceptual considerations I think are crucial by bracketing out these matters for a time. Brown errs in the opposite direction. As noted above, he begs vital conceptual questions by identifying revelation with scripture and hence perpetuates the mistakes which have bedevilled the discussion. I provide an account of canon in *Canon and Criterion in Christian Theology: From the Fathers to Feminism*, forthcoming.
11. Hebrews 1:1–3.

Bibliography

Abraham, William J., *The Divine Inspiration of Holy Scripture*, Oxford, Oxford University Press, 1981.

——, *Divine Revelation and the Limits of Historical Criticism*, Oxford, Oxford University Press, 1982.

Barr, James, *The Scope and Authority of the Bible*, London, SCM Press, 1980.

Dulles, Avery, *Models of Revelation*, New York, Doubleday, 1985.

Farrer, Austin, 'Revelation', in Basil Mitchell, ed., *Faith and Logic*, London, Allen and Unwin, 1957.

Mavrodes, George, *Revelation in Religious Belief*, Philadelphia, Temple University Press, 1988.

Swinburne, Richard, *Revelation*, Oxford, Clarendon, 1992.

Thiemann, Ronald F., *Revelation and Theology*, Notre Dame, University of Notre Dame Press, 1985.

Williams, Rowan, 'Trinity and Revelation', in *Modern Theology* 2 (1986), pp.197–212.

Wolterstorff, Nicholas, *Divine Discourse*, Cambridge, Cambridge University Press, 1995.